Max Leopold Moltke, Robert Gericke

Shakespeare's Hamlet-Quellen

Saxo Grammaticus, Belleforest und the Hystorie of Hamblet

Max Leopold Moltke, Robert Gericke

Shakespeare's Hamlet-Quellen
Saxo Grammaticus, Belleforest und the Hystorie of Hamblet

ISBN/EAN: 9783337412197

Printed in Europe, USA, Canada, Australia, Japan

Cover: Foto ©Thomas Meinert / pixelio.de

More available books at **www.hansebooks.com**

SHAKESPEARE'S
HAMLET-QUELLEN:

SAXO GRAMMATICUS
(LATEINISCH UND DEUTSCH)

BELLEFOREST und THE HYSTORIE OF HAMBLET.

ZUSAMMENGESTELLT

UND

MIT VORWORT, EINLEITUNG UND NACHTRÄGEN

VON

Weiland Dr. ROBERT GERICKE

HERAUSGEGEBEN

VON

MAX MOLTKE.

LEIPZIG,
VERLAG VON JOHANN AMBROSIUS BARTH.
1881.

NACHRUF

AN

DR. ROBERT GERICKE

(GEST. AM 5. APRIL 1880).

Dem Edlen Edles! — Drum ein Edelwort,
Des Kraft auch Du, verklärter Freund, empfunden
In kurzen Lebens langen Leidensstunden,
Ruf' ich Dir nach von Deinem Grabesport.

Reif sein ist alles! — dieses Edelwort
Des Dichters, dessen Dienst uns hielt verbunden,
Nachruf' ich's, meine Trauer zu bekunden,
Dir als Geleitwort zu der Sel'gen Ort.

Ein Leidender seit Deines Lebens Mitten,
Hast Du doch rastlos thätig es durchschritten,
Das Wonn- und Jammerthal des Erdenseins. —

Reif und bereit sein! — weil dies Wort Dein Stecken,
So konnt' auch jenes andre Dich nicht schrecken:
Ein Menschenleben ist, als zählt man Eins!

Leipzig, am 8. April 1880.

Max Moltke.

„*Dem Edlen Edles!*" — vgl. Hamlet, Act V, Sc. 1; Rede 93, Z. 1: „*Sweets to the sweet*" (Queen).
„*Reif und bereit sein ist alles!*" — vgl. Lear, Act V, Sc. 2; Rede 5, Z. 3: „*Ripeness is all*" (Edgar); und Hamlet, Act V. Sc. 2; Rede 77, Z. 4: „*The readiness is all*" (Hamlet).
„*Ein Menschenleben ist, als zählt man Eins!*" — vgl. Hamlet, Act V, Sc. 2; Rede 19, Z. 2: „*And a man's life's no more than to say 'one'*" (Hamlet).

VORWORT.

Eine kurze Entstehungsgeschichte des Vorliegenden mufs erklären, warum es so ist, wie es ist.

Die Quellen (S. IX—C) sind bereits vor nahezu einem Jahrzehnt von Herrn Max Moltke zusammengestellt und unter seiner Leitung für seinen damaligen eigenen Verlag gedruckt worden, mit der Bestimmung, in der von ihm begonnenen, umfassend angelegten englisch-deutschen Ausgabe von Shakespeare's Hamlet (Heft 1 und 2, gr. 8°, 64 S., Leipzig 1871 — Text, Übersetzung und Commentar des Stücks bis Act I Sc. 4 enthaltend) als Heft 3 und 4 zu erscheinen. Allein ehe es dazu kam, brachten widrige äufsere Verhältnisse das Unternehmen ins Stocken, und die in Rede stehenden fast ganz fertig gedruckten Bogen blieben unveröffentlicht liegen. Und so ruhten sie, in Erwartung besserer Zeiten, die langen Jahre daher, bis Herr Moltke sie neuerdings aus seinem Selbstverlage abgab, und der gegenwärtige Verleger, in dankenswerter Willigkeit für die Sache, ihre Veröffentlichung als besonderes Werkchen übernahm. Mir, dem Unterzeichneten, der ich seinerzeit an der Herstellung der Hamlet-Quellen ein — wenn auch nicht selbständig eingreifendes, nur im stillen mithelfendes — thätiges Interesse genommen, ihren Urheber in den Druckcorrecturen unterstützt, auch die Übersetzung des Saxo sowie Anmerkungen und Anmerkungszeichen beigesteuert hatte: mir fiel infolge dessen jetzt die Aufgabe zu, für Herrn Moltke, durch andere Arbeiten verhindert, als Herausgeber der harrenden Bogen einzutreten.

Das jedoch konnte ich, obgleich es sich zunächst blofs um eine zu liefernde Einleitung handelte, nicht wohl auf mich nehmen, ohne das vor so vielen Jahren Gedruckte und mir unterdes ziemlich fremd Gewordene einer nochmaligen genaueren Durchsicht zu unterwerfen. Ich musste zu diesem Zwecke herbeiziehen, was mir an altem und neuem (neuerdings erschienenem oder früher unzugänglichem oder übersehenem) Material

erreichbar war. Auf Grund dessen nun an die Revision gehend, mufste ich aber bald erkennen, dafs ich für mein Pflegekind nachträglich noch Verschiedenes zu thun hatte, wenn ich es mit gutem Gewissen vertreten wollte. Bei Saxo, für den als neu Simrock in zweiter Auflage und Ettmüller zu berücksichtigen waren, fand sich Einiges in Übersetzung und Schlufsanmerkung zu verbessern und beizufügen; für Belleforest — was die Hauptsache ist — lag mir jetzt, neben der von Moltke benutzten Lyoner Ausgabe von 1581, auch die Pariser von 1582 zur Vergleichung vor, und diese bot viele für die Beurteilung der Hystorie of Hamblet mafsgebende Varianten; von dieser selbst endlich war mittlerweile ein neuer, von Hazlitt besorgter, nicht unbeachtet zu lassender Abdruck erschienen; dazu kamen noch einige, wenn auch verhältnismäfsig sehr wenige und kleine Druckfehler. Das alles legte mir die Nötigung auf, den Quellen aufser der von vornherein beabsichtigten Einleitung auch einen nicht unbeträchtlichen Anhang an Nachträgen mitzugeben. Durch letztere wurde nun allerdings das Ganze unangenehm zwiespältig. Indes dem formellen Nachteil stand doch der überwiegende materielle Vorteil gröfserer inhaltlicher Abgeschlossenheit gegenüber. Und, wie die Dinge einmal lagen, war dieser nur durch jenen zu erreichen. Auch sonstige, kleinere (wohl nicht störende) weitere Unzuträglichkeiten in äufserlichen — typographischen und orthographischen — Dingen mussten in den Kauf genommen werden, weil es hier hiefs: Sint ut sunt, aut non sint.

Dafs bei solcher Alternative Verleger und Herausgeber das einmal Vorhandene lieber, so gut es eben ging, wahren, als nutzlos verkommen lassen wollten, rechtfertigt sich hoffentlich von selbst. Neben ihren Mängeln haben unsere Hamlet-Quellen, denken wir, auch des Guten genug, sie als existenzberechtigt erscheinen zu lassen. Jedenfalls bieten sie in bequemer Vereinigung, was bisher, wenn man es suchte, da und dort zusammengetragen werden mufste und zum Teil nicht ohne Mühe zu beschaffen war; wie letzteres wenigstens für Belleforest gilt, der, in keinem Neudruck vorhanden, auf unseren Bibliotheken — zumal in der vermehrten Ausgabe von 1582 — eine mehr oder minder schwierig zu erlangende Seltenheit ist, deshalb auch, obgleich für Shakespeare gerade am ehesten in Betracht kommend und also am wichtigsten, von dessen Herausgebern und Erklärern nur äufserst selten im Original näher gekannt zu sein scheint. Aufserdem dürfte in der Gegenüberstellung des Belleforest und der Hystorie ein wesentliches Erleichterungsmittel für eine eingehendere Benutzung beider liegen. Selbst die Übersetzung des Saxo — wenn auch von dem ursprünglichen Plane einer zweisprachigen Hamlet-Ausgabe bedingt und jetzt viel-

leicht überflüssig erscheinend — wird, neben das oft wunderliche Latein des alten Chronisten gestellt, doch wohl von manchem Leser als nicht abzuweisender Vorteil empfunden werden.

Und so mögen denn die Hamlet-Quellen nun wirklich ins Dasein treten und denen, die der Vorgeschichte von Shakespeare's Meisterwerk ein genaueres Studium widmen wollen, nicht unerwünscht kommen und ihre in manchen erwähnten Beziehungen zu übende Nachsicht in anderen nicht allzusehr in Anspruch nehmen!

Leipzig, im Februar 1880.

Robert Gericke.†

NACHWORT ZUM VORWORT.

Durch den beklagenswerten Tod Dr. Gericke's, der mir ein hochherziger Freund und eifriger Mitarbeiter gewesen, ist nicht nur das Herausgeberamt an mich zurückgefallen, sondern auch die Herausgabe selbst abermals um Jahr und Tag verzögert worden; denn erst jetzt, im dreizehnten Monat nach dem Hinscheiden Dr. Gericke's, hat sich in seinem literarischen Nachlaſs das Concept der im obigen Vorwort erwähnten „Einleitung" und „Nachträge" auffinden lassen. Indem ich aus Pietät und Dankbarkeit gegen den lieben Verstorbenen diese seine letzte Shakespeare-Arbeit unverkürzt und unerweitert hiermit zum Abdruck bringe, enthülle ich gleichsam ein Denkmal, das er als ein Pfadfinder in der Shakespeare-Literatur sich selbst errichtet hat und das gewiſs manchem Hamletforscher zum Wegweiser dienen wird.

Somit übergebe ich denn, als Herausgeber meines Herausgebers, eine vor zehn Jahren von mir unternommene Arbeit, aus dem literarischen Nachlasse meines verewigten Freundes ergänzt und bis auf weitere Ermittelungen ohne selbständige Zusätze aus meiner eigenen Feder vorläufig abgeschlossen, der deutschen und ausländischen Shakespeare-Gemeinde, fest überzeugt, daſs damit wirklich eine Lücke in der Hamlet-Literatur wenigstens notdürftig ausgefüllt werde.

Welche Einblicke in die geistige Werkstätte Meister Shakespeare's, welche Aufschlüsse über den Plan und Bau, Inhalt und Wortlaut der Hamlet-Tragödie, ja selbst über das Verhältnis der beiden Quartos von 1603 und 1604 sich aus dieser Zusammenstellung des lateinischen, französischen und englischen Textes der Hamletsage gewinnen lassen, und anderseits wie wenig und ungenügend für diesen Zweck mit bloſsen Auszügen aus den in Betracht kommenden Saxo-Kapiteln und mit der Heranziehung der „Hystorie of Hamblet" ohne die Gegenüberhaltung des französischen Originals der letzteren, das jedenfalls Shakespeare's unmittelbare Quelle gewesen, seither den selbständigen Shakspeare-Forschern gedient und geholfen sein konnte: dies meinerseits zu erörtern, muſs ich für eine andere Ort- und Zeitgelegenheit mir vorbehalten. Den Kennern der ganz eigentümlichen Schöpfens- und Schaffensweise Shakespeare's wird diese Zusammenstellung seiner mittel- und unmittelbaren Quellen gewiſs ein willkommener Behelf sein, um von einem neuen Standpunkt aus nicht nur gewisse ältere Auffassungen sei es zu verteidigen, sei es zu bekämpfen, sondern auch ganz neue Ansichten zu gewinnen.

Was schlieſslich die in Dr. Gericke's Vorwort erwähnten „Unzuträglichkeiten in orthographischen Dingen" betrifft, so hat für die neugedruckten Partieen dieser Edition (für das Titelblatt und die Textseiten I—VIII und CI—CIV) die neue deutsche Schulrechtschreibung, hingegen für die variantenreichen Namen der Hamlet-Quellen gewiſs die Schreibung der Deutschen Shakespeare-Gesellschaft als Richtschnur gedient. Die vom Wortlaut des Werktitels abweichende sogenannte Norm (Titel-Angabe am Fuſse jeder ersten Bogenseite) erklärt sich aus der ursprünglichen Zugehörigkeit der Textbogen zu meiner unvollendet gebliebenen groſsen Hamlet-Biglotte.

Leipzig, im Mai 1881.

Max Moltke.

EINLEITUNG.

Unser Interesse an den Hamlet-Quellen — Saxo, Belleforest und die Hystorie vorläufig gemeinschaftlich und als gleichberechtigt so zu nennen, — gilt wesentlich den näheren oder ferneren Beziehungen, in welchen sie zu Shakespeare's Hamlet stehen. Deshalb wird ihr Verhältnis zu diesem hier orientirend zu besprechen sein.

Die Frage ist, ob und inwieweit Shakespeare diese und jene der genannten Quellen bei Abfassung seines Stückes gekannt habe und von ihr etwa zu demselben angeregt worden sei.

Dafs der Dichter die Erzählung bei Saxo Grammaticus gelesen habe, wie Theobald und Andere nach ihm meinten, ist höchst unwahrscheinlich. Denn wenn auch zu seiner Zeit bereits drei Ausgaben der Historia Danica (Paris 1514, Basel 1534, Frankfurt 1576) gedruckt waren, so lagen ihm dieselben doch nach den Orten und Zeiten ihres Erscheinens wenig nahe. Und wie immer es mit seiner Kenntnis des Lateinischen gestanden haben möge, das Latein des Saxo wird ihm schwerlich hinreichend geläufig gewesen sein. Man kann sich wohl zufällige Möglichkeiten denken, durch welche die dänische Chronik Shakespeare in die Hände gefallen und er gerade auf die Geschichte von Amleth geraten wäre: fest steht, dafs ihm der Stoff anderwärts, mindestens in der französischen Bearbeitung des Belleforest, viel leichter zugänglich war, und dafs sich in seinem Stücke nicht die geringste Spur zeigt, welche uns direct an die älteste Quelle wiese.

Sind somit bezüglich Saxo's freilich nur allgemeine und blofs negative Gründe der Unwahrscheinlichkeit geltend zu machen, so sprechen positive gegen die von Capell und Farmer herrührende, neuerdings von Collier, Delius, White, Dyce mehr oder weniger bestimmt vertretene Annahme, dafs die Hystorie of Hamblet dem Dichter für sein Stück vorgelegen habe. Von dem alten Drucke, in dem uns dieselbe erhalten ist, existirt nur noch ein einziges Exemplar (in der Capell'schen Sammlung zu Cambridge), und dieses trägt die Jahreszahl 1608, während Shakespeare's Hamlet spätestens 1602 entstanden ist, wie aus dem Eintrag in die Stationers' Registers vom 26. Juli 1602 und bald folgenden Ausgaben von 1603 und 1604 hervorgeht. Zwar hat Collier[1]), wie vor ihm schon Capell, als kaum zweifelhaft hingestellt, dafs ein älterer, uns völlig verloren gegangener Druck der Hystorie bereits ziemlich lange vor 1608, um 1585, erschienen sein müsse; allein diese Annahme schwebt so gut wie ganz in der Luft. Wenn auch Collier, erst nachträglich, eine Beweisstelle dafür in den 1863 von ihm herausgegebenen Trevelyan Papers gefunden hat, wo erzählt wird, dafs 1595 'a servant laid out for his master, for Tarleton Jests, Robin Goodfellow and Hamlet's History 6ᵈ each', so ist doch 'bei der bekannten Unzuverlässigkeit Colliers dieser Angabe bis auf weiteres kein Gewicht beizu-

---

1) Shakespeare's Library (1843), vol. I, The History of Hamlet, Introduction IV, VI. — Was Capell darüber gesagt s. bei Furnefs, Hamlet, 1877 vol. II, 87. Letzterem Bande und der Einleitung zu Shakespeare's Hamlet 1857, herausgeg. von Elze, ist so Vieles im Folgenden entnommen, dafs jener und diese immer nur kurz mit: 'Furnefs' und 'Elze' angeführt werden sollen.

legen'[1]), und selbst, wenn es seine Richtigkeit damit haben sollte, liefse sich aus ihr durchaus nichts Sicheres schliefsen, da 'Hamlet's History' eine Ballade, eine Erzählung, ein Drama, und was sonst noch bedeuten könnte, also keineswegs gerade auf unsere Hystorie of Hamblet irgend bestimmt hinwiese. Und weiter ist für Collier's Behauptung nicht das Mindeste anzuführen. Sie ist nur aus der durch gar nichts haltbaren, rein willkürlichen Voraussetzung geflossen, dafs die Hystorie of Hamblet nicht blofs Shakespeare's Hamlet von 1602, sondern auch dem alten Hamlet-Drama, für welches seit 1589 Zeugnisse vorliegen, zur Quelle gedient habe.[2])

Diese von Gervinus und Delius (E. XV) acceptirte Voraussetzung ist aber nicht allein in sich ganz grundlos, sondern es sind gute Gründe da, die für ihr gerades Gegenteil sprechen. Was Elze (H. XV Einl. 4—5) zunächst als Möglichkeit hingestellt hat, ist wohl mehr als solche und beinahe Gewifsheit: „dafs die prosaische Bearbeitung des Stoffes der dichterischen erst gefolgt, erst durch sie veranlafst worden ist." Denn „dafs ein Dichter die Geschichte von H.'s verstelltem Wahnsinn und seiner Rache aus dem Belleforest auswählte und dichterisch bearbeitete, läfst sich erklären; wie aber ein talentloser Übersetzer darauf gekommen sein sollte, diese einzelne Erzählung herauszugreifen, ohne durch eine vorhergegangene und Aufsehen erregende Dichtung darauf hingeführt worden zu sein, ist schwerer zu begreifen. Damit trifft noch der Umstand zusammen, dafs in demselben Jahr (1608) auch die prosaische Bearbeitung des Pericles von George Wilkins erschien, welche sich eingestandenermafsen auf Sh.'s Stück gründet.

Diesen meiner Ansicht nach schlagenden Ausführungen Elze's ist nun hinzuzufügen, dafs durch eine Vergleichung der Hystorie mit der Pariser Ausgabe des Belleforest die durchgehende sklavische Treue des Übersetzers noch deutlicher hervortritt, als sie Elze, der die weniger vollständige Rouener Ausgabe benutzt hat, erscheinen konnte, dafs also die von Elze hervorgehobenen Abweichungen, die sich nun geradezu als einzige zu erkennen gegeben haben, um so mehr Gewicht gewinnen.

Ob freilich jener Ausruf „A rat, a rat" nicht vielleicht schon in dem alten Stücke Hamlet vorgekommen und von Sh. nur beibehalten worden sei, läfst sich nicht ausmachen; jedenfalls klingt er sehr dramatisch. Und ebenso weist die Änderung des „lodier" in hangings und arras sehr entschieden auf die Bühne hin, wo sich der Vorgang mit der Matratze des Belleforest nicht wohl darstellen liefs, die Vorhänge dagegen eine sehr naheliegende Aushilfe boten. Und so wird es wohl als nahezu feststehend betrachtet werden können, dafs die Hystorie of Hamblet erst nach und aus Sh.'s Hamlet entstanden ist, also sicher keine Quelle Sh.'s war.

Demnach bliebe uns nur noch die Erzählung des Belleforest übrig. Und diese nun ist jedenfalls als eigentliche Quelle zu betrachten, insofern sie es ohne Zweifel gewesen, die als Vermittlung und Veranlassung der dramatischen Behandlung des Stoffes gedient hat. Wie die wiederholten Ausgaben der Histoires tragiques zeigen, waren sie gegen das Ende des XVI. Jahrh. ein beliebtes Buch, und als solches sind sie gewifs auch in England ziemlich verbreitet gewesen[3]). Die französische Sprache war für viele Leser gewifs kein Hindernis. Auch für Sh. ist sie gewifs die bestgekannte fremde Sprache gewesen, so dafs er den Belleforest lesen konnte. Und aller Wahrscheinlichkeit nach hat er ihn gelesen, wie ihm die gesamte Erzählungsliteratur seiner Tage, auch die italienische, ohne Zweifel wohlbekannt war. Vgl. Elze, William Shakespeare, p. 441. Bestimmt scheinen darauf einige Einzelheiten in der französischen Amleth-Erzählung

---

[1]) Elze, Einleitung zu Hamlet, in der Schlegel-Tieck'schen Übersetzung, herausgeg. durch die Deutsche Shakespeare-Gesellschaft. Berlin 1869, Bd. VI, 5.
[2]) Wenn man aus Farmer's Notiz, dafs er „ein Fragment der Hystorie of Hamblet in Blackletter gesehen habe", den Beweis für ein höheres Alter derselben hat gründen wollen, (Elze Hamlet XVII u. 267), so wird dieser einfach dadurch hinfällig, dafs Capell von seinem einzig noch vorhandenen Exemplar von 1608 ausdrücklich sagt: 'it is in Quarto, and black letter'. (Furnefs 87).
[3]) Für Warton's Angabe, (s. Drake 264), dafs nach den Stationers' Registers die Histoire tragiques 1596 teilweise oder ganz ins Englische übersetzt worden seien, hat sich keine Bestätigung gefunden.

hinzuweisen, die wie Keime aussehen, aus denen sich Shakespeare's Auffassung des Hamletcharakters entwickelt hat. So S. LXII unseres Abdrucks: Et dequoy sert vivre ... durable? — LXII, Marginalie: Vie miserable qui est accompagnée d'infamie. — Ferner LXVI: Je n'ay affaire icy ... impressions etc. — Andererseits LVIII, Marg.: Es grandes entreprises ne faut rien precepiter. Sind das alles auch sehr schwache Anklänge, aus denen an und für sich nichts zu schliefsen sein würde, so können sie doch recht wohl dienen, eine bereits vorhandene Wahrscheinlichkeit zu verstärken.

Nur fragt es sich, ob Sh. aus Belleforest die erste Anregung zu seinem Stücke nahm, oder ob er diese von anderer Seite her erhielt und erst darauf hin sich die französische Quelle ansah. Und in dieser Frage glaube ich mich für das Letztere als das Wahrscheinlichere entscheiden zu müssen.

Als Sh. um das Jahr 1602 seinen Hamlet schrieb, war ganz sicher schon ein älterer dramatischer Hamlet vorhanden. Bereits 1589 (oder wie Dyce vermutete vor 1587) spricht Thomas Nash in seiner Rob. Greene's Menaphon vorgedruckten Epistle von 'whole Hamlets, I should say, handfuls of tragical speeches', womit er, auch dem übrigen Inhalt der Stelle nach, nur einen Bühnen-Hamlet meinen kann. Dann findet sich in Henslowe's Tagebuche unterm 9. Juni 1594 die (in Newington Bath stattgefundene) Aufführung eines Hamlet vermerkt, der damals wohl keine Neuigkeit mehr war, wie aus der angegebenen verhältnismäfsig geringen Einnahme, die er erzielte, hervorgeht. Im Jahre 1596 endlich heifst es in Thomas Lodge's Wits Miserie von einem Kritiker: he walks for the most part in black under colour of gravity, and looks as pale as the vizard of the ghost which cried so miserably at the theatre, like an oyster wife, Hamlet revenge [1]).

An der Existenz eines alten Hamlet lange vor 1602 ist also nicht zu zweifeln, und wohl kein Kritiker je hat an ihr gezweifelt; nur über die Autorschaft des alten Stücks sind die Meinungen verschieden. Während die meisten Herausgeber und Erklärer dasselbe einem Vorgänger Shakespeare's zuschreiben, Malone und Collier sogar mit mehr oder minderer Bestimmtheit auf Thomas Kyd als Autor schliefsen [2]), vertreten dagegen besonders Knight und Elze, auch Brown (F. 6) die Ansicht, dafs Shakespeare selbst der Verfasser auch des alten, später von ihm ein- oder mehrmals umgearbeiteten Hamlet gewesen sei.

Und wenngleich letztere Ansicht gewifs hauptsächlich in dem Wunsche begründet ist, unserm Dichter die Urheberschaft seines Hauptwerkes so voll als möglich zu wahren, so hat sie doch auch — abgesehen von sehr fraglichen, da und dorther genommenen Mutmafsungen (Elze H. XVII f. XX—XXIV) — einen positiven Anhalt, der sie sehr entschieden zu stützen scheint. Denn Steevens fand in einem Exemplar von Speght's Ausgabe des Chaucer, welches dem Dr. Gabriel Harvey (dem Gegner des Thomas Nash) gehört hatte, die handschriftliche Notiz desselben: „The younger sort take much delight in Sh.'s Venus and Adonis; but his Lucrece, and his tragedy of Hamlet, Prince of Denmarke, have it in them to please the wiser sort. 1598." Danach zu schliefsen, müfste wenigstens soviel als feststehend betrachtet werden, dafs ein Hamlet von Shakespeare bereits 1598 vorhanden war.

Nur ist leider die Beweiskraft der angeführten Notiz bei weitem nicht so sicher, als es nach Steevens' Angabe aussieht. Denn jene Ausgabe des Chaucer ist im Jahre 1598 erschienen, Malone — der den betreffenden Band sah und auf dessen Zuverlässigkeit wir wohl trauen dürfen — „on an attentive examination, found reason to believe, that the note in question may have been written in the latter end of the year 1600. Harvey doubtless purchased this volume in 1598, having, both at the beginning and end of it, written his name. But it by no means follows that all the intermediate remarks which are scattered throughout were put down at the same time. He speaks of translated Tasso (Furnefs 10) in one passage, and the first edition of Fairfax, which is doubtless alluded to, appeared in 1600. Könnte sich auch die Erwähnung des Tasso, wie Singer bemerkt hat,

---

[1]) Dafs 1596 auch Joseph Taylor die Titelrolle in einem Hamlet gespielt haben soll, wie Drake 203 (ohne Gewährsmann) angiebt, scheint auf einem Irrtum zu beruhen; s. Elze W. Sh. 305.
[2]) Aber s. Elze Übers. 6: „Lowndes ... alle Beweise".

auf eine Übersetzung der ersten 5 Bücher des „Jerusalem, published by R. C[arew] in 1594" beziehen, so wird doch nach Malone die Tragweite der Notiz Harvey's im höchsten Grade fraglich; es ist sogar möglich, dafs Harvey sie erst viel später („in any one of the thirty years which he lived after the book came into his possession") — Hamlet, ed. by Clark and Wright, Clarendon Press books 1872, Preface IX) geschrieben habe, wie ja Malone das Jahr 1600 gewifs nur angenommen hat, weil er aus andern Gründen die Entstehung von Shakespeare's Hamlet in dieses Jahr setzte. Leider hat Malone nicht angegeben, ob er die Jahreszahl 1598 unmittelbar hinter der Notiz geschrieben fand oder nicht. Und, leider! ist es nicht mehr möglich, die Sache weiter zu prüfen, da der in Rede stehende Band in der Bibliothek des Bischofs Percy mit dieser durch einen Brand zu Grunde gegangen ist, ein für die definitive Festsetzung der Hamlet-Chronologie schwerer Verlust.

Somit ist der positive Anhalt für die Ansicht Knight's und Elze's, dafs Sh. selbst der Verfasser des alten Hamlet, jedenfalls doch nur ein überaus schwacher. Und andererseits sind gute, weit überwiegende Gründe für die entgegengesetzte Ansicht vorhanden; dafs Francis Meres in der bekannten Stelle aus seiner Palladis Tamia, 1598, unter den 12 Stücken, die er von Sh. aufführt, Hamlet nicht erwähnt, ist gewifs von einem Gewicht, das allen Bemühungen, es zu verringern, standhalten dürfte. (Elze, H. XIX f.) Hat Meres den Titus Andronicus der Erwähnung wert gehalten, warum soll er den Hamlet übergangen haben? Stellt doch Elze selbst (XXI) beide auf ganz gleiche Wertstufe; nach den Anspielungen aber bei Nash und Lodge war Hamlet ungleich gegebener. Worin hätte also Meres, wenn er aus einer gröfseren Anzahl ihm bekannter Stücke Sh.'s nur eine Auswahl treffen wollte, nicht lieber diesen statt jenen als „Zeugen" für den Dichter aufgerufen? Und welche bereits 1598 vorhandenen, von Meres aber bei der Auswahl unberücksichtigt gelassenen Stücke kann denn Elze angeben, aufser Pericles und Heinrich VI.? Dadurch, dafs der alte Hamlet so mit Pericles und Heinrich VI. in einer Linie zu stehen kommt, gewinnt er keineswegs einen höheren Anspruch an Shakespeare's Autorschaft. Im Gegenteil beweist Meres' Schweigen betreffs jener zwei Stücke nur seine Gewissenhaftigkeit und dafs er wohl auch bezüglich Hamlets in vollem Rechte war, ihn nicht unter Shakespeare's Werken zu nennen. Kurz, ich kann die Stelle durchaus nicht mit Elze als „durchaus unerheblich für die Zeit der Abfassung des Hamlet" betrachten. Wenn gegen die von Elze vertretene Ansicht ferner geltend gemacht worden ist, dafs die bei Nash-Lodge sich findenden Citate „Blood is a beggar und Hamlet revenge in Shakespeare's (uns vorliegendem) Stück nicht vorkommen, und dafs Shakespeare, wenn er schon 1589 oder gar 1587 einen Hamlet geschrieben hatte, damals erst 25 oder 23 Jahr alt gewesen wäre: so kann ich diesen Gründen allerdings kein sonderliches Gewicht beimessen. Wohl aber scheint es mir noch sehr der Beachtung wert zu sein, vgl. Malone (F. 5), dafs wir für kein Stück Sh.'s nachweisen können, dafs der Dichter es nach einem früheren eigenen, für mehrere dagegen, dafs er sie auf Grundlage von älteren Stücken anderer Verfasser umgearbeitet habe; dafs also die Wahrscheinlichkeit auch für Hamlet auf fremde Autorschaft der Vorlage hinweist. Und obgleich es Elze für bei weitem naturgemäfser hält, dafs der Dichter erst durch mehrfache Überarbeitungen den ursprünglich rohen Stoff allmählich zum vollendetsten Meisterwerk umgebildet habe: mir meinesteils will es zu Sh.'s (nach allem, was wir von ihm wissen,) praktischer, leichtschaffender, um das Geschaffene nicht weiter ängstlich sorgender Art viel besser stimmen, dafs auch sein Hamlet, im wesentlichen, auf einen Wurf entstanden und so zu sagen „fertig aus dem Haupte des Dichters hervorgesprungen" sei.

Somit ist es nun, meines Erachtens, höchst wahrscheinlich und fast sicher, dafs der alte Hamlet, der schon 1589 auf der Bühne war, nicht Shakespeare, sondern einen Vorgänger desselben — wohl einen Nacheiferer Kyd's, nicht diesen selbst — zum Verfasser gehabt hat.

Dies angenommen, spricht aber auch alle Wahrscheinlichkeit dafür, dafs der Vor-Shakespearische Hamlet die nächste, eigentliche Quelle des Shakespearischen gewesen sei. War ersterer doch vielleicht — wie aus dem Datum des oben erwähnten Vermerks in Henslowe's Tagebuch zu schliefsen — im Jahre 1596 von Shakespeare selbst und

seiner Gesellschaft, die damals zeitweise in Newington Bath spielte, zur Aufführung gebracht worden. Jedenfalls lag ihm das alte Drama viel näher und bot ihm den bereits dramatisirten Stoff viel handlicher als die ungefüge, langatmige Erzählung des Belleforest, die von Shakespeare, als er an die Erneuerung des aus ihr geflossenen Stückes ging, nicht ganz unberücksichtigt geblieben sein mag, aus der er sich aber schwerlich viel nehmen konnte, höchstens, wie gesagt, einige Winke für seinen Hamlet-Charakter.

Und so wäre denn das schliefsliche Resultat, dafs wir die anfangs gestellte Frage im wesentlichen nur negativ beantworten können. Belleforest's Amleth ist gewifs eine Hamlet-Quelle, insofern er dem Vor-Shakespearischen Bühnen-Hamlet zu Grunde gelegen hat und also gewissermafsen Grofsvaterstelle bei Shakespeare's Hamlet vertritt. Ebenso, nur noch einen Grad weiter zurück, ist der Amlethus des Saxo als Vorfahre des Shakespearischen Hamlet zu betrachten, weil Belleforest jedenfalls aus Saxo schöpfte. Aber als direkte, nächste Shakespeare-Quelle kann ersterer wohl höchstens nur in sehr beschränktem Mafse, letzterer wohl gar nicht gelten. Und die Hystorie of Hamblet hat aller Wahrscheinlichkeit nach auf den Namen einer Hamlet-Quelle sogar nur insoweit Anspruch, als sie lange mehr oder minder allgemein für eine solche gehalten worden ist, während es jetzt ziemlich feststehen dürfte, dafs sie dies nicht, vielmehr erst ein Nach-Shakespearisches Produkt ist.

Damit ist nun freilich unseren Hamlet-Quellen das Interesse der direkten Einwirkung auf Shakespeare abgesprochen. Allein das wird ihnen ihr Interesse überhaupt nicht nehmen können. Denn immerhin stehen sie doch in näherer oder fernerer Beziehung zu dem Haupt- und Meisterwerke unseres Dichters, und niemand, der sich ein bestimmtes Urteil über die Entstehung, über die wirkliche Quelle desselben bilden will, wird umhin können, ihnen eine gründliche Beachtung zu widmen; so negativ deren Ergebnis auch ausfallen mag, so unbedingt nötig ist es doch zur Gewinnung einer positiven Ansicht.

Das alte Stück, auf welches unsere Auseinandersetzungen als mutmafslich eigentliche Quelle Sh.'s geführt haben, ist uns leider verloren gegangen, es wurde gewifs nie gedruckt. Nur eine Nachbildung, eine Art schwacher Wiederschein desselben, scheint uns übrig geblieben zu sein in der alten deutschen Tragoedia: Der bestrafte Brudermord oder Prinz Hamlet aus Dännemark, die wir freilich nur in einem erst von 1710 datirten Manuscript, abgedruckt in Reichards Olla potrida (1781) und in Cohns Shakespeare in Germany (1865) besitzen, die aber wohl in der Hauptsache identisch ist mit der von den englischen Comödianten 1626 in Dresden aufgeführten Tragoedia von Hamlet einem printzen in Dennemark. Auf ihre Bedeutung in der angegebenen Beziehung haben schon Bernhardi (Sh.'s Hamlet, Hamburger literarisch-kritische Blätter, 1857) und Latham (Two Dissertations, London 1812) hingewiesen; aber sie ist doch vielleicht noch nicht genug gewürdigt worden, insofern sie uns wohl bestimmtere Anhaltspunkte für die Entwickelung der Shakespearischen Neugestaltung sowohl als auch für die Entstehung des aus Altem und Neuem zusammengeflickten Textes der Quarto von 1603 geben konnte. Doch dies zu verfolgen ist hier nicht der Ort.

Ebenso kann hier schliefslich nur noch kurz erwähnt werden, dafs Stoll (s. Furnefs II, 79) meint, Shakespeare habe seinen Hamlet einer auf Saxo beruhenden Historia des Hans Sachs (Ausg. v. Keller VIII, 591) entnommen, die ihm auf seinen Reisen in Deutschland bekannt geworden; und dafs Büchner (Hamlet le Danois, Paris 1878, S. 81—95) in einer alten (ebenfalls Saxo folgenden) Dänischen Reimchronik von Pedersen oder Niels eine Quelle des Vor-Shakespearischen Hamlet zu sehen glaubt.

R. G.

QUELLEN.

I.

Aus des Saxo Grammaticus Dänischer Geschichte.[1]

...Horvendillus et Fengo, quorum pater Gervendillus, Jutorum praefectus, extiterat, eidem a Rorico in Jutiae praesidium subrogantur. At Horvendillus, triennio tyrannide gesta, per summam rerum gloriam piraticae incubuerat, cum Rex Norvagiae Collerus, operum ejus ac famae magnitudinem aemulatus, decorum sibi fore existimavit, si tam late patentem piratae fulgorem superior armis obscurare quivisset. Cujus classem varia fretum navigatione scrutatus offendit. Insula erat medio sita pelago, quam piratae collatis utrinquesecus navigiis obtinebant. Invitabat duces jucunda littorum species; hortabatur exterior locorum amoenitas interiora nemorum verna perspicere lustratisque saltibus secretam sylvarum indaginem pererrare. Ubi forte Collerum Horvendillumque invicem sine arbitris obvios incessus reddidit. Tunc Horvendillus prior regem percontari nisus, quo pugnae genere decernere libeat, praestantissimum affirmans, quod paucissimorum viribus ederetur. Duellum siquidem ad capessendam fortitudinis palmam omni certaminis genere efficacius fore, quod propria virtute subnixum, alienae manus opem excluderet. Tam fortem juvenis sententiam admirans Collerus, cum mihi, inquit,

... Horvendil und Fengo, die Söhne Gervendils, wurden von Rorik, König von Dänemark, an ihres verstorbenen Vaters Stelle zu Statthaltern über Jütland gesetzt. Nach dreijähriger Herrschaft hatte sich Horvendil einen so groszen Ruhm als Seeheld erworben, dass der König von Norwegen, Koller, ihm diesen Ruhm beneidete und sich einen nicht geringen Zuwachs seines eigenen versprach, wenn es ihm gelänge, den weitgepriesenen Nebenbuhler im Waffenkampfe zu überwinden. Auf langen Meerfahrten suchte er dessen Flotte, bis er sie endlich traf. An einer Insel mitten im Meer waren die beiden Seehelden, von zwei Seiten her, mit ihren Schiffen gelandet; die reizenden Gestade luden die Führer ein, sie zu betreten; die Freundlichkeit der Umgebungen lockte sie in das Innere der Haine und tiefer und tiefer in das Dunkel des Waldes: da stieszen Koller und Horvendil, beide ohne Gefährten, von ungefähr auf einander. Horvendil zuerst stellte an den König die Frage, welche Art des Kampfes er wähle; er selbst ziehe diejenige vor, welche die Kräfte von möglichst Wenigen in Anspruch nehme; der Zweikampf werde am besten geeignet sein, um durch ihn den Ruhm der Tapferkeit zu gewinnen, weil er sich auf die eigene Kraft stütze und die Hülfe eines fremden Armes ausschliesze. Diese kräftige Meinung des Jünglings bewundernd, antwortete Koller: Da du mir die Wahl des Kampfes

---

[1] Saxonis Grammatici Historia Danica, ed. Müller et Velschow, Havniae 1839—58, Vol. I, Liber III p. 135—149, Liber IV p. 150—161. — Dieser Ausgabe sind auch die

pugnae delectum permiseris, maxime utendum judico, quae tumultuationis expers duorum operam capit. Sane et audacior et victoriae promptior aestimatur. In hoc communis nobis sententia est, hoc ultro judicio convenimus. At quoniam exitus in dubio manet, invicem humanitati deferendum est, nec adeo ingeniis indulgendum, ut extrema negligantur officia. Odium in animis est; adsit tamen pietas, quae rigori demum opportuna succedat. Nam etsi mentium nos discrimina separant, naturae tamen jura conciliant. Horum quippe consortio jungimur, quantuscunque animos livor dissociet.[2]) Haec itaque pietatis nobis conditio sit, ut victum victor inferiis prosequatur. His enim suprema humanitatis officia inesse constat, quae nemo pius abhorruit. Utraque acies id munus, rigore deposito, concorditer exequatur. Facessat post fatum livor simultasque funere sopiatur. Absit nobis tantae crudelitatis specimen, ut, quanquam vivis odium intercesserit, alter alterius cineres persequamur. Gloriosum victori erit, si victi funus magnifice duxerit. Nam qui defuncto hosti justa persolverit, superstitis sibi favorem adsciscit, vivumque beneficio vincit, quisquis extincto studium humanitatis impenderit. Est et alia non minus luctuosa calamitas, quae vivis interdum damnata corporum parte contingit. Huic non segnius quam ultimae sorti succurrendum existimo. Saepe enim incolumi spiritu membrorum clades pugnantibus incidit; quae sors omni fato tristior duci solet, quod mors omnium memoriam tollat, vivens vero proprii corporis stragem negligere nequeat. Hoc quoque malum ope excipiendum est. Conveniat igitur, alterius ab altero laesionem denis auri talentis sarciri.[3]) Nam si pium est alienis calamitatibus compati, quanto

überlässest, so wähle ich den, welcher, ohne viel Lärmens, unter Zweien allein ausgemacht wird. Gewiss ist er der kühnste und entscheidet am besten den Sieg. Darin stimmen wir überein. Aber weil der Ausgang in Zweifel bleibt, müssen wir auch auf das bedacht sein, was die Menschlichkeit fordert, damit nicht der Sieger sich vom Stolze hinreissen lasse, der letzten Pflichten gegen den Besiegten zu vergessen. Wir mögen uns innerlich hassen, aber doch muss eine fromme Rücksicht da sein, welcher die Härte endlich, zur rechten Zeit, weicht. Denn wenn uns auch die Verschiedenheit des Geistes trennt, so versöhnen uns doch die Rechte der Natur; ihre Gemeinschaft macht uns einig, welche Misgunst uns auch scheide. Das also sei die Rücksicht unserer Frömmigkeit, dass der Sieger dem Besiegten Todtenopfer weihe. Denn darin liegen die höchsten Pflichten der Menschlichkeit, die kein Frommer vernachlässigt. Jeder Teil vollbringe friedlich, den Hass vergessend, dieses Amt; mit dem Tode weiche der Neid, im Grabe schlafe aller Groll. Fern von uns sei es, solche Grausamkeit zu zeigen, dass wir, obgleich im Leben Feinde, der Eine des Andern Asche ein Leid antue. Für den Sieger wird es ruhmwürdig sein, wenn er des Besiegten Leiche ehrt. Denn wer dem todten Feinde sein Recht giebt, erwirbt sich die Gunst der Hinterbliebenen; den Lebenden besiegt durch seine Wohltat, wer dem Geschiedenen den Zoll der Menschlichkeit zahlt. — Und ein anderes nicht minder trauriges Leiden ist es, das bisweilen dem Lebenden zustöszt, durch die Einbusze eines Teiles seines Körpers. Dafür müssen wir, meine ich, nicht geringere Sorge tragen, als für den Fall des Todes. Denn oft befällt den Kämpfenden bei heilem Geiste ein Verlust von Gliedern, und das achtet Jedermann für ein traurigeres Geschick als den Untergang, weil der Tod alles Gedächtnis endet, der Lebende aber die Niederlage des eigenen Körpers nicht vergessen und verwinden kann. Auch für dies Uebel ist eine Vorsorge nötig. Es möge also festgesetzt sein, dass jeder die Verletzung des Anderen mit zehn Mark Goldes büsze. Denn wenn es recht ist, Mitgefühl zu haben mit fremden Leiden, um

---

hier in Auszug und Übersetzung gegebenen Noten entlehnt.

Saxo Grammaticus lebte um 1150—1220 und schrieb sein Werk um 1180—1208. Ausgaben desselben, vor der angeführten, erschienen: Parisiis 1514 (Editio princeps), Basileae 1534, Francofurti a. M. 1576, Sorae 1644 sq. (ed. Stephanius), Lipsiae 1771 (ed. Klotz). Handschriften sind nicht vorhanden.

[2]) Die Ed. pr. hat animo livor dissociet; wohl nur Druckfehler.

[3]) Der Vertrag zwischen Horvendil und

magis propriis misereri? Nemo naturae non consulit; quam qui negligit, sui parricida est.

In haec data acceptaque fide, pugnam ineunt. Neque enim eis aut mutui occursus novitas, aut vernantis loci jucunditas, quo minus inter se ferro occurrerent, respectui fuit. Horvendillus, appetendi hostis, quam muniendi corporis nimio animi calore avidior redditus, neglecta clypei cura, ambas ferro manus injecerat. Nec audaciae eventus defuit. Collerum siquidem, scuto crebris ictibus absumpto spoliatum, desecto tandem pede exanimem occidere coegit. Quem, ne pacto abesset, regio funere elatum magnifici operis tumulo ingentique exequiarum apparatu prosequutus est. Deinde sororem ejus, Selam nomine, piraticis exercitam rebus ac bellici peritam muneris, persequutus occidit. Triennium fortissimis militiae operibus emensus opima spolia delectamque praedam Rorico destinat, quo sibi propiorem amicitiae ejus gradum conscisceret. Cujus familiaritate fultus filiae ejus Geruthae connubium impetravit, ex qua filium Amlethum sustulit.

Tantae felicitatis invidia accensus Fengo fratrem insidiis circumvenire constituit. Adeo ne a necessariis quidem secura est virtus. At ubi datus parricidio locus, cruenta manu funestam mentis libidinem satiavit. Trucidati quoque fratris uxore potitus, incestum parricidio adjecit. Quisquis enim uni se flagitio dederit, in aliud mox proclivior ruit; ita alterum alterius incitamentum est. Idem atrocitatem facti tanta calliditatis audacia texit, ut sceleris excusationem benevolentiae simulatione componeret parricidiumque pietatis nomine coloraret. Gerutham siquidem, quanquam tantae mansuetudinis esset, ut neminem vel tenui laesione commoverit, incitatissimum

*

Koller weicht ab von dem was sonst beim Zweikampfe Gebrauch war, wonach der zuerst Verwundete ein Lösegeld an den Sieger zu zahlen hatte.

wie viel mehr, sich der eigenen zu erbarmen! Niemand ist, der nicht für sich selbst sorgte; wer es unterlässt, wird sein eigener Mörder.

Nachdem sie sich darauf das Wort gegeben, schritten sie zum Kampfe; denn weder das Ungewöhnliche ihrer zufälligen Begegnung, noch die Lieblichkeit des blühenden Ortes hatte Macht über ihr Vorhaben. Horvendil, im Feuer seines Mutes mehr auf den Angriff des Feindes als auf die Wahrung des Leibes bedacht, liesz den Schild bei Seite und fasste das Schwert mit beiden Händen. Und der Kühnheit fehlte nicht der Erfolg. Schlag auf Schlag gegen Koller seine Streiche führend, entblöszte er ihn des Schildes, und stürzte ihn endlich, ihm das Bein abhauend, entseelt zu Boden. Treu dem Vertrage gab er ihm eine königliche Bestattung und ein prächtiges Grabmal und eine glänzende Leichenfeier; dann wandte er sich gegen Kollers Schwester, Sela mit Namen, eine im Seekampf gewaltige Kriegerin, und besiegte und erschlug sie. Nach den herrlichsten Kriegstaten, drei Jahre hindurch, brachte Horvendil dem König Rorik die Waffen der Besiegten und eine erlesene Beute zum Geschenk, um sich dessen Gunst in noch höherem Grade zu erwerben. Und er machte sich ihn so zum Freunde, dass er seine Tochter Geruthe zur Gemahlin erhielt, die ihm einen Sohn, Amleth, gebar.

Solches Glück liesz Fengo von Neid entbrennen und auf den Tod des Bruders sinnen. So ist der Tugendhafte selbst vor den Nächstangehörigen nicht sicher. Als Ort und Zeit sich dem Morde günstig erwiesen, sättigte er mit blutiger Hand das entsetzliche Gelüste des Herzens. Und indem er des erschlagenen Bruders Gattin gewann, fügte er zum Morde noch Blutschande. Denn wer sich der einen Schuld ergeben, stürzt bald um so jäher in die andere; die erste ist der Anreiz zur zweiten. Und Fengo bedeckte die Schändlichkeit der Tat mit so vermessener Schlauheit, dass er das Verbrechen mit dem Vorwand wohlwollender Absicht beschönigte und den Brudermord zum Liebesdienste färbte: er sagte, Geruthe, obgleich sie in ihrer Sanftmut Niemand das kleinste Leid zugefügt hätte, sei von ihrem Gemahl mit dem

2*

tamen mariti odium expertam, salvandaeque ejus gratia fratrom a se interfectum dicebat, quod mitissimam et sine felle foeminam gravissimum viri supercilium perpeti indignum videretur. Nec irrita propositi persvasio fuit. Neque enim apud principes fides mendacio deest, ubi scurris interdum gratia redditur, obtrectatoribus honos. Nec dubitavit Fengo parricidales manus flagitiosis inferre complexibus, geminae impietatis noxam pari scelere prosequutus. Quod videns Amlethus, ne prudentius agendo patruo suspectus redderetur, stoliditatis simulationem amplexus extremum mentis vitium finxit, eoque calliditatis genere non solum ingenium texit, verum etiam salutem defendit. Quotidie maternum larem pleno sordium torpore complexus, abjectum humi corpus obscoeni squaloris illuvie respergebat. Turpatus oris color illitaque tabo facies ridiculae stoliditatis dementiam figurabant. Quicquid voce edebat, deliramentis consentaneum erat; quicquid opere exhibuit, profundam redolebat inertiam. Quid multa? Non virum aliquem, sed delirantis fortunae ridendum diceres monstrum. Interdum foco assidens favillasque manibus verrens ligneos uncos creare [4]) eosdemque igni durare solitus erat; quorum extrema contrariis quibusdam hamis, quo nexuum tenaciores existerent, informabat. Rogatus, quid ageret, acuta se referebat in ultionem patris spicula praeparare. Nec parvo responsum ludibrio fuit, quod ab omnibus ridiculi operis vanitas contemneretur, quanquam ea res proposito ejus postmodum opitulata fuerit. Quae solertia apud altioris ingenii spectatores primam ei calliditatis suspicionem injecit. Ipsa namque exiguae artis industria arcanum opificis ingenium figurabat. Nec credi poterat obtusi cordis esse, qui tam exculto manus artificio calluisset. Denique

bittersten Hass verfolgt worden, und um sie zu retten, habe er den Bruder getötet, da es ihm unerträglich gewesen, dass ein so liebe- und gütevolles Weib dem wilden Groll ihres Mannes ausgesetzt sein sollte. Und sein Vorgeben ermangelte nicht des erwünschten Erfolges; denn bei den Groszen findet die Lüge leicht Eingang, wie ja Narren bei ihnen oft Gunst, und Verlaümder Ehre gewinnen. So hatte denn Fengo kein Bedenken, sich mit von Brudermord befleckten Händen in verbrecherische Umarmungen zu stürzen und die Schuld doppelten Frevels auf sich zu laden. Als Amleth das sah, griff er, damit er nicht durch kluges Handeln dem Oheim verdächtig werde, zu erkünstelter Geistesschwäche und stellte sich, als sei er vollkommen von Sinnen; auf diese Weise verdeckte er seinen Verstand und wahrte sein Heil. Täglich erschien er von Schmutz starrend und warf sich zur Erde und besudelte sich mit dem Unrat des Bodens; die entstellte Farbe des Gesichtes, das er mit widriger Feuchtigkeit bestrich, liesz auf den Wahnwitz eines Verrückten schlieszen; was er sprach, klang blödsinnig; was er vornahm, sah nach völliger Geistesabwesenheit aus. Kurz, nicht einen Menschen, sondern ein von der Natur vernachlässigtes, zu Spott und Hohn gebornes Misgeschöpf musste man in ihm erblicken. Oft, am Herde sitzend und die Asche mit den Händen zusammenkehrend, schnitzte er krumme Stäbchen aus Holz, die er am Feuer härtete und an der Spitze mit Widerhaken versah, wodurch sie um so geeigneter zum festen Zusammenheften wurden; und wenn man ihn fragte, was er da mache, sagte er, er sorge für scharfe Spiesze, den Tod seines Vaters zu rächen. Diese Antwort trug ihm nicht wenig Spott ein, weil man fast allgemein die Eitelkeit des scheinbar törichten Beginnens verlachte, das ihm doch nachher bei der Ausführung seines Vorhabens grosze Hülfe leistete. „Bei schärferen Beobachtern aber erregte diese Tätigkeit zuerst den Argwohn listiger Verstellung gegen ihn; denn das Geschick selbst bei so geringfügiger Arbeit deutete auf verborgene Anlagen, und der, dessen Hand eine so kunstreiche Spielerei schuf, konnte kaum ein Stumpfsinniger sein.

---

[4]) Es liegt vielleicht ein Wortspiel zu Grunde; denn im Isländischen bedeutet Krokr (dänisch Krog) zugleich Haken und Hinterlist, zweideutiges Wesen.

exactissima cura praeustorum stipitum congeriem asservare solebat. Fuere ergo, qui illum vegetioris ingenii asserentes, sapientiam simplicitatis praetextu occulere profundumque animi studium calliditatis commento obscurare putarent, nec aptius astum deprehendi posse, quam si illi inter latebras usquam excellentis formae foemina applicaretur, quae animum ejus ad amoris illecebras provocaret. Naturae siquidem tam praeceps in venerem esse ingenium, ut arte dissimulari non possit; vehementiorem quoque hunc motum fore, quam ut astu interpellari queat, ideoque, si is inertiam fingeret, futurum, ut occasione suscepta voluptatis illico viribus obtemperaret. Procurantur igitur, qui juvenem in longinquas nemorum partes equo perductum eo tentamenti genere aggrederentur. Inter quos forte quidam Amlethi collacteus aderat, a cujus animo nondum sociae educationis respectus exciderat. Hic praeteriti convictus memoriam praesenti imperio anteponens, Amlethum inter deputatos comites instruendi potius quam insidiandi studio prosequebatur, quod eum ultima passurum non dubitaret, si vel modicum sensati animi indicium praebuisset, maxime vero, si veneris palam rebus uteretur. Quod ipsi quoque Amletho obscurum non fuit. Equum siquidem conscendere jussus, ita se de cervice industria collocavit,[5]) ut suum ipsius cervici dorsum obvertens adversa cauda fronte spectaret. Quam frenis quoque complecti coepit, perinde atque ea parte ruentis equi impetum moderaturus. Qua astutiae meditatione patrui commentum elusit, insidias expugnavit. Ridiculum satis·spectaculum fuit, cum idem, habenae expers, regente cauda sessore procurreret.

Procedens Amlethus, cum obvium inter arbusta lupum habuisset, comitibus tene-

---

[5]) cervice ist von Stephanius (wohl mit Recht) gestrichen.

Dann wandte er auch die gröszte Sorge darauf, die gehärteten und zugeschnitzten Stäbchen zu sammeln und aufzubewahren. Es kamen also Einige zu der Überzeugung, dass er gesunden Geistes sei und wohl nur seine Klugheit unter dem Vorwande der Einfalt verberge, ein tiefes Streben mit erdichteter Torheit verhüllend; und dass das beste Mittel zur Entdeckung der List sein würde, wenn man ihm irgendwo im Verborgenen ein schönes Weib zuführe, die sein Herz zu Liebeslust entzünde; denn zu fleischlichem Genusse sei der Sinn so geneigt, dass dagegen keine Kunst der Verstellung Stand halte, und diesen Antrieb werde keine Schlauheit zu bewältigen im Stande sein; deshalb dürfe man erwarten, dass Amleth, wenn sein Wahnwitz ein angenommener sei, die dargebotene Gelegenheit ergreifen und sich sogleich der Wollust hingeben werde. So wurden denn Etliche bestellt, die den Jüngling zu Pferde in einen entlegenen Teil des Waldes geleiten und ihn auf die angegebene Art prüfen sollten. Zufällig war unter ihnen ein Milchbruder des Prinzen, in dessen Herzen die Rücksichten der Freundschaft gegen den Gefährten der Kindheit noch nicht ihre Geltung verloren hatten. Dieser, das Andenken des früheren Zusammenlebens höher achtend als das Gebot seines gegenwärtigen Herrn, hatte sich den gewählten Begleitern Amleth's angeschlossen, als Warner und Berater vielmehr denn als Versucher, weil er nicht zweifelte, dass ihm das Ärgste geschehen werde, wenn er das geringste Zeichen klaren Verstandes gäbe, vorzüglich aber, wenn er sich offen der sinnlichen Lust überliesze. Und Amleth selbst wusste das; deswegen setzte er sich, als er das Pferd besteigen sollte, absichtlich so, dass er seinen Rücken gegen den Nacken des Pferdes kehrte und den Schwanz mit dem Gesicht ansah; er zäumte es an demselben, als wolle er so den Lauf des Pferdes lenken. Durch diese List wich er dem Anschlag des Oheims aus und entkräftete seine Nachstellungen. Ein lächerlicher Anblick war es, als das Pferd, der Zügel ledig, mit seinem Reiter, der es am Schwanze hielt, davonlief.

Im Fortgange der Reise stiesz man im Gebüsch auf einen Wolf, und als seine Be-

rioris aetatis equum occurrisse dicentibus, perpaucos hujusmodi in Fengonis grege militare subjunxit, ut modesto, ita faceto imprecationis genere⁶) patrui divitias insequutus. Qui cum illum prudenti responso usum astruerent, ipse quoque se de industria locutum asseverabat, ne aliqua ex parte mendacio indulgere videretur. Falsitatis enim alienus haberi cupiens, ita astutiam veriloquio permiscebat, ut nec dictis veracitas deesset nec acuminis modus verorum indicio ⁷) proderetur.

Idem littus praeteriens, cum comites, invento periclitatae navis gubernaculo, cultrum a se eximiae granditatis repertum dixissent, eo, inquit, praegrandem pernam secari convenit, profecto mare significans, cujus immensitati gubernaculi magnitudo congrueret. Arenarum quoque praeteritis clivis, sabulum perinde ac farra aspicere jussus⁸), eadem albicantibus maris procellis permolita esse respondit. Laudato a comitibus responso, idem a se prudenter editum asseverabat. Ab iisdem, quo majorem exercendae libidinis audaciam sumeret, de industria relictus, immissam a patruo foeminam, perinde ac fortuito oblatam, obscuro loco obviam recepit, constuprassetque, ni collacteus ejus tacito consilii genere insidiarum indicium detulisset. Considerans enim, quonam aptius modo occultum monitoris officium exequi periculosamque juvenis lasciviam praecurrere posset, repertam humi paleam oestri praetervolantis caudae submittendam curavit. ⁹) Egit deinde ipsum in ea potissimum loca, quibus Amlethum inesse cognovit; eoque facto maximum incauto beneficium attulit. Nec callidius transmissum indicium, quam cognitum fuit. Siquidem Amlethus, viso oestro simulque stramine, quod caudae insitum gestabat,

gleiter zu Amleth sagten, es sei ein junges Pferd gewesen, erwiderte er, derartige Streitrosse gebe es sehr wenige in Fengos Gestüten, womit er ebenso versteckt als witzig den Reichtümern seines Oheims den Untergang anwünschte. Und auf die Bemerkung der Begleiter, dass er da sehr klug geantwortet, versicherte er, mit voller Absicht gesprochen zu haben; damit er sich auf keine Weise der Lüge schuldig mache. Denn indem er sich immer fern von Trug zu halten wünschte, paarte er dergestalt List mit Wahrheit, dass diese seinen.Worten stets zum Grunde lag, und das Masz seines Scharfsinns sich doch nicht durch Anzeichen des Wahren verriet.

Ebenso, als sie weiter an das Ufer des Meeres kamen und die Begleiter das Steuer eines gestrandeten Schiffes, das sie fanden, für ein mächtig groszes Messer ausgaben, äuszerte Amleth, mit dem müsse ein ungeheurer Schinken geschnitten werden; womit er in der Tat das Meer meinte, dessen unermesslicher Ausdehnung die Grösze des Steuerruders entspreche. Dann, als sie auf Dünen trafen und er den Sand für Mehl ansehen sollte, antwortete er, das sei von den Wogen des Meeres gemahlen worden; und da die Begleiter auch diese Antwort lobten, versicherte er wieder, sie mit bewusster Klugheit gegeben zu haben. Endlich wurde er von jenen absichtlich, damit er um so kühner seiner Lust nachgebe, allein gelassen und ihm das von seinem Oheim bestimmte Mädchen, als ob es ihm zufällig begegne, an einem dunklen Orte in den Weg gebracht; und er hätte sich diese Gelegenheit auch zu Nutze gemacht, wenn ihm nicht sein Milchbruder auf versteckte Art einen Wink hätte zukommen lassen über den ihm gelegten Hinterhalt. Darauf bedacht, wie am besten er ihm eine geheime Warnung geben und einer gefährlichen Ausschreitung des Jünglings zuvorkommen könne, befestigte derselbe einen am Boden gefundenen Halm an den Schwanz einer vorbeifliegenden Bremse und trieb diese dann dahin, wo Amleth, wie er wusste, war. Und dadurch erzeigte er dissem, den seine Vorsicht verlassen wollte, den gröszten Dienst. Der Wink wurde so scharfsinnig verstanden, als er erteilt war; Amleth, die Bremse sehend und den Halm an ihrem

---

⁶) Amleth wünscht nämlich dem Fengo Wölfe als Zerstörer seines Glücks, indem er sagt, derselbe habe sehr wenige (d. h. zu wenige) solcher Pferde, wie ihm seine Begleiter eines gezeigt.
⁷) indicio ist die Verbesserung Madvigs für judicio der Ausgaben.
⁸) Dieser Scherz der Begleiter Amleths kann mit veranlasst sein durch die Ähnlich-

curiosius pernotato, tacitum cavendae fraudis monitum intellexit. Igitur insidiarum suspicione conterritus, quo tutius voto potiretur, exceptam amplexibus foeminam ad palustre procul invium protrahit. Quam etiam peracto concubitu, ne rem cuiquam proderet, impensius obtestatus est. Pari igitur studio petitum ac promissum est silentium. Maximam enim Amletho puellae familiaritatem vetus educationis societas conciliabat, quod uterque eosdem infantiae procuratores habuerit. Demum itaque reductus, cunctis, an voneri indulsisset, per ludibrium interrogantibus, puellam a se constupratam fatetur. Interrogatus rursum, quo rem loco egerit quove pulvino usus fuerit, ungulae jumenti cristaeque galli, laquearibus quoque tecti innixum se dixit. Horum enim omnium particulas, vitandi mendaci gratia, cum tentandus proficisceretur, contraxerat. Quae vox multo circumstantium risu excepta est, quanquam nihil rerum veritati per jocum detraxerit. Puella quoque ea de re interrogata, nihil eum tale gessisse perhibuit. Fides negationi habita est, eo quidem pronius, quo minus satellites facti conscios fuisse constabat. Tum is, qui praestandi indicii gratia oestrum signaverat, ut salutem Amlethi vaframenti sui beneficio constitisse monstraret, nuper se ejus unice studiosum extitisse dicebat. Nec inepta juvenis responsio fuit. Ne enim indicis meritum negligere putaretur, quiddam straminis gerulum subitis adlapsum pennis, quodque paleam posteriore corporis parte defixam gestaret, sibi conspectum retulit. Quod dictum ut ceteros cachinno concussit, ita Amlethi fautorem prudentia delectavit.

Superatis [10]) omnibus arcanamque juvenilis industriae scram patefacere nequeuntibus, quidam amicorum Fengonis, praesumptione

Schwanze bemerkend, erkannte darin eine Warnung, sich vor Verrat zu hüten; deshalb, weil er Gefahr ahnte und damit er seine Lust in Sicherheit befriedigen könne, nahm er das Mädchen in seine Arme und führte sie weit weg an einen unwegsamen sumpfigen Ort. Nachdem er bei ihr zum Ziel seiner Wünsche gelangt war, beschwor er sie auch iuständig, die Sache Niemand zu verraten; und so dringend er darum bat, so bereitwillig versprach sie ihm ihr Stillschweigen; denn das Mädchen war ihm von Kindheit an zugetan, da beide gemeinschaftlich erzogen werden waren.

Als nun Amleth bei der Heimkehr von Allen wie im Scherze gefragt wurde, ob er das Mädchen genossen habe, gestand er das frei und offen zu; und auf die weitere Frage, wo er es getan und was für eines Polsters er sich dabei bedient, antwortete er, er habe auf dem Huf eines Rindes, dem Kamm eines Hahnes und den Balken eines Daches gelegen. Denn Teilchen und Splitter aller dieser Dinge hatte er, um nicht lügen zu müssen, zu sich gesteckt als er die Reise, die ihn versuchen sollte, antrat. Die Rede erregte ein groszes Gelächter der Umstehenden, obgleich auch dieser Scherz der Wahrheit keinen Abbruch tat. Als man auch das Mädchen über die Sache befragte, behauptete sie, nichts derartiges mit ihm getrieben zu haben; und man glaubte ihrem Laügnen um so eher, da es feststand, dass Amleths Begleiter nichts von dem Vorfall wussten. Derjenige, welcher der Warnung wegen die Bremse mit dem Zeichen versehen hatte, sagte, um anzudeuten, wieviel Amleth seiner List zu verdanken habe: er sei in der letzten Zeit nur für ihn besorgt gewesen. Und die Antwort des Jünglings war nicht unpassend. Denn, damit er nicht gleichgültig gegen das Verdienst des Warners scheine, erzählte er, dass er einen gewissen Strohträger gesehen, der plötzlich auf ihn losgeflogen sei, mit einem Halm hinten am Leibe. Diese Rede reizte die Übrigen zum Lachen, erfreute aber den Beschützer Amleths durch ihre Klugheit.

So hatte er Alle, die ihm nachstellten, getäuscht, und Keiner konnte den Schlüssel zu des Jünglings Benehmen finden: da erklärte Einer von Fengos Freunden, der

---

keit der isländischen Wörter mél oder miöl, Mehl und mellr oder möllr, Sand.

⁹) Vielleicht sollte der Strohhalm am Schwanze der Bremse Amleth andeuten, dass ihm auch in der scheinbaren Einöde List und Nachstellung nahe sei. Und die Bremse als Sinnbild wilder Aufregung sollte ihn vielleicht mahnen, seine aufgeregte Lust zu zügeln.

¹⁰) Die Ed. pr. hat Superatisque.

quam solertia abundantior, fore negabat, ut inextricabile calliditatis ingenium usitato insidiarum genere proderetur. Majorem quippe ejus pervicaciam esse, quam ut levibus experimentis attingi debeat. Quamobrem multiplici illius astutiae simplicem tentationis modum afferri non oportere. Subtiliorem itaque rationis viam altiore animi sensu a se repertam dicebat, executioni non incongruam et propositae rei indagationi efficacissimam. Fengone siquidem per ingentis negotii simulationem de industria absentiam praestante, solum cum matre Amlethum cubiculo claudi oportere, procurato antea viro, qui ambobus insciis in obscura aedis parte consisteret, quid illis colloquio [11]) foret, attentius excepturus. Futurum enim, ut, si quid filius saperet, apud maternas aures eloqui non dubitaret, nec se genitricis fidei credere pertimesceret. Idem se explorationis ministrum cupidius offerebat, ne potius autor consilii, quam executor videretur. Delectatus sententia Fengo facta longinquae profectionis simulatione discedit. Is vero, qui consilium dederat, conclave, quo cum matre Amlethus recludebatur, tacite petivit submissusque stramento delituit. Nec insidiarum Amletho remedium defuit. Veritus enim, ne clandestinis cujuspiam auribus exciperetur, primum ad ineptae consuetudinis ritum decurrens, obstrepentis galli more occentum edidit, brachiisque pro alarum plausu concussis, consenso stramento corpus crebris saltibus librare coepit, si quid illic clausum delitesceret, experturus. At ubi subjectam pedibus molem persensit, ferro locum rimatus, suppositum confodit egestumque latebra trucidavit. Cujus corpus in partes conscissum aquis ferventibus coxit, devoran-

sich auf seine Klugheit mehr einbildete als wirklich an ihr war, es sei unmöglich, die undurchdringliche Schlauheit des Prinzen mit gewöhnlichen Mitteln zu fangen; seine Beharrlichkeit sei zu fest, als dass man ihr durch leichte Versuche beikommen sollte; deshalb dürfe man gegen seine vielfache und vielgewandte Verschlagenheit nicht ein einfaches Masz der List, ihn auf die Probe zu stellen, in Anwendung bringen. Er selbst nun, sagte Jener, habe mit Aufwendung gröszeren Scharfsinns ein feineres Mittel entdeckt, leicht in der Ausführung und zur Erforschung des vorliegenden Rätsels gewiss sehr wirksam. Wenn sich nämlich Fengo, ein wichtiges Geschäft vorgebend, absichtlich entferne, dann solle man Amleth allein mit seiner Mutter, der Königin, in ein Gemach einschlieszen, nachdem vorher für einen zuverlässigen Mann gesorgt worden, der sich in dem Zimmer verstecke und unbemerkt Alles angehen mit anhören könne, was zwischen den Beiden zur Sprache komme. Denn sich der Mutter auszusprechen werde der Sohn, wenn er irgend bei Verstande wäre, kein Bedenken tragen; ihrer Treue sich anzuvertrauen werde ihn kaum keine Furcht abhalten. Der Ratgeber, um nicht blos als solcher zu erscheinen, sondern die Sache auch auszuführen, bot sich sehr dienstfertig an, das Amt des Lauschers selbst zu übernehmen. Fengo, mit dem Vorschlage ganz einverstanden, gab eine weite Reise vor und entfernte sich. Der Ratgeber aber schlich sich heimlich in das Zimmer, in dem Amleth mit seiner Mutter eingeschlossen wurde, und verbarg sich dort unter einer Decke. Amleth fehlte es jedoch nicht an einer Gegenmaszregel. Da er fürchtete, heimlich behorcht zu werden, blieb er vorerst seinem angenommenen Wesen getreu und krähte wie ein Hahn und schlug mit den Armen wie mit Flügeln auf und nieder und sprang auf die Decke und auf ihr herum, um zu erforschen, ob da etwas verborgen sei. Als er aber unter seinen Füszen einen Körper fühlte, stiesz er mit dem Schwerte in die Decke und durchbohrte den Versteckten und zog ihn hervor, ihn vollends zu töten. Den Leichnam zerschnitt er in Stücke und kochte diese in heiszem Wasser; dann warf er sie durch

---

[11]) Wohl zu lesen: colloquii, nach Madvig.

XVII

dumque porcis per os cloacae patentis effudit, atque ita miseris artubus coenum putre construxit. Taliter elusis insidiis conclave repetit. Cumque mater magno ejulatu questa praesentis filii socordiam deflere coepisset, quid, inquit, mulierum turpissima, gravissimi criminis dissimulationem falso lamenti genere expetis, quae scorti more lasciviens, nefariam ac detestabilem tori conditionem secuta, viri tui interfectorem pleno incesti sinu amplecteris et ei, qui prolis tuae parentem extinxerat, obscoenissimis blandimentorum illecebris adularis? Ita nempe equae conjugum suorum victoribus maritantur; brutorum natura haec est, ut in diversa passim conjugia rapiantur; hoc tibi exemplo prioris mariti memoriam exolevisse constat. Ego vero non ab re stolidi speciem gero, cum haud dubitem, quin is, qui fratrem oppresserit, in affines quoque pari crudelitate debacchaturus sit. Unde stoliditatis quam industriae habitum amplecti praestat, et incolumitatis praesidium ab extrema deliramentorum specie mutuari. In animo tamen paternae ultionis studium perseverat, sed rerum occasiones aucupor, temporum opportunitates opperior. Non idem omnibus locus competit. Contra obscurum immitemque animum altioribus ingenii modis uti convenit. Tibi vero supervacuum sit meam lamentari desipientiam, quae tuam justius ignominiam deplorare debueras. Itaque non alienae, sed propriae mentis vitium defleas necesse est. Caetera silere memineris. Tali convicio laceratam matrem ad excolendum virtutis habitum revocavit praeteritosque ignes praesentibus illecebris praeferre docuit.

Reversus Fengo, insidiosae explorationis auctorem nusquam repertum diutinae inquisitionis studio prosequebatur, nemine se eum uspiam conspexisse dicente. Amlethus quoque, an ullum ipsius vestigium

die Öffnung einer Abzugsrinne den Schweinen zum Fressen vor, den stinkenden Kot mit den Gliedern des Unglücklichen dicht bedeckend. Nachdem er sich so der Nachstellungen erwehrt hatte, kehrte er in das Zimmer zurück; und da seine Mutter mit heftiger Wehklage über den Wahnsinn ihres Sohnes zu weinen anfing, wandte er sich gegen sie: Wie, Unseligste der Weiber! Willst du deine schmachvolle Missetat hinter falschem Jammer verbergen? die du, nach geiler Metzen Art, einem sündlichen, abscheulichen Ehebett dich hingiebst, den Mörder deines Gatten blutschänderisch am Busen hegst und ihm, der den Vater deines Sohnes tötete, mit ekelhaften Liebkosungen schmeichelst? Ja, so geben sich Stuten dem jedesmaligen Sieger hin; wilder Tiere Art ist es, in ihrer Neigung bald hierhin bald dorthin zu schweifen; an ihnen hast du dir sicherlich ein Beispiel genommen, um den früheren Gemahl ganz zu vergessen. Ich aber trage nicht umsonst das Kleid der Torheit; denn ich zweifle nicht, dass der, welcher seinen Bruder mordete, auch gegen dessen Angehörige mit gleicher Grausamkeit wüten werde. Deshalb ist es besser, für einen Narren als für einen Klugen zu gelten und Schutz und Sicherheit von dem Schein äuszerster Geistesverwirrung zu borgen. Im Herzen lebt mir das Streben, den Vater zu rächen; ich warte nur auf die günstige Gelegenheit und die richtige Zeit. Nicht jeder Ort passt zu jedem Unternehmen; gegen einen finsteren, wilden Sinn muss man mit überlegenen Kräften des Geistes handeln. Du aber brauchst nicht meine Torheit zu bejammern, da du lieber deine eigene Schande beweinen solltest. Also beklage, was dir, nicht was einem Andern fehlt. Im Übrigen wirst du zu schweigen wissen.

Mit solch vorwurfsvoller Rede rief er die im Innersten erschütterte Mutter auf den Weg der Tugend zurück und mahnte sie, die frühere Liebe den Lockungen der Gegenwart vorzuziehen.

Als der König heimkehrte und jenen Späher nirgends fand, liesz er Tag für Tag eifrig nach ihm suchen; aber Niemand wusste etwas von ihm. Auch Amleth wurde, Scherzes halber, gefragt, ob er nicht eine

XVIII

deprehenderit, per jocum rogatus, in cloacam illum ivisse retulit, perque ejus ima collapsum ac nimia coeni mole obrutum a subeuntibus passim porcis esse consumptum. Quod dictum tametsi veri confessionem exprimeret, quia specie stolidum videbatur, auditoribus ludibrio fuit.

Cumque Fengo privignum indubitatae fraudis [12]) suspectum tollere vellet, sed id tum ob avi ejus Rorici tum ob conjugis offensam exequi non auderet, Britanniae regis officio necandum duxit, innocentiae simulationem. alieno ministerio quaesiturus. Ita dum occultare saevitiam cupit, amicum inquinare, quam sibi infamiam consciscere maluit. Discedens Amlethus matri tacite jubet, textilibus aulam nodis instruat, suasque post annum inferias falso peragat, eoque tempore reditum pollicetur. Proficiscuntur cum eo bini Fengonis satellites, literas ligno insculptas (nam id celebre quondam genus chartarum erat) secum gestantes, quibus Britannorum regi transmissi sibi juvenis occisio mandabatur. Quorum Amlethus quietem capientium loculos perscrutatus, literas deprehendit. Quarum perlectis mandatis, quicquid chartis illitum erat, curavit abradi, novisque figurarum apicibus substitutis, damnationem suam in comites suos, mutato mandati tenore, convertit. Nec mortis sibi sententiam ademisse et in alios periculum transtulisse contentus, preces hujusmodi falso Fengonis titulo subnotatas adjecit, ut Britanniae rex prudentissimo ad se juveni misso filiam in matrimonium erogaret.

At ubi in Britanniam ventum, adeunt legati regem, literasque, quas alienae cladis instrumentum putabant, propriae mortis indices obtulerunt. Quo dissimulato

Spur von ihm entdeckt habe; und darauf erzählte dieser, der Vermisste sei in eine Abzugsrinne gegangen, dort in den Schlamm geraten, und, in der Masse des Unrats erstickt, von herumschweifenden Schweinen gefressen worden. Obgleich dieser Bericht die Wahrheit sagte, wurde er doch, weil scheinbar aberwitzig, von denen, die ihn hörten, gründlich verlacht.

Fengo indess hegte doch starken Verdacht, dass sein Stiefsohn ihn hintergehe, und hätte ihn gern aus dem Wege geräumt. Da er dies aber, aus Rücksichten auf dessen Grossvater Rorik sowohl als auf seine Gemahlin Geruthe, nicht selbst zu tun wagte, so beschloss er, Amleth durch den König von Britannien beseitigen zu lassen, um sich so den Schein der Unschuld zu wahren, indem er einen Andern zum Täter machte; damit er seine Schlechtigkeit verberge, wollte er lieber einen Freund mit schwerem Unrecht beladen, als sich selbst einen bösen Ruf zuziehen.

Bei der Abreise nach England trägt Amleth insgeheim der Mutter auf, sie möge die Halle des Schlosses mit einem netzartigen Gewebe bekleiden und nach Jahresfrist zum Schein sein Todesfest feiern; er verspricht ihr, zur selben Zeit zurückzukehren. Mit ihm reisen Zwei vom Hofe des Königs, Runentafeln (die damals die Briefe ersetzten) bei sich führend, in welchen dem König von Britannien aufgetragen war, den Jüngling, den man ihm schicke, zu töten. Während aber die Begleiter schliefen, untersuchte Amleth ihre Taschen und fand die Runentafeln; und als er den Auftrag gelesen, schabte er das Geschriebene aus, setzte dafür neue Zeichen und änderte so den Auftrag dahin, dass er das ihm zugedachte Verderben gegen seine Begleiter kehrte. Und nicht zufrieden, sich dem Todesurteile entzogen und die Gefahr auf Andere gewälzt zu haben, fügte er unter Fengos Namen die Bitte hinzu, dass der König von Britannien dem klugen Jüngling, den man ihm sende, seine Tochter zur Gemahlin geben wolle.

In Britannien angekommen, verfügten sich die Gesandten zum König und überreichten ihm den Brief, den sie zu Amleths Untergang geschrieben glaubten, der aber in der Tat ihren eigenen Tod

---

[12]) Die Ed. pr. hat fraudi.

XIX

rex hospitali illos humanitate prosequitur. Tunc Amlethus omnem regiarum dapum apparatum perinde ac vulgare edulium aspernatus, summam epularum abundantiam miro abstinentiae genere aversatus est, nec minus potioni quam dapibus pepercit. Admirationi omnibus erat, quod alienigenae gentis juvenis accuratissimas luxu epulas tanquam agreste aliquod obsonium fastidiret. Soluto convivio, rex, quum amicos ad quietem dimitteret, per quendam cubiculo immissum nocturna hospitum colloquia clandestino explorationis genere cognoscenda curavit. Interrogatus igitur a sociis Amlethus, quid ita [13]) hesternis epulis perinde ac venenis abstinuisset, panem cruoris contagio respersum, potioni ferri saporem inesse, carneas dapes humani cadaveris oliditate perfusas ac veluti quadam funebris nidoris affinitate corruptas dicebat. Addidit quoque, regem servilibus oculis esse, reginam tria ancillaris ritus officia prae se tulisse, non tam coenam quam ejus auctores plenis opprobrii conviciis insecutus. Cui mox socii, pristinum mentis vitium exprobrantes, variis petulantiae ludibriis insultare coeperunt, quod probanda culparet, causaretur idonea, quod insignem regem excultamque moribus foeminam parum honesto sermone lacesseret, laudemque meritos extremi dedecoris opprobrio respersisset.

Quibus rex ex satellite cognitis, talium auctorem supra mortalem habitum aut sapere aut desipere testatus est, tam paucis verbis perfectissimam industriae altitudinem complectendo. Accersitum deinde villicum, unde panem adsciverat, percontatur, Qui quum eum domestici pistoris opera confectum assereret, sciscitatur item, ubi materiae ejus seges crevisset, et an ullum illic humanae stragis indicium extaret.

forderte. Der König, ohne sich etwas merken zu lassen, nahm sie mit groszer Gastfreundschaft auf. Da verschmähte aber Amleth die Pracht des königlichen Mahles, als sei es das gewöhnlichste Essen; mit merkwürdiger Enthaltsamkeit wandte er sich ab vom Überflusse der Speisen und war nicht weniger enthaltsam im Trinken. Das war Allen ein Wunder, dass der fremde Jüngling die Kostbarkeiten der königlichen Tafel, die üppigst zubereiteten Gerichte, verachtete, als habe er das Zubrot eines Bauern vor sich. Nach Aufhebung der Tafel entliesz der König die Gäste zur Ruhe, sorgte aber dafür, dass sich Jemand in ihrem Schlafgemache verstecke, durch den er die nächtlichen Gespräche der Fremden erforsche. Als nun Amleth von den Gefährten gefragt wurde, warum er sich heute aller Speisen, als ob es Gift sei, enthalten habe, sagte er, das Brot habe etwas von Blut an sich gehabt, das Getränk nach Eisen geschmeckt, und die Fleischspeisen seien mit einem gewissen Geruch nach Verwesung, wie eines menschlichen Leichnams, behaftet gewesen. Auch fügte er hinzu, die Augen des Königs seien die eines Knechtes, und die Königin habe dreierlei an sich, was nur einer Magd gezieme; so haüfte er Vorwürfe und Schmähungen nicht sowohl auf das Mahl, als auf die Geber desselben. Seine Begleiter warfen ihm seine Sinnesverkehrtheit vor und spotteten seiner mit mutwilligem Hohne, dass er das Gute schmähe, das Schickliche verunglimpfe, einen vortrefflichen König und eine Königin von den reinsten Sitten mit schnöden Reden antaste, und sie, die nur Lob verdienten, mit ärgstem Schimpfe begeifere.

Als der König das von seinem Kundschafter erfuhr, musste er gestehen, dass, wer so spreche, entweder übermenschlich klug oder völlig unklug sein müsse; mit diesen wenigen Worten umfasste er die ganze Höhe und Tiefe von Amleths Geistesschärfe. Nun wird zunächst der Verwalter herbeigeholt und gefragt, woher das Brot stamme; und dieser, da er nur die Auskunft geben kann, dass der Hofbäcker es gebacken, forscht hierauf bei dem weiter nach, wo das Korn dazu gewachsen sei und ob sich dort nicht Spuren von Men-

---

[13]) Die Ed. pr. hat quid igitur ita, und 3 Zeilen weiter humana cadaveris, beide Fehler von Stephanius verbessert.

3*

Qui respondit, haud procul abesse campum vetustis interfectorum ossibus obsitum et adhuc manifesta antiquae stragis vestigia prae se ferentem, quem a se, perinde ac caeteris feraciorem, opimae ubertatis spe verna fruge consertum dicebat. Itaque se nescire, an panis hoc tabo vitiosi quicquam saporis contraxerit. Quo audito rex, Amlethum vera dixisse conjectans, unde lardum quoque allatum fuisset, cognoscere curae habuit. Ille sues suos, per incuriam custodia elapsos, putri latronis cadavere pastos asseverabat, ideoque forte eorum carnibus corruptioni affinem incessisse saporem. Quum rex in hoc quoque veracem Amlethi sententiam comperisset, quonam liquore potionem miscuisset, inquirit. Ut farre et aqua temperatam cognovit, demonstratum sibi scaturiginis locum in altum fodere aggressus, complures gladios rubigine adesos reperit, ex quorum odore lymphas vitium traxisse existimatum est. Alii ideo potionem notatam referunt, quod in ejus haustu apes abdomine mortui alitas deprehenderit, vitiumque referri gustu, quod olim favis inditum extitisset. A quo rex culpati saporis causas competenter editas videns, quum ab eodem exprobratam sibi oculorum ignominiam ad generis foeditatem pertinere cognosceret, clam conventa matre, quis sibi pater extitisset, inquirit. Qua neminem se praeter regem passam dicente, rem quaestione ex ea cognoscendam minatus, quod servo ortus esset, accepit, notatae originis ambiguitatem extorto confessionis indicio perscrutatus. Igitur ut conditionis suae rubore confusus, ita juvenis prudentia delectatus, eundem, cur reginam servilium morum exprobratione maculasset, interrogat.

schenleichen fänden; worauf derselbe antwortet, in der Nähe sei ein Feld, mit alten Knochen bedeckt und allen Anzeichen nach der Schauplatz einer früheren Schlacht, das er in der Hoffnung, es werde besonders fruchtbar sein, im Frühjahre bestellt und eingesäet habe; möglich also, dass das Brot daher etwas nach Verwesung schmecke. Als der König das hörte und Amleths Ausspruch in dieser Hinsicht bestätigt fand, stellte er weitere Erkundigungen an, woher man den Speck genommen habe; da erfuhr er, dass die Schweine durch Unachtsamkeit des Hüters aus dem Stalle gebrochen wären und die verwesende Leiche eines Raubers gefressen hätten, dass deshalb ihrem Fleische also wohl ein etwas fauler Geschmack anhaften könne. Jetzt, da der König Amleths Urteil auch darin richtig befunden, fragte er, woraus das Getränk bereitet worden; man sagte ihm, es sei gebraut aus Getraide und Wasser; nun liess er sich die Quelle zeigen, aus der das Wasser genommen, und liess dort nachgraben und fand mehre verrostete Schwerter, von denen jener falsche Geschmack des Wassers wahrscheinlich herrührte. — Andere erzählen, Amleth habe am Getränk getadelt, dass er beim Truken Bienen verspürt hätte, die vom Leib eines toten Menschen gefressen; so sei ein Fehler von ihm heraus geschmeckt worden, der dem zum Met verwendeten Honig angehaftet habe. — Da der König also sah, dass Amleth in Betreff des tadelnswerten Geschmacks jener Dinge ganz richtig geurteilt hatte, und da er in dem Vorwurf, den derselbe seinen Augen gemacht, einen Zweifel an der Reinheit seiner Abstammung erkannte, sprach er insgeheim mit seiner Mutter und fragte sie aufs Gewissen wer sein Vater wäre. Sie behauptete anfangs, von keinem Manne auszer dem König zu wissen; als er ihr aber mit einer öffentlichen Untersuchung drohte, gestand sie ihm, dass er einem Knechte sein Leben verdanke; und nach dem Zeugnisse dieses Bekenntnisses konnte er die Schande seines Ursprungs nicht bezweifeln. Ebenso beschämt über den Makel seines Herkommens, wie erfreut über die Klugheit des Jünglings, stellte er nun an diesen die Frage, warum er der Königin die Sitten

Sed dum conjugis comitatem nocturno hospitis sermone lacessitam doluit, eandem ancilla matre creatam didicit. Siquidem ille tria se circa eam servilis ritus vitia denotasse dicebat, unum, quod ancillae more pallio caput obduxerit, alterum, quod vestem ad gressum succinxerit [14]), tertium, quod ciborum reliquias deutium angustiis inhaerentes stipite eruerit erutasque commanducaverit. Matrem quoque ejus in servitutem captivitate redactam memorabat, ne potius servili more, quam genere esse videretur.

Cujus industriam rex perinde ac divinum aliquod ingenium veneratus, filiam ei in matrimonium dedit; affirmatiouem quoque ejus tanquam coeleste quoddam testimonium amplexatus est. Caeterum comites ipsius, ut amici mandatis satisfaceret, proxima die suspendio consumpsit. Quod beneficium Amlethus tanquam injuriam simulata animi molestia prosecutus, aurum a rege compositionis nomine recepit, quod postmodum igni liquatum clam cavatis baculis infundendum curavit.

Apud quem annum emensus, impetrata profectionis licentia, patriam repetit, nihil secum ex omni regiarum opum apparatu praeter gerulos auri bacillos deportans. Ut Jutiam attigit, praesentem cultum pristinis permutavit moribus, quibus ad honestatem usus fuerat, in ridiculae consuetudinis speciem de industria conversis. Cumque triclinium, in quo suae ducebantur exequiae, squalore obsitus intrasset, maximum omnibus stuporem injecit, quod obitum ejus falso fama vulgaverat. Ad ultimum horror in risum concessit, exprobrantibus sibi mutuo per ludibrium conviviis, vivum affore, quem ipsi perinde ac defunctum inferiis prosequerentur. Idem super comitibus interrogatus, ostensis, quos gestabat, baculis,

einer Magd vorgeworfen. Aber während es ihn schon bekümmerte, dass der Anstand seiner Gemahlin von dem Gaste im nächtlichen Gespräche angegriffen worden, musste er jetzt erfahren, dass sie eine Magd zur Mutter gehabt. Amleth sagte nämlich, er habe an ihr in dreierlei Hinsicht ein unadeliges Benehmen bemerkt: erstens, dass sie wie eine Magd ein Tuch über den Kopf trage; zweitens, dass sie das Kleid beim Gehen aufnehme; drittens, dass sie die Überbleibsel der Speisen aus den Zähnen gestochert und dann noch einmal gekaut habe. Auch sei ihm kund geworden, dass ihre Mutter einmal durch Kriegsgefangenschaft in Dienstbarkeit geraten, so dass der Grund ihrer Fehler mehr in der Abstammung als in der Erziehung zu liegen scheine.

Nun bewunderte der König Amleths Verstand als etwas Übermenschliches und gab ihm seine Tochter zur Gemahlin; dass Amleth gern einwilligte, nahm er als ein Zeichen des Himmels. Die Begleiter desselben liesz er, um dem Auftrage des Freundes nachzukommen, folgenden Tages aufknüpfen. Amleth aber stellte sich über diese ihm geschehene Wohltat sehr aufgebracht und ungehalten, als sei ihm ein Unrecht widerfahren, und empfing vom König zur Sühne eine Summe Goldes, das er nachher schmelzen und in heimlich ausgehöhlte Stöcke gieszen liesz.

Nach Verlauf eines Jahres nahm Amleth Urlaub und kehrte in sein Vaterland zurück, von allem Reichtum der königlichen Schätze nichts als seine goldgefüllten Stöcke mit sich führend. Sobald er in Jütland angelangt war, vertauschte er das zeitherige Benehmen mit dem früheren, so ehrenhaft durchgeführten, indem er wieder den Schein eines lächerlichen Wahnsinns anlegte. Und als er nun, mit Schmutz bedeckt, die Speisehalle des Königspalastes betrat, wo man eben sein Leichenfest feierte, erfüllte er Alle mit Staunen und Entsetzen, weil das Gerücht fälschlich seinen Tod verbreitet hatte. Schlieszlich löste sich der Schrecken in Gelächter auf, und die Gäste verspotteten einander gegenseitig, dass der lebend unter ihnen sei, den sie als tot feierlich betrauerten. Wegen der Begleiter befragt, zeigte Amleth auf die Stöcke, die er trug, und sagte: Hier ist der Eine,

---

[14]) Nur freie Frauen trugen eine Kopfbedeckung, Mägde ersetzten dieselbe durch Übernehmen des Kleides; jene gingen in langen Kleidern, diese, um sich bei der Arbeit leichter bewegen zu können, schürzten dieselben auf.

hic, inquit, et unus et alius est. Quod utrum verius an jocosius protulerit, nescias. Siquidem ea vox, quanquam a plerisque vana existimata fuerit, a veri tamen habitu non descivit, quae peremptorum loco pensationis eorum pretium demonstrabat. Pincernis deinde, quo majorem convivis hilaritatem afferret, conjunctus, curiosiore propinandi officio fungebatur. Et ne gressum laxior vestis offenderet, latus gladio cinxit, quem plerumque de industria distringens supremo digitos acumine vulnerabat. Quamobrem a circumstantibus curatum, ut gladius cum vagina ferreo clavo trajiceretur. Idem quo tutiorem insidiis aditum strueret, petitam poculis nobilitatem crebris potionibus oneravit, adeoque cunctos mero obruit, ut, debilitatis temulentia pedibus, intra regiam quieti se traderent, eundemque convivii et lecti locum haberent. Quos quum insidiis opportunos animadverteret, oblatam propositi facultatem existimans, praeparatos olim stipites sinu excipit, ac deinde aedem, in qua proceres passim fusis humi corporibus permixtam somno crapulam ructabantur, ingressus, compactam a matre cortinam, quae etiam interiores aulae parietes obducebat, rescissis tenaculis decidere coegit. Quam stertentibus superjectam, adhibitis stipitum curvaminibus, adeo inextricabili nodorum artificio colligavit, ut nemo subjectorum, tametsi validius adniteretur, consurgendi effectum assequi posset. Post haec tectis ignem injicit, qui crebrescentibus flammis late incendium spargens totos involvit penates, regiam consumpsit, omnesque aut profundum carpentes somnum aut frustra assurgere conantes cremavit. Inde petito Fengonis cubiculo, qui prius a comitibus in tabernaculum perductus fuerat, gladium forte lectulo cohaerentem arripuit, suumque ejus loco defixit. Excitato deinde patruo, proceres ejus igne perire retulit; adesse Amlethum veterum uncorum suorum ope succinctum et jam debita paternae cladis supplicia exigere avidum. Ad hanc vocem Fengo lectulo desiliens, dum proprio de-

und hier der Andere; — ebenso scherzhaft als wahr, da diese Rede, so eitel sie den Meisten schien, doch von der Wahrheit nicht abwich, insofern sie auf das hinwies, was er nach ihrem Tode für sie als Busze erhalten hatte. Dann, um die Gäste noch trunkener und fröhlicher zu machen, mischte er sich unter die Schenken und kredenzte sehr eifrig. Und damit das weite Gewand ihn nicht beim Gehen hindere, gürtete er sich mit einem Schwert, das er absichtlich öfters herauszog, bis er sich die Fingerspitzen an ihm verwundete. Darauf hin sorgten die Umstehenden dafür, dass das Schwert und die Scheide mit einem eisernen Keil durchstochen und jenes so an diese festgeheftet wurde. Nun hatte Amleth, zur Sicherung seines Vorhabens, den edlen Gästen so mit dem Becher zugesprochen und Alle so trunken gemacht, dass sie nicht mehr auf ihren Füszen zu stehen vermochten und sich im Königssaale selbst hinlegten und die Speisehalle in ein Schlafgemach verkehrten. Da sah Amleth seine Zeit gekommen; er sammelte die früher vorbereiteten Stäbchen in seinem Busen und kehrte mit ihnen in die Halle zurück, wo die Groszen des Reiches, überall herumliegend, ihren Rausch verschliefen, und löste das von der Mutter um die inneren Wände der Halle gezogene Gewebe von den Haften, so dass es herabfiel. Nun befestigte er dasselbe mit Hilfe der Hakenstäbchen über den Schlafenden und verknotete es so künstlich, dass Keiner der Darunterliegenden mit aller Anstrengung sich vom Boden erheben konnte. Hierauf legte er Feuer an den Palast; und die mächtig züngelnden Flammen ergriffen den ganzen Bau und brannten die Halle nieder und in ihr Alle, die dort noch in tiefem Schlafe lagen oder vergeblich sich abmühten gegen ihre Fesseln. Dann aber begab er sich in das Schlafgemach Fengos, der sich früher zurückgezogen hatte, und nahm das am Bett hängende Schwert desselben weg und hing dafür seines hin; worauf er den Oheim weckt mit dem Rufe: die Gäste verzehre das Feuer, Amleth aber sei da mit seinen Hakenstäbchen, um die Rache für den Mord des Vaters einzufordern. Das hörend, springt Fengo aus dem Bett, und indem er, seines eigenen Schwertes

fectus gladio nequicquam alienum distringere conatur, opprimitur. Fortem virum aeternoque nomine dignum, qui, stultitiae commento prudenter instructus, augustiorem mortali ingenio sapientiam admirabili ineptiarum simulatione suppressit, nec solum propriae salutis obtentum ab astutia mutuatus, ad paternae quoque ultionis copiam eadem ductum praebente pervenit. Itaque et se solerter tutatus, et parentem strenue ultus fortior an sapientior existimari debeat, incertum reliquit [15]).

Peracta vitrici strage, Amlethus, facinus suum incerto populariam judicio offerre veritus, latebris utendum existimavit, donec, quorsum inconditae plebis vulgus procurreret, didicisset. Igitur vicinia, quae noctu incendium speculata fuerat, mane causam conspecti ignis nosse cupiens, collapsam in cineres regiam animadvertit, ruinasque ejus adhuc tepidas perscrutata, nihil praeter informes combustorum corporum reliquias reperit. Adeo autem vorax flamma omnia perederat, ut ne index quidem extaret, ex quo tantae cladis causa accipi posset. Corpus quoque Fengonis ferro confossum inter cruentas spectabatur exuvias. Aliis indignatio patens, aliis moeror, quibusdam gaudium occultum incesserat. Hi ducis lamentabantur interitum, hi sopitam parricidae tyrannidem gratulabantur. Ita regiae necis eventus dividua spectatorum sententia excipiebatur.

Ea vulgi tranquillitate Amlethus relinquendarum latebrarum fiduciam adeptus, accersitis, quibus arctiorem patris memoriam inhaerere cognoverat, concionem petit, in qua orationem hujusmodi habuit: Non vos moveat, proceres, praesens calamitatis facies, si quos miserabilis Horvendilli exitus movet; non vos, inquam, moveat, quibus in regem

beraubt, das fremde nicht aus der Scheide ziehen kann, fällt er von Amleths Hand. So handelte Amleth als Mann der Tat, ewigen Ruhmes wert. Klugerweise Dummheit erkünstelnd, verbarg er eine fast übermenschliche Weisheit hinter bewundernswürdiger Erdichtung scheinbaren Blödsinns. Durch Geistesgewandtheit erwarb er nicht allein sich selbst Heil, sondern wurde durch sie auch dazu geführt, dass er volle Rache nehmen konnte für seinen Vater. Indem er so sich geschickt schützte und den Vater kräftig rächte, lässt er uns ungewiss, was wir höher an ihm schätzen sollen, seine Kraft oder seine Weisheit.

Nach Vollstreckung der Tat an seinem Stiefvater hielt Amleth, weil ihm die Gesinnung des Volkes zu unsicher war, zunächst für geraten, sich in einem Versteck zu verbergen, bis er erkannt hätte, wohin die Stimmung der schwankenden Menge sich neige. Die Nachbarschaft, die den Brand in der Nacht wahrgenommen hatte und sich am nächsten Morgen nach der Ursache des Feuers umsah, fand den Königspallast in Asche gelegt und beim Durchsuchen der rauchenden Trümmer nichts weiter als unförmliche Überreste verbrannter Leichen. Die Flamme hatte alles so gründlich verzehrt, dass nichts übrig geblieben war, was auf die Veranlassung der jammervollen Verheerung schlieszen liesz. Auch der Leichnam Fengos wurde, vom Schwerte durchbohrt, unter den blutigen Resten aufgefunden. Die Einen ergriff Entsetzen und Unwillen, die Anderen Trauer, Manche empfanden auch geheime Freude; jene beklagten den Tod ihres Fürsten, diese wünschten sich Glück zu dem Ende der Herrschaft des Brudermörders. So wurde der Tod des Königs mit geteilter Stimmung aufgenommen.

Aus dieser Ruhe des Volkes schöpfte Amleth das Vertrauen, sein Versteck zu verlassen; und nachdem er diejenigen, deren Anhänglichkeit an das Gedächtnis seines Vaters ihm bekannt war, zu sich entboten, berief er eine Versammlung und redete zu ihr wie folgt: Werte Freunde! der Anblick des gegenwärtigen Jammers kann euch nicht wehe tun, wenn euch der jammervolle Untergang Horvendils wehetut; euch, sage ich, kann der nicht wehe

---

[15]) Hier schlieszt das dritte Buch des Saxo Grammaticus.

fides, in parentem pietas servata est. Parricidae, non regis intueamini funus. Luctuosior siquidem illa facies erat, quum ipsi regem nostrum ab iniquissimo parricida, ne dicam fratre, flebiliter jugulatum vidistis. Ipsi laceros Horvendilli artus, ipsi corpus crebris vulneribus absumptum plenis miserationis oculis aspexistis. Quem ab atrocissimo carnifice spiritu spoliatum, ut patria libertate exueretur, quis dubitet? Una manus ei fatum et vobis servitutem injecit. Quis igitur tam amens, ut Fengonis crudelitatem Horvendillianae praeferat pietati? Mementote, qua vos Horvendillus benevolentia foverit, justitia coluerit, humanitate dilexerit. Memineritis, ademptum vobis mitissimum regem, justissimum patrem, subrogatum tyrannum, suffectum parricidam, erepta jura, contaminata omnia, pollutam flagitiis patriam, impositum cervicibus jugum, ereptum libertatis arbitrium. Et nunc his finis, quum suis auctorem criminibus obrutum, suorum poenas scelerum parricidum pependisse cernatis. Quis mediocriter prudens spectator beneficium injuriae loco duxerit? Quis mentis compos proprium in auctorem scelus recidisse condoleat? Quis cruentissimi lictoris cladem defleat aut crudelissimi tyranni justum lamentetur interitum? Praesto est auctor rei, quem cernitis. Ego quidem et parentem et patriam ultione prosequutum me fateor. Opus, quod vestris pariter manibus debebatur, exercui. Quod vos mecum communiter condecebat, solus implevi. Adde, quod neminem tam praeclari facinoris socium habui, nec cujuspiam mihi comes opera fuit. Quanquam haud ignorem, vos huic manum daturos negotio, si petissem, a quibus fidem regi, benevolentiam principi servatam non

tun, die ihr Treue eurem Fürsten, Liebe eurem Vater bewahrt habt. Eines Brudermörders, nicht eines Königs Leiche habt ihr vor euch. Das war ein beklagenswerterer Anblick, als ihr unsern König vom verruchtesten Meuchelmörder — um nicht Bruder zu sagen — elendiglich umgebracht saht. Ihr selbst habt den verstümmelten, wundenbedeckten Leib Horvendils mit tränenvollen Augen geschaut. Wer von euch zweifelt, dass der grausame Henker ihn des Lebens beraubt hat, um das Vaterland in Ketten zu schlagen? Dieselbe Hand tat Jenem den Tod und euch die Knechtschaft an. Wer wäre nun so verblendet, dass er Fengos Schlechtigkeit der Güte und Milde Horvendils vorzöge? Gedenkt wie Horvendil euch mit Wohlwollen hegte, mit Gerechtigkeit schützte, mit Milde liebte. Erinnert euch, dass euch der gütigste Fürst, der gerechteste Vater genommen und ein Tyrann, ein Mörder an seine Stelle gekommen ist, der eure Rechte euch entrissen hat, Zucht und Sitte geschändet, das Vaterland mit Schändlichkeiten besudelt, euere Nacken ins Joch gebeugt, euch eueren freien Willen geraubt hat. Und jetzt seht ihr dem ein Ende gesetzt; der Urheber dieser Schmach ist seinen Verbrechen erlegen, der Brudermörder hat seine Schandtaten gebüszt. Wer, der nur halbwegs klug ist, könnte die Wohltat für ein Unrecht halten? Wer, der seines Verstandes mächtig, wollte betrauern, dass die Missetat auf den Verbrecher zurückgefallen ist? Wer wird den Tod des blutigsten Henkers beweinen, wer den gerechten Untergang des grausamsten Tyrannen bejammern? Hier steht der, der die Tat getan; hier seht ihr ihn vor euch. Ich bin es; ich bekenne mich dazu, dem Vater und dem Vaterlande die Schuld der Rache abgetragen zu haben. Das Werk, das gleicherweise euren Händen zukam, ich habe es vollbracht. Was euch mit mir zugleich geziemte, habe ich allein ausgeführt. Ich habe auch keinen Genossen der groszen Tat gehabt, Niemandes Hilfe war mir ein Beistand. Obgleich ich wohl weisz, dass ihr mir eure Teilname nicht versagt haben würdet, wenn ich darum gebeten hätte; denn ich zweifle nicht, dass ihr euerem Könige Liebe und Treue be-

dubito. Sed sine vestro discrimine nefarios puniri placuit. Neque enim alienos humeros oneri subjiciendos putabam, cui sustentando proprios suffecturos credebam. Incineravi ego alios, solum Fengonis truncum vestris manibus concremandum reliqui, in quo saltem justae ultionis cupidinem exsatiare possitis. Concurrite alacres, extruite rogum, exurite impium corpus, decoquite scelestos artus, spargite noxios cineres, disjicite immites favillas; non urna, non tumulus nefandas ossium reliquias claudat. Nullum parricidii vestigium maneat, nullus contaminatis artubus intra patriam locus existat, nulla contagium vicinia contrahat; non mare, non solum damnati cadaveris hospitio polluatur. Caetera ego praebui, id solum vobis pietatis officium relictum est. His exequiis prosequendus tyrannus, hac pompa parricidae funus ducendum. Sed neque ejus cineres, qui patriam libertate nudaverit, a patria tegi convenit. Praeterea quid meas revolvam aerumnas? calamitates recenseam? retexam miserias? quas ipsi me plenius nostis. Ego a vitrico ad mortem quaesitus, a matre contemptus, ab amicis consputus, annos flebiliter exegi, dies calamitose duxi, incertum vitae tempus periculis ac metu refertum habui. Postremo omnem aetatis partem maxima cum rerum adversitate miserabiliter emensus sum. Saepe me tacitis intra vos questibus sensu vacuum gemebatis; deesse ultorem patri, parricidio vindicem. Quae res occultum mihi vestrae caritatis indicium attulit, in quorum animis necdum regiae cladis memoriam exolevisse cernebam. Cujus itaque tam asperum pectus, tam saxeus rigor, quem non passionum mearum compassio molliat, aerumnarum miseratio non flectat?

wahrt habt. Aber ich wollte die Schuldigen strafen, ohne euch einer Gefahr auszusetzen; ich glaubte, fremden Schultern nicht eine Last aufbürden zu dürfen, der ich selbst und allein mich gewachsen fühlte. Alle die Andern habe ich zu Asche verbrannt, nur den Leib Fengos sparte ich euren Händen auf, ihn dem Feuer zu übergeben, damit ihr an ihm wenigstens die Lust gerechter Rache sättigen könnt. Eilt, richtet einen Scheiterhaufen, verbrennt den Leichnam des Schändlichen, lasst die verruchten Glieder in Flammen untergehen, streut die schuldbeladene Asche, den schnöden Staub in alle Winde; nicht Urne, nicht Grab umschliesze dieser Gebeine nichtswürdige Überreste. Keine Spur soll bleiben von dem Brudermörder, keine Stätte im Vaterlande seinen blutbefleckten Gliedern zuteil werden, dass sie nicht die Nachbarschaft verpesten; nicht das Meer, nicht der Schoosz der Erde darf verunreinigt werden mit der Beherbergung des verdammten Leibes. Alles Übrige habe ich getan; dieser Dienst allein ist eurem Pflichteifer überlassen. Das sind die Ehren, die der Leiche des Tyrannen gebühren, so soll das Begängnis des Brudermörders gefeiert werden. Selbst seine Asche darf das Land nicht decken, das er seiner Freiheit entblöszte. — Was mich betrifft, wozu soll ich von meinen Kümmernissen sprechen, euch erzählen, was ich gelitten und geduldet? Ihr wisst es besser als ich. Vom Stiefvater mit dem Tode bedroht, von der Mutter verachtet, von den Freunden verspottet, habe ich Jahre des Jammers, unselige Tage dahingelebt, mein ganzes Dasein voll von Unsicherheit und Gefahr und Angst. Einen ganzen Teil meines Lebens habe ich elendiglich verbringen müssen im Kampfe gegen die Widrigkeit der Verhältnisse. Oft beklagtet ihr unter euch mit stillen Seufzern meinen Stumpfsinn; dass dem Vater kein Rächer, dem Mörder kein Strafer da sei. Das war mir ein heimliches Zeichen eurer Treue, da ich die Erinnerung an den schmählichen Tod eures Königs in euch noch nicht erstorben sah. Wessen Herz wäre auch so hart, wessen Starrheit so steinern, dass er nicht Mitleid mit meinen Leiden, nicht Kummer mit meinen Kümmernissen empfände? Erbarmt

Miseremini alumni vestri, moveamini infortuniis meis, qui ab Horvendilli nece immunes goritis manus. Miseremini quoque afflictae genitricis meae, et reginae quondam vestrae extincto congaudete dedecori, quae viri sui fratrem interfectoremque complexa, geminum ignominiae pondus foemineo perpeti corpore cogebatur. Quamobrem ut ultionis studium occultarem, obscurarem ingenium, adumbratum, non verum inertiae habitum amplexatus sum; stoliditatis figmento usus, sapientiae commentum texui, quod nunc an efficax fuerit, utrum finis sui complementum attigerit, vestro conspectui patet; vos tantae rei arbitros habere contentus sum. Ipsi parricidales favillas pedibus proculcate [10]); despicamini cineres ejus, qui jugulati fratris uxorem polluit, flagitio temeravit, dominum laesit, majestatem proditionis scelere lacessivit, acerbissimam vobis tyrannidem intulit, libertatem ademit, incesto parricidium cumulavit. Me tam justae vindictae ministrum, tam piae ultionis aemulum, patricio suscipite spiritu, debito prosequimini cultu, benigno refovete contuitu. Ego patriae probrum dilui, matris ignominiam extinxi, tyrannidem repuli, parricidam oppressi, insidiosam patrui manum mutuis insidiis elusi; cujus, si superesset, indies scelera percrebescerent. Dolebam et patris et patriae injuriam; illum extinxi vobis atrociter et supra, quam viros decuerat, imperantem. Recognoscite beneficium, veneramini ingenium meum, regnum, si merui, date; habetis tanti auctorem muneris, paternae potestatis haeredem non degenerem, non parricidam, sed legitimum regni successorem et pium noxae parricidalis ultorem. Debetis mihi

[10]) Aus proculcatis der Ed. pr. von Stephanius geändert.

euch — ihr, die ihr schuldlos seid an Horvendils Tode — erbarmt euch des Jünglings, der in eurer Hut aufgewachsen; last euch rühren von meinem Unglück. Erbarmt euch auch meiner tiefgebeugten Mutter und freut euch mit mir und ihr, dass die Schmach eurer ehemaligen Königin getilgt ist, die in den Umarmungen des Bruders und Mörders ihres Gemahls ein doppeltes Gewicht der Schande tragen musste mit der Schwäche des Weibes. Deshalb, um mein Rachestreben zu verhehlen, das Licht meines Geistes zu verbergen, habe ich mich zum Toren erniedrigt, der ich nicht war; unter der Maske des Blödsinns habe ich einen Plan der Klugheit gesponnen; und ob er wirksam gewesen, ob er die Erfüllung seines Zweckes erreicht, das liegt euch nun vor Augen; ihr sollt in so groszer Sache Schiedsrichter sein. Tretet die Reste des Mörders mit Füszen, stoszt seine Asche mit Abscheu von euch, der des erschlagenen Bruders Gemahlin verunehrte und beschimpfte, seinen Herrn und König verriet und verdarb, und euch, eure Freiheit raubend, die schwerste Knechtschaft auferlegte, der zum schändlichsten Mord noch Blutschande häufte. Mich, den Handhaber so gerechten Gerichts, den Vollstrecker so frommer Rache, mich nehmt auf mit gewogenem Sinn, ehrt mich mit verdienter Achtung, lasst mich wieder aufleben an eurem Wohlwollen. Ich habe das Land vom Schimpfe reingewaschen, die Unehre der Mutter gelöscht, eure Knechtschaft gelöst, den Mörder zu Boden geworfen, mit List die Hinterlist des Oheims entwaffnet, der, wenn er am Leben geblieben wäre, von Tag zu Tag mehr Bosheiten verübt hätte. Mich jammerte des dem Vater und dem Vaterlande angetanen Unrechts; ich vertilgte den, der euch unter einem erbarmungslosen, für Männer nicht zu tragenden Joche hielt. Erkennt diese Wohltat, ehrt meinen Unternehmungsgeist, gebt mir, wenn ich ihrer würdig, die Herrschaft; ihr habt in mir den Erfinder und Vollbringer eines groszen Werkes, den echten Erben der väterlichen Gewalt, nicht einen Brudermörder, sondern den rechtmäszigen Nachfolger der Krone und den frommen Rächer der Mordschuld. Mir verdankt ihr das Glück der wiederer-

recuperatum libertatis beueficium, exclusum afflictantis imperium, ademptum oppressoris jugum, excussum parricidae dominium, calcatum tyrannidis sceptrum. Ego servitute vos exui, indui libertate, restitui culmen, gloriam reparavi, tyrannum sustuli, carnificem triumphavi. Praemium penes vos est; ipsi meritum nostis; a vestra merces virtute requiritur. Flexerat hac oratione adolescens omnium animos; quosdam ad miserationem, alios ad lachrymas usque perduxit. At ubi quievit moeror, rex alacri cunctorum acclamatione censetur. Plurimum quippe spei in ejus industria ab universis reponebatur, qui tanti facinoris summam profundissimo astu texuerat, incredibili molitione conclyserat. Mirari illum complures videres tanto temporis tractu subtilissimum texisse consilium.

His apud Daniam gestis, ternis navigiis impensius adornatis, socerum visurus ac conjugem Britanniam repetit. In clientelam quoque armis praestantem juventutem adsciverat, exquisito decoris genere cultam, ut, sicut cuncta despicabili dudum habitu gesserat, ita nunc magnificis ad omnia paratibus uteretur, et, quicquid olim paupertati tribuerat, ad luxuriae impensam converteret. In scuto quoque, quod [17]) sibi parari jusserat, omnem operum suorum contextum, ab ineuntis aetatis primordiis auspicatus, exquisitis picturae notis adumbrandum curavit. Quo gestamine perinde ac virtutum suarum teste usus, claritatis incrementa contraxit. Istic depingi videres Horvendilli jugulum [18]), Fengonis cum incestu parricidium, flagitiosum patruum, fratruelem ridiculum, aduncas stipitum formas, suspicionem vitrici, dissimulationem privigni, procurata tentamentorum genera, adhibitam insidiis foeminam, hiantem lupum, inventum gubernaculum, praeteritum sabulum, initum

---

[17]) In der Ed. pr. fehlt das von Stephanius eingefügte quod.
[18]) Stephanius schlug vor zu lesen Horvendilli jugulum confossum od. abscis-

langten Freiheit, und dass die Herrschaft des Wütrichs gebrochen, das Joch des Bedrückers abgeschüttelt, die Gewalt des Mörders beseitigt, das Scepter des Tyrannen niedergetreten ist. Ich habe eure Ketten von euch genommen und euch die Freiheit gegeben, eure Hoheit, euren Ruhm wieder hergestellt, euch befreit von dem Zwingherrn, euch den Sieg gewonnen über den Henker. Bei euch steht der Lohn; ihr wisst, was ich verdient; von eurer Tugend erwarte ich den Dank.

Mit dieser Rede hatte der Jüngling Aller Herzen zu Mitleid gerührt, Viele bis zu Tränen. Und als der erste Schmerz sich beruhigt, wurde die Angelegenheit mit schneller, allseitiger Zustimmung erledigt. Denn Alle setzten die gröszte Hoffnung in dessen Kraft und Klugheit, der eine so gewaltige Tat allein und mit der tiefsten Überlegung erdacht, mit unglaublicher Kühnheit ausgeführt hatte; Alles war voll Bewunderung seines so lange Zeit hindurch mit solcher Feinheit gesponnenen Unternehmens.

Nachdem er solches in Dänemark vollbracht und drei Schiffe kostbar ausgerüstet hatte, segelte Amleth wieder zu seinem Schwiegervater und seiner Gemahlin nach Britannien. Zu Begleitern hatte er sich die im Waffendienst vorzüglichsten Jünglinge erlesen und auch sie aufs glänzendste ausgerüstet, um, wie er bisher stets in äuszerster Niedrigkeit aufgetreten war, so nun in höchster Pracht zu erscheinen, seine frühere Armseligkeit in glänzenden Reichtum zu verkehren. Auf dem Schilde, der auf sein Geheisz angefertigt worden war, hatte er alles, was er von erster Jugend an getan in ausgezeichneter Bildnerei darstellen lassen; so diente ihm derselbe, seine Mannestugend zu bezeugen, und verhalf ihm zu noch gröszerem Ruhme. Da konnte man abgebildet sehen: Horvendils Ermordung, Fengos doppelte Blutschuld, den schändlichen Oheim, den verlachten Neffen, die zu Haken gekrümmten Stäbchen, den Argwohn des Stiefvaters, die Verstellung des Sohnes, die verschiedenen Versuche ihn auszuforschen, das Mädchen mit dem man ihn hatte fangen wollen, den offenrachigen Wolf, das aufgefundene Steuerruder, den Sandhügel an dem man

nemus, insitam oestro paleam, instructum indiciis adolescentem, elusis comitibus rem seorsum cum virgine habitam. Cerneres itaque adumbrari regiam, adesse cum filio reginam, trucidari insidiatorem, trucidatum decoqui, cloacae coctum infundi, infusum suibus objici, coeno artus insterni, instratos belluis absumendos relinqui. Videres etiam, ut Amlethus dormientium comitum secretum deprehenderit, ut obliteratis apicibus alia figurarum elementa substituerit, ut dapem fastidierit potionemque contempserit, ut vultum regis arguerit, ut reginam sinistri moris notaverit. Aspiceres quoque legatorum suspendium, adolescentis nuptias figurari, Daniam navigio repeti, inferias convivio celebrari, comitum loco baculos percontantibus ostendi, juvenem pincernae partes exequi, discricto per industriam ferro digitos exulcerari, gladium clavo pertundi, convivales plausus augeri, increbrescere tripudia, aulaeam dormientibus injici, injectam uncorum nexibus obfirmari, pertinacius sopitos involvi, tectis torrem immitti, cremari convivas, depastam incendio regiam labefactari, Fengonis cubiculum adiri, gladium eripi, inutilem erepti loco constitui, regem privigni manu proprii mucronis acumine trucidari. Haec omnia excultissimo rerum artificio militari ejus scuto opifex studiosus illeverat, res formis imitatus et facta figurarum adumbratione complexus. Sed et comites ipsius, quo se nitidius gererent, oblitis tantum auro clypeis utebantur.

Quos Britanniae rex benignissime exceptos regii apparatus impensis prosequitur. Qui inter epulandum, an Fengo viveret integrisque fortunis esset, cupide percontatus, cognoscite genero, ferro periisse,

---

sum, oder Horvendillum jugulatūm, oder Horvendilli jugulationem.

vorbeikam, den Hain in den man ihn führte, wie dann der Bremse ein Strohhalm angehängt wurde und wie der Jüngling diese Warnung verstand und den Begleitern entging und sich mit dem Mädchen vergnügte. Da konnte man auch das königliche Gemach schauen, wo die Königin mit dem Sohne beisammen war, und wie der Lauscher getötet und der Getötete gekocht und die gekochten Glieder in die Abzugsrinne vor die Schweine geworfen, im Kote verstreut, den Tieren zum Frasze preisgegeben wurden. Da sah man ferner, wie Amleth den schlafenden Begleitern ihr Geheimnis entwendete, die Schrift der Runentafeln löschte und durch andere Zeichen ersetzte; wie er am Hofe von Britannien Speise und Trank verschmähte und am Gesicht des Königs einen Makel fand und die Königin niedriger Sitten bezichtigte. Auch der Tod der Gesandten war dargestellt und Amleths Vermählung; und wie er wieder nach Dänemark schiffte, wie dort das Totenmahl gefeiert wurde und der Ankommende den Fragenden die Stöcke statt der Begleiter zeigte, dann den Schenken machte und sich absichtlich mit dem herausgezogenen Schwerte an den Fingern verwundete, wie sein Schwert in der Scheide befestigt wurde; wie die Trunkenheit und der Lärm der Gäste zunahm, wie Amleth die Decke über die Schlafenden warf, diese mit den Haken anheftete, die Darunterliegenden fester und fester einhüllte, Feuer anlegte, die Gäste verbrannte, die Halle, von der Flamme verzehrt, in Schutt legte, sich dann in Fengos Schlafgemach begab, ihm sein Schwert nahm, an dessen Stelle ein unbrauchbares hinhing, wie endlich der König von der Hand seines Stiefsohnes durch sein eignes Schwert fiel. — Das Alles hatte der geschickte Verfertiger mit höchster Kunst auf dem Kriegsschild Amleths angebracht, die Wirklichkeit nachahmend und alles Geschehene in seiner Abschilderung umfassend. — Aber auch Amleths Begleiter, damit sie in grösstem Glanze erschienen, hatten mit Gold überzogene Schilde.

Der König von Britannien nahm sie freundlichst auf und ehrte sie mit fürstlichem Aufwand. Beim Mahle fragte er, ob Fengo lebe und wohlauf sei, und erfuhr von seinem Schwiegersohn, dass der durchs

de cujus frustra salute perquireret. Cumque interfectorem ejus crebris percontationibus investigaret, eundem cladis ejus auctorem ac nuncium extare didicit. Quo audito, tacitum animi stuporem contraxit, quod ad se promissam quondam Fengonis ultionem pertinere cognosceret. Ipse siquidem [19]) ac Fengo, ut alter alterius ultorem ageret, mutua quondam pactione decreverant. Trahebat itaque regem hinc in filiam pietas, in generum amor, inde caritas in amicum et praeterea jurisjurandi firmitas, ipsa quoque mutuae obtestationis religio, quam violare nefarium erat. Tandem cum affinitatis contemptu juratoria praeponderavit fides, conversusque ad ultionem animus necessitudini religionem anteposuit. Sed quoniam hospitalitatis sacra violare nefas credebatur, aliena manu ultionis partes exequi praeoptavit, innocentiae speciem occulto facinore praetenturus. Igitur insidias officiis texit, laedendique curam adumbratis benevolentiae studiis obscuravit. Et quia conjunx ejus nuper morbo consumpta fuerat, Amlethum reparandarum nuptiarum legationem suscipere jubet, admodum se singulari ipsius industria delectatum praefatus. Regnare siquidem in Scotia foeminam asserebat, cujus vehementer connubium affectaret. Sciebat namque, eam non modo pudicitia coelibem, sed etiam insolentia atrocem, proprios semper exosam procos, amatoribus suis ultimum irrogasse supplicium, adeo ut ne unus quidem e multis extaret, qui procationis ejus poenas capite non luisset.

Proficiscitur itaque Amlethus, quanquam periculosa legatio imperaretur, injuncti muneris obsequium non detrectans, sed partim domesticis servis, partim regis vernaculis fretus. Ingressusque Scotiam, quum haud procul reginae penatibus abesset, recreandorum equorum gratia junctum viae pratum accessit, ibique, loci specie delectatus, quieti consuluit, jucundiore rivi strepitu

Schwert umgekommen sei, nach dessen Wohlergehen er sich erkundige. Und als er nun mit weiterem Forschen in Amleth drang, hörte er, dass der Urheber des Todes jetzt in dem, der ihn meldete, vor ihm stehe. Diese Kunde erregte ihm geheimen Schauder, weil er wusste, dass es ihm, einem früheren Versprechen zufolge, obliege, Fengo zu rächen; denn er und Fengo hatten sich einst gegenseitig das Wort gegeben, dass der Eine des Andern Rächer werde. So zog nun den König hierhin die Liebe zur Tochter und zum Schwiegersohn, dorthin die Anhänglichkeit an den Freund und die Heiligkeit des Eides und die Mahnung des Gewissens, die er nicht misachten dürfte. Zuletzt überwog die Eidestreue, und die Verwandtschaft hintansetzend, seinen Sinn der Rache zuwendend, liesz er die Rücksicht auf den Freund siegen über die Liebe zu den Seinen. Da er aber für Unrecht hielt, das heilige Gastrecht zu verletzen, wünschte er, dass eine fremde Hand die Rache vollstrecke und er durch die Heimlichkeit der Tat sich den Schein der Unschuld wahre. So hüllte er seine Pläne in Freundlichkeit und verbarg die böse Absicht unter eifrig an den Tag gelegtem Wohlwollen. Und weil seine Gemahlin kürzlich gestorben war, beauftragte er Amleth, auf eine neue Brautwerbung für ihn auszuziehen, indem er denselben des grössten Vertrauens in seine Klugheit versicherte. Es herrsche in Schottland, sagte er, eine Jungfrau, die er heisz zur Ehe begehre. Denn er wusste, dass dieselbe nicht nur spröde jede Ehe verschmähe, sondern auch, in wildem Stolze alle Freier hassend, jede Bewerbung um sie mit dem Tode strafe, so dass Keiner sie zu gewinnen versucht habe, der es nicht mit dem Leben gebüszt hätte.

So begiebt sich nun Amleth auf die Reise, und unterzieht sich der wenn auch gefährlichen Sendung, indem er sich dabei auf die Diener verlässt, die er, teils seine eigenen, teils solche des Königs, mitnimmt. In Schottland angekommen und nicht fern mehr von der Burg der Königin, machte er, um den Pferden eine Erholung zu gönnen, Rast auf einer am Wege gelegenen Wiese; und hier, wo die Lieblichkeit des Ortes und das lustige Plätschern eines Baches

---

[19]) siquidem ist Verbesserung Madvigs für equidem der früheren Ausgaben.

XXX

somni cupidinem provocante, ordinatis, qui stationem eminus observarent. Quo audito regina denos juvenes exterorum adventum apparatumque speculaturos emittit. Quorum unus vegetioris ingenii, eitisis vigilibus, pervicacius subiens clypeum Amlethi, quem capiti forte dormiturus affixerat, tanta lenitate submovit, ut ne superjacentis quidem quietem turbaret, aut cujuspiam ex tanto agmine somnum perrumperet, dominam non modo nuncio, sed etiam rerum indicio certiorem redditurus. Delegatas quoque ei literas loculis, quibus asservabantur, pari calliditate subduxit. Quibus regina ad se perlatis, clypeum curiosius contemplata, ex affixis notulis totius argumenti summam elicuit, eumque affore intellexit, qui, exactissimo prudentiae consilio fretus, de patruo paternae cladis poenas acceperit. Literas quoque nuptiarum suarum petitionem continentes intuita, totos obliteravit apices, quod sonum admodum connubium abhorreret, juvenum complexus appeteret. Inscripsit autem mandatum perinde atque a Britanniae rege sibi transmissum et ejus titulo pariter ac nomine consignatum, quo se latoris peti conjugio simularet. Quin etiam facta, quae ex ejus scuto cognoverat, scripto complectenda curavit, ut et clypeum literarum testem et literas clypei interpretes existimares. Deinde eos, quorum exploratione usa fuerat, scutum referre literasque loco suo restituere jubet, eodem fallaciae genere Amlethum insequuta, quo eum in cavillandis comitibus usum acceperat.

Interea Amlethus clypeum capiti fraude subductum expertus, occlusis de industria oculis quietem callidius simulat, quod vero sopore amiserat, ficto recuperaturus. Alteram quippe fallendi vicem hoc pronius ab insidioso quaerendam putavit, quo solam pro-

ihn zur Ruhe aufforderte, überliesz er sich dem Schlafe, nachdem er vorher Wachen ausgestellt hatte. Auf die Kunde hiervon schickte die Königin zehn Jünglinge aus, die Ankunft und die Ausrüstung der Fremden zu erforschen. Einer unter diesen, besonders gewandten Geistes, schlich sich, die Wachen umgehend, zum Schilde Amleths, den dieser sich zum Schlafen unter das Haupt gelegt hatte, und zog ihn so leise hervor, dass er des Schlafenden Ruhe nicht störte, noch sonst irgend Jemand aus der groszen Menge weckte; er wollte der Herrin nicht blos Botschaft sondern auch ein handgreifliches Zeugnis bringen. Und auszerdem entwandte er mit gleicher Geschicklichkeit, aus der Tasche Amleths, die demselben mitgegebenen Briefschaften. Die Königin, als ihr beides gebracht wurde, betrachtete aufmerksam den Schild und entnahm aus den den Bildern beigegebenen Worten, dass sie den vor sich habe, der mit höchster Klugheit am Oheim den Tod des Vaters gerächt. Und nachdem sie auch die Briefe, welche die Werbung enthielten, eingesehen hatte, löschte sie deren Inhalt, weil sie sich keinem Greise, sondern einem Jünglinge vermählen wollte. Sie schrieb aber an Stelle des Gelöschten einen Auftrag, ihr scheinbar vom König von Britannien zugeschickt und mit seinem Titel und Namen unterzeichnet, als ob derselbe um ihre Hand für den Überbringer bitte. Auch die Taten, von denen sie durch den Schild Kenntnis erhalten hatte, waren in dem Schreiben erwähnt, so dass man den Schild für eine Bestätigung der Schrift, die Schrift für eine Erklärung des Schildes halten konnte. Darauf hiesz sie diejenigen, welche sie als Kundschafter gebraucht, den Schild zurückbringen und die Briefe wieder an ihren Ort stecken, indem sie so Amleth in ganz gleicher Weise täuschte, wie sie erfahren, dass er es mit seinen Begleitern nach England getan.

Unterdess hatte aber Amleth gemerkt, dass ihm der Schild heimlich unterm Haupte weggezogen worden, und stellte sich nun, die Augen geschlossen haltend, als ob er noch schliefe; was er im wirklichen Schlafe verloren hatte, wollte er durch verstellten wiedergewinnen. Er glaubte, dass der Dieb um so eher einen zweiten Versuch machen

sperius egerit. Nec eum opinio fefellit. Speculatorem quippe clandestino aditu scutum ac chartam pristino loco reponere cupientem prosiliens corripit, captumque vinclorum poena coercuit. Deinde, excitatis comitibus, reginae penates accedit. Cui, ex soceri persona consalutatae scriptum ejusdem sigillo obsignatum porrexit. Quod quum accepisset Hermuthruda[20] (Reginae id nomen erat) perlegissetque, operam Amlethi industriamque verbis impensioribus prosequuta, justas Fengonem poenas pependisse dicebat, ipsum vero Amlethum rem humana aestimatione majorem incomprehensae profunditatis ingenio molitum, quod non solum paterni exitii maternique concubitus ultionem inscrutabili sensus altitudine commentus fuisset, verum etiam regnum ejus, a quo crebras insidias expertus fuerat, conspicuae probitatis operibus occupasset. Quamobrem mirari se tam eruditi ingenii virum uno nuptiarum errore labefactari potuisse, qui, quum humanas paene res claritate transscendat, in ignobilem obscuramque copulam prolapsus videatur. Quippe conjugem ejus servis parentibus esse, quanquam eos fortuna regiis honoribus exornasset. In expetendis siquidem conjugiis prudenti non formae fulgorem, sed generis metiendum. Quapropter si rite copulam appetat, prosapiam aestimet nec specie capiatur, quae quum illecebrarum irritamentum sit, multorum candorem inaniter fucata detersit. Esse vero, quam sibi nobilitate parem asciscere possit. Se siquidem, nec rebus tenuem nec sanguine humilem, ejus amplexibus idoneam fore, utpote quam nec regiis opibus vincat nec avito splendore praecellat. Quippe reginam se esse, et, nisi refragaretur sexus, regem existimari posse; imo, quod verius est, quemcunque toro suo dignata fuerit, regem existere, regnumque se cum amplexibus dare. Ita et nuptiis sceptrum et sceptro

würde, je besser ihm der erste gelungen. Und dieser Glaube betrog ihn nicht. Als der Kundschafter, heimlich heranschleichend, Schild und Brief wieder hinlegen wollte, von wo er sie genommen, sprang Amleth auf und ergriff ihn und warf ihn in Ketten. Dann weckte er sein Gefolge und zog nach der Burg der Königin. Sie im Namen seines Schwiegervaters begrüszend, überreichte er ihr das mit dessen Siegel versehene Schreiben. Als Hermuthruda — so hiesz die Königin — es in Empfang genommen und gelesen hatte, ehrte sie Amleths Tat und seine Gewandtheit mit sehr lobenden Worten und sagte, Fengo sei der gerechten Strafe verfallen, Amleth aber habe mit unfassbarer Tiefe des Geistes ein unschätzbares Werk vollführt, indem er nicht nur unerforschlich klug eine Rache ersonnen für den Mord des Vaters und die Entehrung der Mutter, sondern sich auch mit offenbarem Recht der Herrschaft seines Feindes bemächtigt. Deshalb nehme es sie Wunder, wie ein so bedächtiger Mann den einen Fehler hinsichtlich seiner Verheiratung habe begehen können, da er, in allem Übrigen fast übermenschlich hoch stehend, durch eine unedle und unwürdige Eheverbindung erniedrigt erscheine. Denn die er seine Gemahlin nenne, stamme von knechtischen Eltern, wenn auch das Glück dieselben mit königlichen Ehren geschmückt habe. Bei Schlieszung einer Ehe aber sehe der Kluge nicht auf den Glanz der Schönheit, sondern auf den der Abkunft. Wenn er also eine ihm geziemende Verbindung wünsche, so müsse er auf edle Sippschaft achten und sich nicht von der äuszern Erscheinung bestechen lassen, die ein Reiz der Verlockung, mit ihrer eitlen Schminke schon viele Männer zu Grunde gerichtet habe. Eine ihm an Adel Ebenbürtige aber gebe es, die er wählen könne. Das sei sie selbst: sowohl ihre Glücksgüter als ihr edles Blut machten sie seiner würdig, da sie ihm weder an königlichen Reichtümern noch an Glanz der Ahnen nachstehe. Sie sei eine Königin und könne, wenn nicht ihr Geschlecht dem entgegen wäre, für einen König geachtet werden; jedenfalls werde der ein König, dem sie sich zur Gemahlin gebe; mit ihrer Hand schenke sie ein Reich. So entspreche

---

[20] Hermuthruda (weiterhin Hermutruda geschrieben) ist kein schottischer, sondern ein germanischer Name.

nuptias respondere. Nec parvi beneficii esse, eam proprios offerre amplexus, quae circa alios ferre repulsam exequi consveverat. Hortatur itaque, placendi studium in se transferat, in se votum nuptiale deflectat, genusque formae praeferre discat. Haec dicens astrictis in eum complexibus ruit. Ille, tam comi virginis eloquio delectatus, in mutua prorumpit oscula, alternos complexuum nodos conserit, sibique, quod virgini, placitum protestatur. Fit deinde convivium, accersuntur amici, corrogantur primores, nuptiae peraguntur. Quibus expletis, cum nupta Britanniam repetit, valida Scotorum manu propius subsequi jussa, cujus opera adversum varios insidiarum objectus uteretur. Redeunti Britannici regis filia, quam in matrimonio habebat, occurrit. Quae quanquam se superductae pellicis injuria laesam quereretur, indignum tamen ajebat, maritali gratiae pellicatus odium anteferri, neque se adeo virum aversaturam, ut, quod ei fraudulentius intentari sciat, silentio occultare sustineat. Habere enim se pignus conjugii filium, cujus saltem respectus conjugalem matri caritatem commendare debuerat. Ipse enim, inquit, matris suae pellicem oderit, ego diligam; meos in te ignes²¹) nulla calamitas sopiet, nullus livor extinguet, quin et in te sinistre excogitata detegam et, quas deprehenderim insidias, pandam. Quamobrem cavendum tibi socerum putes, quod ipse legationis proventum carpseris, omnemque ejus fructum in temet, eluso mittentis voto, pervicaci usurpatione transtuleris. Qua voce se conjugali quam paternae caritati propiorem ostendit.

ihre Würde ihrer Vermählung mit ihm und ihre Vermählung mit ihm ihrer Würde. Und nichts Kleines sei es, dass sich die ihm freiwillig anbiete, die bisher alle Bewerber nicht nur abgewiesen, sondern mit dem Tode gestraft habe. — So dringt sie in ihn, ihr seine Liebe und sein Ehegelübde zuzuwenden und edle Geburt der bloszen Schönheit vorzuziehen. Und damit wirft sie sich, ihn fest umfangend, in seine Arme.

Amleth, von so liebreichen Reden der Jungfrau entzückt, fühlt sich hingerissen, ihre Küsse zu erwidern, umschlingt sie auch seinerseits mit Umarmungen und beteuert ihr, dass ihr Wille sein Wille sei. Nun wird ein Fest veranstaltet, die Freunde werden herbeigerufen, die Groszen des Reichs versammelt, die Hochzeit gefeiert. Nachdem aber die Feier zu Ende, kehrt er mit seiner Neuvermählten nach Britannien zurück, eine starke schottische Macht, zum Schutze gegen feindliche Überfälle, als Gefolge mit sich nehmend. Bei seiner Ankunft in der Heimat kommt ihm die Tochter des Königs von Britannien, seine erste Gemahlin, entgegen. Wohl beklagte sie sich über das ihr durch seine zweite Verbindung angetane Unrecht: aber sie sagte, sie halte es für unwürdig, wenn sie den Hass gegen die Nebenbuhlerin die Oberhand gewinnen lasse über ihre eheliche Liebe, und sie könne ihrem Gemahl nicht so übel wollen, dass sie ihm nicht entdeckte, was gegen ihn heimlich im Werke sei. Denn sie habe als Pfand ihrer Ehe einen Sohn und die Rücksicht auf ihn wenigstens müsse die Mutter bestimmen zur Treue gegen ihren Gatten. Mein Sohn, sagte sie, mag die Nebenfrau seiner Mutter hassen, ich will sie lieben; keine Widerwärtigkeit soll das Feuer meiner Liebe zu dir dämpfen, kein Neid es löschen; ich will vielmehr aufdecken, was Böses man gegen dich sinnt und dich wissen lassen, welche Nachstellungen ich erkundet. Sei denn darauf bedacht, deinen Schwiegervater zu meiden, weil du den Erfolg deiner Sendung für dich selbst eingeheimst und alle Frucht derselben, den Wunsch des Absenders taüschend, fester Hand dir angemaszt hast. — Diese Worte zeigten, dass sie dem Gatten in Liebe näher stand als dem Vater.

---

²¹) So Stephanius, während die Ed. pr. hat tuos in me ignes.

XXXIII

Haec loquente ea adest Britanniae rex, generumque arctius quam affectuosius amplexatus, convivio excipit, liberalitatis specie fraudis propositum celaturus. Amlethus, cognita fraude, metum dissimulanter habuit, ducentisque equitibus in comitatum receptis, subarmalem vestem indutus obsequitur invitanti, maluitque regiae simulationi periculose parere, quam turpiter repugnare. Adeo honestatem in cunctis observandam putabat. Quem cominus obequitantem rex sub ipsa bipatentium portarum testudine adortus jaculo transegisset, ni ferrum subarmalis togae durities repulisset. Amlethus, levi recepto vulnere, eo loci se contulit, ubi Scoticam juventutem exspectandi officio fungi jusserat, captivo novae conjugis speculatore ad regem remisso, qui se destinatas dominae literas loculorum custodiae furtim exemisse testando crimen in Hermutrudam refunderet, ipsumque accurato genere excusationis reatu proditionis absolveret. Quem rex avidius fugientem insequi non moratus, majore copiarum parte privavit, ita ut Amlethus die postero, salutem praelio defensurus, desperatis admodum resistendi viribus, ad augendam multitudinis speciem exanima sociorum corpora, partim subjectis stipitibus fulta, partim propinquis lapidibus affixa, alia viventium more equis imposita nullo armorum detracto, perinde ac praeliatura seriatim in aciem cuneumque digesserit. Nec rarius mortuorum cornu erat, quam viventium globus. Stupenda siquidem illa facies erat, quum extincti rape-

Während sie noch solches redete, kam der König von Britannien herbei und umarmte den Schwiegersohn, freundlicher als es ihm ums Herz war, und lud ihn zum Festmahl; er wollte die verrätherische Absicht mit dem Schein des Wohlwollens verdecken. Amleth, sein böses Vorhaben wohl kennend, liesz doch nichts von Furcht blicken, und nachdem er sich 200 Reiter zur Begleitung genommen und ein Panzerhemd unter seinem Gewand angelegt hatte, folgte er der Einladung; er wollte dem Vorgeben des Königs lieber mit Gefahr seines Lebens Folge leisten, als ihm ungeziemend widersprechen; so sehr glaubte er unter allen Umständen die Wohlanständigkeit beobachten zu müssen. Als er nun neben dem König daherritt, wandte sich dieser unter dem Bogen des weitoffenstehenden Burgtores plötzlich gegen ihn und hätte ihn mit seinem Wurfspeer durchbohrt, wenn nicht das Panzerhemd gewesen wäre, dessen Härte das Eisen abspringen liesz. Amleth, leicht verwundet, eilte nach dem Orte, an dem er seine schottische Schutzwache zurückgelassen hatte, und schickte jenen damals gefangen genommenen Kundschafter seiner neuen Gemahlin an den König ab, damit er durch sein Zeugniss, dass er die für seine Herrin bestimmten Briefe heimlich aus Amleth's Tasche entwendet habe, die Schuld auf Hermuthruda zurückschiebe und Amleth vollkommen von dem Vorwurfe des Verrates reinige. Allein der König wartete nicht so lange, sondern verfolgte sofort den eilig Fliehenden und tötete ihm einen groszen Teil seiner Reiterschaar; so dass, als Amleth am nächsten Tage sein Heil in einem Treffen versuchen wollte, seine Streitkräfte ihm aber keine Hoffnung auf gehörigen Widerstand lieszen, er, um seiner Macht den Schein einer gröszeren Stärke zu geben, die Leichen seiner erschlagenen Krieger, als zögen sie mit in den Kampf, reihenweise und in Schlachtordnung aufstellte, die Einen durch angestemmte Pfähle, die Anderen durch daliegende Steine gestützt, noch Andere wie lebend auf's Pferd gesetzt, Alle in voller Waffenrüstung. Der Toten, die den Flügel bildeten, waren nicht weniger als der Lebenden im Mitteltreffen. Ein schrecklicher Anblick, wo Leichen eine

rentur ad praelia, defuncti decernere cogerentur. Quae res auctori otiosa non fuit, quum ipsae extinctorum imagines lacessentibus solis radiis immensi agminis speciem darent. Ita enim inania illa defunctorum simulacra pristinum militum numerum referebant, ut nihil ex eorum grege hesterna strage deminutum putares. Quo aspectu territi Britanni pugnam praecurrere fuga, a mortuis superati, quos vivos oppresserant. Quae victoria nescio callidior an felicior existimanda sit. Rex dum segnius fugam intendit, ab imminentibus perimitur Danis. Victor Amlethus, ingenti praeda acta convulsisque Britanniae spoliis, patriam cum conjugibus petit. Interea, defuncto Rorico, Vigletus regnum adeptus, Amlethi matrem omni petulantiae genere fatigatam regiis opibus vacuefecerat, filium ejus, fraudato Lethrarum [21]) rege, cui dignitatum jura dandi tollendique jus esset, Jutiae regnum occupasse conquestus. Quam rem Amlethus tanta animi moderatione excepit, ut, Vigleto splendidissimis victoriae suae manubiis donato, calumniam beneficio rependere videretur. Quem postmodum, exigendae ultionis occasione suscepta, bello lacessitum devicit, atque ex occulto hoste, manifestus evasit. Fiallerum Scaniae praefectum exilio adegit; quem ad locum, cui Undensakre [22]) nomen est, nostris ignotum populis, concessisse est fama. Post haec quum a Vigleto, Scaniae Sialandiaeque viribus recreato, per legatos ad bellum provocaretur, mirifica animi industria duascirca se res, quarum alteri probrum, alteri periculum inesset, fluctuari pervidit. Sciebat quippe sibi, si provocationem sequeretur, imminere vitae periculum si refugeret, instare militiae probrum. Praeponderavit tamen in contemplatore virtutum animo

Schlacht schlagen mussten! Die List brachte aber ihrem Erfinder groszen Vorteil, da die Gestalten der Entseelten im Glanze der Sonnenstrahlen den Heerhaufen gewaltig grosz erscheinen lieszen; die toten Körper der Erschlagenen stellten die frühere Kriegeranzahl wieder her, so dass es aussah, als sei sie im gestrigen Kampfe um keinen Mann vermindert worden. Die Britannier, von dem Anblick erschreckt, flohen ehe es zur Schlacht kam und wurden so von denen im Tode überwunden, die ihnen im Leben unterlegen waren. List und Glück hatten gleich groszen Anteil an dem Siege. Der König, während er sich langsam zur Flucht wandte, wurde von den Dänen erschlagen. Der Sieger Amleth aber trieb aus ganz Britannien eine ungeheure Beute zusammen und kehrte mit seinen beiden Gemahlinnen in sein Vaterland zurück.

Hier war unterdess nach Roriks Tode, Viglet auf den Thron gekommen und hatte Amleths Mutter durch Ränke aller Art gequält und sie ihrer königlichen Schätze beraubt, indem er als Grund seines Zornes angab, dass ihr Sohn mit Umgehung des Königs von Lethra, dem das Recht, Ämter und Würden zu erteilen und zu entziehen zustehe, die Herrschaft über Jütland an sich gerissen habe. Amleth nahm das mit so groszer Mäszigung auf, dass er dem Viglet glänzende Geschenke aus seiner Siegesbeute machte und Verläumdung mit Wohlwollen zu vergelten schien. Nachher aber, als sich Gelegenheit zur Rache darbot, überzog er ihn mit Krieg und schlug ihn, und trat ihm auch weiterhin mit offener Feindschaft entgegen. Den Statthalter von Schonen, Fialler, schickte er in die Verbannung; derselbe soll sich, wie die Sage erzählt, nach Undensakre, einem bei uns unbekannten Ort, begeben haben. Unter der Zeit hatte Viglet in Schonen und Seeland neue Streitkräfte gesammelt und liesz Amleth durch Gesandte zum Krieg herausfordern. Da erkannte dieser mit voller Klarheit, dass er zwischen zwei Nothwendigkeiten stehe, von denen ihm die eine Schande, die andere Gefahr drohe; er wusste, dass er, wenn er der Herausforderung folgte, sein Leben, wenn er sie ausschlüge, seine Kriegerehre aufs Spiel setzte. In seinem auf Heldentugend gerichteten Sinn

---

[21]) Lethra (hier Lethrae) war die alte, in der Nähe des heutigen Roeskilde gelegene Residenz der dänischen Könige.

[22]) Undensakre ist wohl der in einigen isländischen Schriften späterer Zeit vorkommende Odains-akr, d. i. ein paradiesisches (in der Nähe Indiens gedachtes) Land, dessen Bewohner unsterblich sind.

servandae honestatis cupido, obtuditque cladis formidinem impensior laudis aviditas, ne solidus gloriae fulgor meticulosa fati declinatione corrumperetur. Animadvertebat quoque, tantum paene inter ignobilem vitam et' splendidam mortem discriminis interesse, quantum dignitas a contemptu distare cognoscitur. Tanta autem Hermutrudae caritate tenebatur, ut majorem futurae ejus viduitatis quam propriae necis solicitudinem animo insitam gestaret, omnique studio circumspiceret, qualiter ei secundas nuptias ante belli ingressum consciseret. Quamobrem Hermutruda, virilem professa fiduciam, ne in acie quidem se eum deserturam spopondit, detestabilem inquiens foeminam, quae marito morte conseri formidaret. Quam promissionis novitatem parum executa est. Nam quum Amlethus apud Jutiam a Vigleto acie interemptus fuisset, ultro in victoris praedam amplexumque concessit. Ita votum omne foemineum fortunae varietas abripit, temporum mutatio dissolvit, et muliebris animi fidem lubrico nixam vestigio fortuiti rerum casus extenuant, quae sicut ad pollicendum facilis, ita ad persolvendum segnis, variis voluptatis irritamentis astringitur, atque ad recentia semper avidius expetenda, veterum immemor, anhela praeceps cupiditate dissultat. Hic Amlethi exitus fuit, qui si parem naturae atque fortunae indulgentiam expertus fuisset, aequasset fulgore superos, Herculea virtutibus opera transscendisset. Insignis ejus sepultura ac nomine campus apud Jutiam extat.[23]

[25] Heutzutage giebt es ein Dorf Amelhede im Amt Randers und einen Flurbezirk (campus) gleichen Namens in der Nähe von Viborg. — Fegge Klit und Fegge Sund auf der Insel Morsö erinnern vielleicht an Fengo.

überwog jedoch das Streben, die Ehre zu wahren, und seine Ruhmbegierde schlug alle Todesfurcht nieder; er wollte den Glanz seines Namens nicht noch zuletzt durch Kleinmut verdunkeln; er sagte sich auch, dass zwischen einem schimpflichen Leben und einem ehrenvollen Tod ein Unterschied sei, wie zwischen der Verachtung und der Hochachtung selbst. Seine Liebe zu Hermuthruda aber war so gross, dass ihn ihre Wittwenschaft im Fall seines Todes mehr bekümmerte als die Gefahr seines eignen Lebens und dass er nur darauf dachte, wie er noch vor Beginn des Kampfes für ihre Wiederverheiratung sorge. Hermuthruda indes rühmte sich männlichen Mutes und gelobte ihm, ihn auch inmitten der Schlacht nicht zu verlassen, indem sie die Frau verächtlich nannte, die ihrem Manne nicht freudig in den Tod folge. Es war das ein unerhörtes und völlig eitles Versprechen. Denn als darauf Amleth in Jütland von Viglet in einem Treffen erschlagen wurde, gab sie sich dem Sieger freiwillig zur Beute und zur Ehe. So wird jedes weibliche Gelübde von einem Glückswechsel, einer Änderung der Zeiten aufgelöst und zu nichte gemacht; die Treue einer Frau steht auf so schlüpfrigem Grunde, dass ein Zufall sie niederwirft; schnell im Versprechen, ist sie träge im Worthalten, läst sich von jeder Lockung der Lust fangen, und stürzt sich mit athemloser Begier auf alles Neue und denkt nicht des Alten. Das war Amleths Ausgang, der, wenn ihn das Glück in gleicher Weise wie die Natur begünstigt hätte, den Göttern an Ruhm gleichkommen wäre und die Arbeiten des Herkules durch seine Grosztaten übertroffen hätte. Ein durch sein Grabmal berühmtes Gefilde in Jütland trägt noch seinen Namen.

Quellen, aus denen Saxo die Amlethsage geschöpft, oder historische Anhaltspunkte für dieselbe, sind nirgends nachzuweisen. Abgesehen von den Anm. 22 angeführten Ortsnamen findet sich eine vereinzelte Spur nur in einem Fragment des isländischen Dichters Snaebiörn (in der Edda Snorroniana), wo das Meer als die Mühle bezeichnet wird, in der neun Nymphen den Ufersand für Amlod gemahlen haben. Hieraus und aus der Erwähnung des, im Isländischen nachweisbaren, Saxo aber unbekannten Undensakre (S. XXXIV) lässt sich vermuten, dass Saxo die Sage in der vorliegenden Gestalt durch Vermittlung isländischer Erzähler erhalten habe. Überdies bedeutet Amlod im Isländischen einen dummen Menschen. Die Sage von Amleth scheint demnach, ebenso wie die ähnliche von L. Iunius Brutus, im engsten Zusammenhange zu stehen mit dem Namen des Helden. (Müller-Velschow, II, S. 132 ff.) — Simrock (Quellen des Shakespeare III, S. 166 ff.) verfolgt die Ähnlichkeit der Amleth- und Brutus-Sage bis in's Einzelne und ist geneigt, eine gemeinsame Grundlage beider anzunehmen.

II.

Aus Belleforests Histoires Tragiques.[1])

Argument.

Le desir de regner conduit les hommes à devenir meurtriers &c. traistres.

Ce n'est a'aujourd'huy,[2]) ny d'un seul jour que l'envie regnant a tellement aveuglé les hommes, que sans respect de sang ny d'obligation, ils se sont oubliez jusques à là, que de souiller leur vertu premiere, en espandant le sang, duquel à plus juste tiltre, ils deussent estre deffenseurs. Car quelle autre impression avoit saisi le coeur de Romule, lors que souz couleur d'une telle quelle loy, il ensanglanta ses mains du sang de son propre frere, sinon ceste abominable convoitise? Laquelle si sagement, et en toutes ses occurrences, bon heurs, et circonstances estoit consideree, je ne sache homme qui n'aymast mieux vivre à son aise, et en son privé, sans charge, qu'estant craint et honoré de tous, avoir aussi les charges de tous sur les espaules, servir aux fantasies d'un peuple, craindre à tous propos, et de mesme se voir exposé à mille occasions de crainte, et le plus souvent assailly, lors qu'il se pense tenir fortune comme l'esclave de ses fantasies. Et toutefois les hommes achetent une telle misere et vie calamiteuse, pour la gloire caduque de ce monde, et au prix de leurs ames, et font prodigue largesse de leur conscience, laquelle ne s'esmeut pour meurtre, trahison, fraude ou meschanceté qu'ils commettent, pourveu que la voye leur soit ouverte, laquelle les face parvenir à ceste miserable felicité, que de commander sur tout un peuple, ainsi que desja j'ay dict de Romule, lequel avec un forfaict abominable, se prepara la voye au ciel, et non avec la Vertu:

---

[1]) Le Cinquiesme Livre des Histoires Tragiques, le succez et evenement desquelles est pour la plus part recueilly des choses advenues de nostre temps, et le reste des histoires anciennes. Le tout faict, illustré et mis en ordre, par François de Belleforest Comingeois. A Lyon, par Benoist Rigaud. 1581. Avec privilege du Roy. (Histoire III, p. 177—274.) — Nach Brunet, Manuel du libraire, erschienen von den Hist. Trag.: Bd. 1 zuerst Paris 1559; Bd. 5 zuerst Paris 1570, dann Lyon 1583 (?) u. 1591; Gesammtausgaben (Bd. 1—7) zuerst Paris 1580—82 u. Rouen 1603—4. — Über Belleforest (geb. 1530 in der Grafschaft Cominge, gest. 1583 zu Paris) s. Nicerons Nachrichten, herausg. v. Baumgarten, Halle 1754, IX, S. 187—212, wo 57 Schriften von ihm aufgeführt sind.

[2]) Soll heiszen d'aujourd'huy; das *a* des schlecht gedruckten Originals ist ein abgesprungenes *d*. Der Fehler ist aber beibehalten, weil er den Fehler der englischen Übersetzung erklärt und vermuten lässt, dass derselben die hier benutzte Ausgabe von 1581 zu Grunde liege. — Überhaupt hält sich vorliegender Abdruck streng an das Original, nur dass jour, envie, sans, hommes, achetent etc. für iour, enuie, fans, hōmes, achetēt etc. gesetzt ist.

III.

The Hystorie of Hamblet.a)

The Argument.

It is not at this present, neither yet a small time since, that envy raigning in the worlde hath in such sort blinded men, that without respect of consanguinitie, friendship, or favour whatsoever, they forget themselves so much as that they spared not to defile their hands with the blood of those men, who by all law and right they ought chiefly to defend and cherish. For what other impression was it that entered into Romulus heart, when, under pretence of I know not what lawe, he defiled his hands with the blood of his owne brother, but the abhominable vice of desire to raigne? which, if in all the accurrences,b) prosperities, and circumstances thereof, it were well wayed and considered, I know not any man that had not rather live at his ease, and privately without charge, then, being feared and honored of all men, to beare all the charge and burden upon his shoulders; to serve and please the fantasies of the common people; to live continually in feare, and to see himself exposed to a thousand occasions of danger, and most commonly assailed and spoiled when hee thinkes verily to hold Fortune as slave to his fantasies and will, and yet buyes such and so great misery for the vaine and fraile pleasures of this world, with the losse of his owne soule; making so large a measure of his conscience, that it is not once mooved at any murther, treason, deceit, nor wickednes whatsoever he committed, so the way may be opened and made plaine unto him, whereby hee may attaine to that miserable felicitie, to command and governe a multitude of men (as I said of Romulus), who, by a most abhominable action, prepared himselfe a way to heaven (but not by vertue).

The desire of rule causeth men to become traytors and murtherers.

The miserable condition of such as rule over others.

Romulus, for small or no cause, killed his brother.

---

a) *London:* Imprinted by Richard Bradocke, for Thomas Pavier, and are to be sold at his shop in Corne-hill, neere to the Royall Exchange. 1608. — Hier abgedruckt aus Payne Collier: Shakespeare's Library, vol. I. p. XI—XVI, 131—182. — Das einzige noch vorhandene Exemplar des alten Drucks von 1608 befindet sich in der Capell'schen Sammlung zu Cambridge. Collier's Annahme einer früher (etwa um 1585) erschienenen Ausgabe ist blosze Vermutung.

b) Lies occurrences. — Derartige, leicht (vorzüglich durch Vergleichung des französischen Originales) erkennbare, unverändert beibehaltene Fehler sind weiterhin einfach durch ein † als solche bezeichnet.

[II.] ainsi que chante l'ambitieux Orateur, et seditieux harangueur de Rome, qui trouvoit les degrez du Ciel, et le chemin de la vertu és trahisons, ravissemens et massacres, faicts par celuy qui le premier posa les fondemens de leur ville. Et sans nous esloigner des Romains, qui incita les enfans d'Ance Martie à massacrer Tarquin ancien, sinon ce desir de regner mesme, lequel avoit esguillonné ledict l'ancien d'en frustrer les vrays et legitimes heritiers? Qui conduit Tarquin le superbe à souiller traitreusement ses mains du sang de son beau pere Servie Tullie, que ce desir sans bride, ny justice d'occuper la principauté de Rome? Ceste façon de faire ne se discontinua onc en la cité chef de l'Empire: veu que, et durant qu'elle estoit gouvernee par les plus grands et plus sages, souz l'election et suffrages du peuple, on y a veu infinité de seditions, troubles, pillages, rançonnemens, confiscations, et massacres, procedans de ce seul fondement, et principe, lequel saisit les hommes allechez de l'esperance de se faire chef de toute une republique. Et apres que le peuple fut privé de sa liberté, et que l'Empire se veit soumis à la volonté et fantasie d'un seul qui commandoit sur tous, je vous prie feuilletez les livres, lisez diligemment les histoires, et regardez les moyens tenus par la plus part, pour parvenir à telle puissance, et verrez

Plusieurs par-venus à l'Empire par meurtre.

les poisons, assassinats, et meurtres secrets faciliter la voye à ceux, qui n'osoyent l'attenter publiquement, et ne pouvoyent y parvenir à guerre ouverte. Et d'autant que l'histoire que je pretens vous reciter, est appuyee sur la trahison de frere contre frere: je ne veux m'esloigner aussi du sujet: voulant neantmoins vous faire voir, qu'encore cela a eu place de long temps, qu'on s'attaquast à son sang le plus proche pour se faire grans: et d'autres, qui ne pouvans attendre le temps juste des succes, ont advancé la mort à leurs parens, ainsi que vouloit faire Absalon au sainct Roy David son pere. Et comme on lit de Domitian, qui empoisonna son frere Tite, le plus courtois, et plus liberal Prince qui jamais tinst l'Empire de Rome. Et Dieu sçait si de nostre temps les exemples de telle meschanceté nous manquent, et si les fils ne conspirent contre le salut de leur pere, veu que Sultan Zelin Roy des Turcs, fut si homme de bien, que de ne pouvoir attendre que Bajazeth son pere mourust de

Soliman fait estrangler son fils Mustapha.

sa belle mort naturelle, si encor il n'y eust aidé, pour s'emparer du Royaume. Sultan Soliman successeur de Zelin, quoy qu'il n'ait rien attenté contre celuy qui l'avoit engendré, si est-ce que solicité d'une frayeur d'estre chassé de son siege, et portant envie à la vertu de Mustapha son fils, esguillonné à ce faire par Rustain Bassa, gaigné par les presens des Juifs, ennemis de ce jeune Prince, il le feit estrangler avec une corde d'arc, sans vouloir ouyr les justifications de celuy qui onc ne luy avoit faict offense. Laissons les Turcs comme Barbares, et le throsne desquels est ordinairement establiy par l'effusion du sang de ceux, qui les atouchent de plus pres de consanguinité, et alliance: pour considerer quelles tragedies ont esté jouees pour ce mesme cas de la memoire de nos peres en Escosse et Angleterre, et avec quelle charité se sont caressez les plus proches parens ensemble: si vous n'aviez les histoires en main, si la

XXXIX

The ambitious and seditious Orator of Rome supposed the degrees and steps to heaven, and the wayes to vertue, to consist in the treasons, ravishments, and massacres committed by him that first layd the foundations of that citty. And not to leave the hystories of Rome, what, I pray you, incited Ancius Martinus† to massacre Tarquin the Elder, but the desire of raigning as a king, who before had bin the onely man to move and solicite the saide Tarquinius to bereave the right heires and inheriters thereof? What caused Tarquinius the Proud traiterously to imbrue his hands in the blood of Servius Tullius, his father in law, but onely that furnish and unbridled desire to be commander over the cittie of Rome? which practise never ceased nor discontinued in the said principall cittie of the empire, as long as it was governed by the greatest and wisest personages chòsen and elected by the people; for therein have been seen infinite numbers of seditions, troubles, pledges, ransommings, confiscations and massacres, onely proceeding from this ground and principle, which entereth into mens hearts, and maketh them covet and desirous to be heads and rulers of a whole common wealh. And after the people were deprived of that libertie of election, and that the empire became subject to the pleasure and fantasie of one man, commanding al the rest, I pray you peruse their bookes, and read diligently their hystories, and do but looke into the meanes used by the most part of their kings and emperours to attaine to such power and authoritie, and you shall see how poysons, massacres, and secret murthers, were the meanes to push them forwards that durst not openly attempt it, or else could not compasse to make open warres. And for that the Hystory (which I pretend to shew unto you) is chiefly grounded upon treason, committed by one brother against the other, I will not erre far out of the matter; thereby desiring to shew you, that it is and hath been a thing long since practised and put in use by men, to spill the blood of their neerest kinsmen and friends to attaine to the honour of being great and in authoritie; and that there hath bin some, that being impatient of staying till their just time of succession, have hastened the death of their owne parents: as Absolon would have done to the holy king David, his father; and as wee read of Domitian, that poysoned his brother Titus, the most curtious and liberall prince that ever swayed the empire of Rome. And God knowes we have many the like examples in this our time, where the sonne conspired against the father; for that Sultan Zelin, emperour of Turkes, was so honest a man, that fearing Baiazeth, his father, would die of his naturall death, and that thereby he should have stayd too long for the empire, bereaved him of his life; and Sultan Soliman, his successor, although he attempted not any thing against his father, yet being mooved with a certaine feare to bee deposed from his emperie, and bearing a hatred to Mustapha, his son (incited therunto by Rustain Bassa, whom the Jewes, enemies to the yong prince, had by gifts procured thereunto), caused him to be strangled with a bowe string, without hearing him (that never had offended his father) once speake to justifie his innocencie. But let us leave the Turkes, like barbarians as they are, whose throne is ordinarily established by the effusion of the blood of those that are neerest of kindred and consanguinitie to the empire, and consider what tragedies have bin plaid to the like effect in the memorie of our ancestors, and with what charitie and love the neerest kindreds and friends among them have bin intertained. One of the other, if you had not the hystories extant before you,

[III.]
Cicero in his Paradoxes.

Tarquin the elder slaine in Rome.

Servius Tullius slaine by his sonne in law.

Wherefore Rome was subject to seditions.

Divers attained to the empire by murther.

Absolon conspired against David his father.

Zelin slew his father, Baiazeth.

Soliman caused Mustapha, his sonne, to be hanged.

Great mischiefe in our age.

[II.]

Grand malheur de nostre temps.

memoire n'en estoit comme toute fresche, si un Roy n'estoit mort hors de saison, et si les plus tyrans, et qui n'ont aucun droit és terres et seigneuries de leurs souverains, si les enfans ne conspiroient la mort de leurs peres, les femmes celles de leurs espoux, si tout cela n'estoit presque cogneu à chacun, j'en ferois un long discours: mais les choses estant si claires, la verité tant descouverte, le peuple presque abreuvé de telles trahisons, je passeray outre pour suivre mon projet, et monstrer que si l'iniquité d'un frere a faict perdre la vie à celuy qui luy estoit si proche, aussi vengeance ne s'en est esloignee: mais quelle vengeance? la plus gaillarde, sagement conduite, et bravement executee, qu'homme sçauroit imaginer, afin que les traistres cognoissent que jaçoit que la punition de leurs forfaicts soit retardee, si se peuvent ils asseurer de jamais ne passer sans sentir la main puissante et vengeresse de Dieu, lequel estant tardif à courroux, ne laisse à la fin de donner les signes effroyables de son ire, sur ceux qui s'oublians en leur devoir espandent le sang innocent, et trahissent les chefs, ausquels ils doivent tout service, honneur et reverence.

Avec quelle ruse Amleth, qui depuis fut Roy de Dannemarch, vengea la mort de son pere Horwendille, occis par Fengon son frere, et autre occurrence de son histoire.

Quoy que j'eusse deliberé des le commencement de ce mien oeuvre de ne m'esloigner, tant peu soit, des histoires de nostre temps, y ayant assez de sujets pleins de succez tragiques, si est-ce que partie pour ne pouvoir en discourir sans chatouiller plusieurs ausquels je ne voudroy desplaire, partie aussi que l'argument que j'ay en main m'a semblé digne d'estre offert à la noblesse Françoise, pour les grandes, et gaillardes occurrences qui y sont deduites, j'ay un peu esgaré mon cours de ce siecle, et sortant de France et pays voisins, suis allé visiter l'histoire Danoise, afin qu'elle puisse servir et d'exemple de vertu, et de contentement aux nostres, ausquels je tasche de complaire, et pour le rassasiement desquels je ne laisse fleur qui ne soit goustee, pour leur en tirer le miel le plus parfait et delicat, afin de les obliger à ma diligence: ne me souciant de l'ingratitude du temps present, qui laisse ainsi en arriere et sans recompence ceux, qui servent au public, et honorent, par leur travail, et diligence leur pays, et illustrent la France. Car je m'estime pour plus que satisfait en ce contentement et grande liberté d'esprit, de laquelle je jouys estant aymé de la noblesse, pour laquelle je travaille avec si peu de relache, caressé des gens de sçavoir pour les admirer, et leur faire reverence, telle que leur excellence merite, et honoré du peuple, duquel jaçoit que je ne cerche le jugement pour ne l'estimer assez suffisant de faire vivre le nom de quelque homme illustre, si me pense je assez heureux d'avoir atteint à ceste felicité, qu'il se trouve peu d'hommes qui desdaignent de lire mes oeuvres, qui est le plaisir plus grand que j'aye, et la richesse la plus abondante de mes coffres, de laquelle toutefois je suis plus content que si sans nom je jouyssois des thresors le plus grands qui soient en l'Asie. Revenant donc à nostre propos, et recueillans un peu de loing le sujet de nostre dire, faut sçavoir que long temps auparavant que le Royaume de Dannemarch receust la foy de Jesus, et embrassast

Contentement de l'auteur de cest oeuvre.

if the memorie were not in a manner fresh, and known almost to every man, I would make a long discourse thereof c); but things being so cleare and evident, the truth so much discovered, and the people almost, as it were, glutted with such treasons, I will omit them, and follow my matter, to shew you that, if the iniquitie of a brother caused his brother to loose his life, yet that vengeance was not long after delayed; to the end that traitors may know, although the punishment of their trespasses committed be stayed for awhile, yet that they may assure themselves that, without all doubt, they shal never escape the puisant and revenging hand of God; who being slow to anger, yet in the ende doth not faile to shew some signes and evident tokens of his fearefull judgement upon such as, forgetting their duties, shed innocent blood, and betray their rulers, whom they ought chiefly to honour, serve, and reverence.

[III.]

God stayeth his wrath, but yet revengeth wrong: read Plutarch Opuscules, of the slownesse of God's judgements.

The Preface.

Although in the beginning of this Hystorie I had determined not to have troubled you with any other matter than a hystorie of our owne time, having sufficient tragicall matter to satisfie the minds of men; but because I cannot wel discourse thereof without touching many personages whom I would not willingly displease, and partly because the argument that I have in hand, seemed unto me a thing worthy to bee offered to our French nobilitie, for the great and gallant accurrences† therein set downe, I have somewhat strayed from my course, as touching the tragedies of this our age, and, starting out of France and over Neitherlanders countries, I have ventured to visit the hystories of Denmarke, that it may serve for an example of vertue and contentment to our nation (whom I specially seeke to please), and for whose satisfaction I have not left any flower whatsoever untasted, from whence I have not drawne the most perfect and delicate hony, thereby to bind them to my diligence herein; not caring for the ingratitude of the time present, that leaveth (as it were rejecteth) without recompence such as serve the common wealth, and by their travell and diligence honour their countrey, and illustrate the realme of France:[so that oftentimes the fault proceedeth rather from them, then * from the great personages that have other affaires which withdraw them from things that seeme of small consequence.] Withall, esteeming my selfe more than satisfied in this contentment and freedome which I now injoy, being loved of the nobilitie, for whom I travell without grudging, favoured of men of learning and knowledge, for admiring and reverencing them according to their worthinesse, and honoured of the common people, of whom, although I crave not their judgement, as not esteeming them of abilitie to eternize the name of a worthy man, yet I account my selfe sufficiently happy to have attained to this felicitie, that few or no men refuse, or disdaine to reade my workes, many admiring and wondering thereat; as there are some that, provoked by envie, blame and condemne it. To whom I confesse my selfe much bound and beholding, for that by their meanes I am tho more vigelant, and so by my travell much more beloved and honored than ever I was; which to mee is the greatest pleasure that I can injoy, and the most abundant treasures in my coffers, wherewith I am more satisfied and contented then (if without comparison) * I enjoyed the greatest treasures in all Asia. Now, returning to our matter, let us beginne to declare the Hystorie.

c) Zu dem Anfange dieses Satzes sowie zu dem weiterhin mit * bezeichneten Stellen vergleiche das französische Original.

[II.]

Danois jadis fort rudes et barbares.

la doctrine et sainct lavement des Chrestiens, comme le peuple fut assez Barbare et mal civilisé, aussi leurs Princes estoient cruels, sans foy ny loyauté, et qui ne jouyoient qu'au boutehors, taschans à se getter de leurs sieges, ou de s'offencer, fust en la robe ou en l'honneur, et le plus souvent en la vie, n'ayans guere de coustume de mettre à rançon leurs prisonniers, ains les sacrifioyent à la cruelle vengeance, imprimée naturellement en leur ame. Que s'il y avoit quel que bon Roy ou Prince, qui poussé des instincts les plus parfaits de nature, voulust s'adonner à la vertu, et usast de courtoisie, bien que le peuple l'eust en admiration (comme la vertu se rend admirable aux vicieux mesme) si est-ce que l'envie de ses voisins estoit si grande, qu'on ne cessoit jamais jusqu'à

Rorikus roy de Dannemarch.

tant que le monde fut depesché de cest homme ainsi de bonnaire. Regnant donc en Dannemarch Rorique, apres qu'il eut apaisé les troubles du pays, et chassé les Sueons et Sclaves de ses terres, il departist les Provinces de son Royaume, y mettant des Gouverneurs, qui depuis (ainsi qu'il en est advenu en France) ont porté tiltre de Ducs, Marquis et Contes: il donna le gouvernement de Jutie (qui s'appelle vulgairement à present Diethmarsen, et est assise sur le Chersonnese des Cimbres, en celle estressisure de terre, qui avoisine la mer comme une pointe, laquelle vers le North regarde le Royaume de Norvege) à deux seigneurs vaillans hommes nommez Horwendille et Fengon, enfans de Gerwendille, lequel avoit esté aussi Gouverneur de celle Province. Or le plus grand honneur que pouvoient acquerir les hommes de sorte en ce temps là, estoit en exerçant l'art d'escumeur et pirate sur mer, assaillans leurs voisins, et ravageant les terres voisines, et tant plus accroissoit leur gloire et reputation, comme ils alloient voltiger par les Provinces, et Isles lointaines: en quoy Horwendille se faisoit dire le premier de son temps, et le plus renommé de tous ceux qui escumoient pour lors la mer, et havres de Septentrion. La grand' renommee de cestuy cy esmeut le cœur du Roy de

Collere roy de Norvege.

Norvege, nommé Collere, lequel se faschoit que Horwendille le surmontast en fait d'armes, et obscurcist la gloire qu'il avoit desja acquise au fait de la marine: car c'estoit l'honneur, plus que les richesses qui esguillonnoit ces Princes Barbares à s'accabler l'un autre, sans qu'ils se souciassent de mourir de la main de quelque vaillant homme. Ce Roy magnanime ayant deffié au combat, corps à corps, Horwendille, y fut receu avec pactes, que celuy qui seroit vaincu perdroit toutes les richesses qui seroient en leurs vaisseaux, et le vainqueur feroit enterrer honnestement celuy qui seroit occis au combat, car la mort estoit le pris et salaire de celuy, qui perdroit la bataille. Que sert de tant discourir? le Roy (quoy que vaillant,

Chap. I.

How Horvendile and Fengon were made Governours of the Province of Ditmarse, and how Horvendile marryed Geruth, the daughter to Roderick, chief K. of Denmark, by whom he had Hamblet: and how after his marriage his brother Fengon slewe him trayterously, and marryed his brothers wife, and what followed.

You must understand, that long time before the kingdome of Denmark received the faith of Jesus Christ, and imbraced the doctrin of the Christians, that the common people in those dayes were barbarous and uncivill, and their princes cruell, without faith or loyaltie, seeking nothing but murther, and deposing (or at the least) offending each other, either in honours, goods, or lives; not caring to ransome such as they tooke prisoners, but rather sacrificing them to the cruell vengeance naturally imprinted in their hearts: in such sort, that if ther were sometime a good prince or king among them, who beeing adorned with the most perfect gifts of nature, would adict himselfe to vertue, and use courtesie, although the people held him in admiration (as vertue is admirable to the most wicked) yet the envie of his neigbbors was so great, that they never ceased untill that vertuous man were dispatched out of the world. King Rodericke, as then raigning in Denmarke, after hee had appeased the troubles in the countrey, and driven the Sweathlanders and Slaveans from thence, he divided the kingdom into divers provinces, placing governours therein; who after (as the like happened in France) bare the names of Dukes, Marqueses, and Earls, giving the government of Jutie (at this present called Ditmarsse) lying upon the countrey of the Cimbrians, in the straight or narrow part of land that sheweth like a point or cape of ground upon the sea, which neithward† bordereth upon the countrey of Norway, two valiant and warlike lords Horvendile and Fengon, sonnes to Gervendile, who likewise had beene governour of that province. Now the greatest honor that men of noble birth could at that time win and obtaine, was in exercising the art of piracie upon the seas, assayling their neighbours, and the countries bordering upon them; and how much the more they used to rob, pill, and spoyle other provinces, and ilands far adjacent, so much the more their honours and reputation increased and augmented: wherin Horvendile obtained the highest place in his time, beeing the most renouned pirate that in those dayes scoured the seas and havens of the north parts: whose great fame so mooved the heart of Collere, king of Norway, that he was much grieved to heare that Horvendile surmounting him in feates of armes, thereby obscuring the glorie by him alreadie obtained upon the seas: (honor more than covetousnesse of riches (in those dayes) being the reason that provoked those barbarian princes to overthrow and vanquish one the other, not caring to be slaine by the handes of a victorious person). This valiant and hardy king having challenged Horvendile to fight with him body to body, the combate was by him accepted, with conditions, that hee which should be vanquished should loose all the riches he had in his ship, and that the vanquisher should cause the body of the vanquished (that should bee slaine in the combate) to be honourably buried, death being the prise and reward of him that should loose the battaile: and to conclude, Collere, king of

The Danes in times past barbarous and uncivill.

The crueltie of the Danes.

Rodericke king of Denmarke.

Jutie at this time, called then Ditmarsse.

Horvendile a king and a pirate.

Collers king of Norway.

XLIV

[II.] courageux, et adextre fut-il) en fin fut vaincu et occis par le Danois, lequel luy feit dresser tout soudain un tombeau, et luy feit des obseques dignes d'un Roy, suivant les façons de faire et superstitions de leur siecle, et selon l'accord du combat, despouillant la suite du Roy de leurs richesses, ayant faict mourir une sœur du Roy defunct, fort gaillarde, et vaillante guerriere, et ayant couru toute la coste de Norvege, et jusques aux Isles Septentrionales, il s'en revinst chargé d'honneur et de richesses, envoyant à son souverain le Roy Rorique, la pluspart du butin et despouilles, à fin de le gaigner, et qu'estant si brave, il peust tenir le lieu des plus favoris de sa majesté. Le Roy alliché de ces presents, et s'estimant heureux, d'avoir un si homme de bien pour subjet, tascha avec une honesteté de se le rendre à jamais obligé, car il luy donna pour femme Geruthe sa fille, de laquelle il sçavoit ce seigneur estre fort amoureux, et voulut luy mesme la conduire, pour plus l'honnorer, jusques en Jutie, où les nopces furent celebrees, selon la façon ancienne: et pour trousser briefvement matiere, de ce mariage sortist Amleth, duquel je pretens parler, et pour lequel j'ay desseigné le discours de l'histoire presente. Fengon frere de ce genre Royal, poussé d'un esprit d'envie, crevant le despit en son cœur, tant pour la grand' reputation aquise par Horwendille au maniement des armes, que solicité d'une sotte jalousie, le voyant honoré de l'alliance et amitié royalle, craignant d'estre depossedé de sa part du gouvernement, ou plustost desirant d'estre seul en la principauté, et obscurcir par ce moyen, la memoire des victoires et conquestes de son frere, delibera, comme que ce fust, de le faire mourir. Ce qui luy succeda assez aisément, nul ne se doubtant de luy, et chacun pensant que d'un tel nœud d'alliance et consanguinité, ne pourroit jamais sortir autre chose, que les effects pleins de vertu et courtoisie: mais comme j'ay dit, le desir de regner, ne respecte sang, ny amitié, et n'a soucy aucun de vertu: voire il est sans respect, ny reverence des loix, ny de la majesté divine, s'il n'y est possible que celuy qui sans aucun droit envahist le bien d'autruy, aye quelque opinion de la divinité. Ainsi Fengon ayant gaigné secretement des hommes, se sentant assez fort pour executer son entreprinse, se rua un jour en un banquet, sur son frere lequel il occist autant traistreusement, comme cautelausement il se purgea devant ses sujets, d'un si detestable massacre: veu qu'avant que mettre la main sanguinolente, et parricide sur son frere, il avoit incestueusement souillé la couche fraternelle, abusant de la femme de celuy, duquel il devoit autant pourchasser l'honneur, comme il en poursuivoit, et effectua la ruine: aussi il est bien vray, que l'homme qui se laisse aller apres un vice, et forfait detestable, estant la liaison des pechez fort grande, il ne se soucie en rien de s'abandonner à un pire, et plus abominable. Or couvrit il avec

Geruthe fille de Rorique femme de Horwendille.

Conspiration de Fengon contre son frere Horwendille.

Norway (although a valiant, hardy, and couragious prince) was in the end vanquished and slaine by Horvendile, who presently caused a tombe to be erected, and therein (with all honorable obsequies fit for a prince) buried the body of king Collere, according to their aunciont manner and superstitions in these dayes, and the conditions of the combate, bereaving the kings shippes of all their riches; and having slaine the kings sister, a very brave and valiant warriour, and over runne all the coast of Norway, and the Northern Ilands, returned home againe layden with much treasure, sending the most part thereof to his soveraigne, king Rodericke, thereby to procure his good liking, and so to be accounted one of the greatest favourites about his majestie.

[III.]
Horvendile slew Collere.

The king, allured by those presents, and esteeming himselfe happy to have so valiant a subject, sought by a great favour and courtesie to make him become bounden unto him perpetually, giving him Geruth his daughter to his wife, of whom he knew Horvendile to bee already much inamored. And the more to honor him, determined himselfe in person to conduct her into Jutie, where the marriage was celebrated according to the ancient manner: and to be briefe, of this marriage proceeded Hamblet, of whom I intend to speake, and for his cause have chosen to renew this present hystorie.

Hamlet sonne to Horvendile.

Fengon, brother to this prince Horvendile, who [not] d) onely fretting and despighting in his heart at the great honor and reputation wonne by his brother in warlike affaires, but solicited and provoked by a foolish jealousie to see him honored with royall aliance, and fearing thereby to bee deposed from his part of the government, or rather desiring to be onely governour, thereby to obscure the memorie of the victories and conquests of his brother Horvendile, determined (whatsoever happened) to kill him; which hee effected in such sort, that no man once so much as suspected him, every man esteeming that from such and so firme a knot of alliance and consanguinitie there could proceed no other issue then the full effects of vertue and courtesie: but (as I sayd before) the desire of bearing soveraigne rule and authoritie respecteth neither blood nor amitie, nor caring for vertue, as being wholly without respect of lawes, or majestie devine; for it is not possible that hee which invadeth the countrey and taketh away the riches of an other man without cause or reason, should know or feare God. Was not this a craftie and subtile counsellor? but he might have thought that the mother, knowing her husbands case, would not cast her sonne into the danger of death e). But Fengon, having secretly assembled certain men, and perceiving himself strong enough to execute his interprise, Horvendile his brother being at a banquet with his friends, sodainely set upon him, where he slewe him as traiterously, as cunningly he purged himselfe of so detestable a murther to his subjects; for that before he had any violent or bloody handes, or once committed parricide upon his brother, hee had incestuously abused his wife, whose honour hee ought as well to have sought and procured as traiterously he pursued and effected his destruction. And it is most certaine, that the man that abandoneth himselfe to any notorious and wicked action, whereby he becommeth a great sinner, he careth not to commit much more haynous and abhominable offences, and covered his boldnesse and

Fengon, his conspiracie against his brother.

Fengon killeth his brother.

---

d) So bei Collier, der also wohl das *not* eingefügt hat.
e) Scheint ein Zusatz des englischen Übersetzers zu Chap. III.

XLVI

[II.] si grande ruse, et cautelle, et souz un voile si fardé de simplicité, son audace, et mechanceté, que favory de l'honneste amitié qu'il portoit à sa belle sœur, pour l'amour de laquelle il se disoit avoir ainsi puny son frere, que son peché trouva excuse à l'endroit du peuple, et fut reputé comme justice envers la noblesse: D'autant qu'estant Geruthe autant douce et courtoise, que Dame qui fut en tout les Royaumes du Septentrion, et tellement que jamais n'avoit tant peu soit, offencé homme de ses sujetz, soit du peuple, ou des courtisans, ce paillard, et infame meurtrier, calomnia le deffunct, d'avoir voulu occir ceste Dame, et que s'estant trouvé sur le poinct qu'il taschoit de la massacrer, il avoit defendu la Dame, et occis son frere, parant aux coups ruez sur la Princesse innocente, et sans fiel, ny malice quelconque. Il n'eut ja faute de tesmoins approuvans son faict, et qui deposerent selon le dire du calomniateur, mais c'estoyent ceux mesmes qui l'avoyent accompagné, comme participans de la conjure, et qu'au reste en lieu de le poursuyvre, comme parricide et incestueux, chacun des courtisans luy applaudissoit, et le flattoit en sa fortune prospere, et faisoyent les Gentilshommes plus de compte des faux rapporteurs, et honnoroyent les calomniateurs, plus que ceux qui mettans en jeu les vertus du deffunct, eussent voulu punir les brigands, et assassineurs de sa vie. Qui fut cause que Fengon enhardy pour telle impunité, osa encor s'assoupler par mariage, a celle qu'il entretenoit execrablement, durant la vie du bon Horwendille, souillant son nom de double vice, et chargeant sa conscience de double impieté, d'adultere incestueux, et de felonnie, et parricide. Et celle mal-heureuse qui avoit receu l'honneur d'estre l'espouse d'un des plus vaillans et sages Princes de Septentrion, souffrit de s'abaisser jusques a telle villenie, que de luy faucer la foy: et qui pis est, espouser encor celuy, lequel estoit le meurtrier tyran de son espoux legitime: ce qui donna à penser à plusieurs, qu'elle pouvoit avoir causé ce meurtre pour jouyr librement de son adultere. Que sçauroit on voir de plus effronté, qu'une grande, depuis qu'elle s'esgare en ses honnestetez? Ceste Princesse, qui au commencement estoit honnoree de chacun, pour ses rares vertus, et courtoisies, et cherie de son espoux, dés aussi tost qu'elle preste l'oreille au tyran Fengon, elle oublia, et le rang qu'elle tenoit entre les et† plus grands, et le devoir d'une espouse honneste, pour le salut de sa patrie. Je ne veux m'amuser contre ce sexe, à cause qu'il en y a assez qui s'estudient à la blasonner, courant sus à toute espace de femmes, pour la faute de quelques unes: Bien diray je que, où il faudroit que nature eust osté l'opinion aux hommes de s'accointer à icelles, ou leur donner l'esprit assez rassis, pour supporter les traverses qu'ils en reçoivent, sans se plaindre si souvent, et tant estrangement, puis que c'est leur bestise qui les acable. Car s'il est ainsi que la femme soit un animal si imparfait, qu'ils le chantent, et qu'ils cognoissent ceste beste si indomptable, comme ils le crient, pourquoy sont ils si sots, que de la poursuyvre, et tant hebetez, et abrutiz, que de se

Marriage incestueux de Fengon avec sa bellesœur.

---

†) Fehler des Originals.

wicked practise with so great subtiltie and policie, and under a vaile of meere simplicitie, that beeing favoured for the honest love that he bare to his sister in lawe, for whose sake, hee affirmed, he had in that sort murthered his brother, that his sinne found excuse among the common people, and of the nobilitie was esteemed for justice: for that Geruth, being as courteous a princesse as any then living in the north parts, and one that had never once so much as offended any of her subjects, either commons or courtyers, this adulterer and infamous murtherer, slaundered his dead brother, that hee would have slaine his wife, and that hee by chance finding him upon the point ready to do it, in defence of the lady had slaine him, bearing off the blows, which as then he strooke at the innocent princesse, without any other cause of malice whatsoever. Wherein hee wanted no false witnesses to approove his act, which deposed in like sort, as the wicked calumniator himselfe protested, being the same persons that had born him company, and were participants of his treason; so that insteed of pursuing him as a parricide and an incestuous person, al the courtyers admired and flattered him in his good fortune, making more account of false witnesses and detestable wicked reporters, and more honouring the calumniators, then they esteemed of those that seeking to call the matter in question, and admiring the vertues of the murthered prince, would have punished the massacrers and bereavers of his life. Which was the cause that Fengon, boldned and incouraged by such impunitie, durst venture to couple himselfe in marriage with her whom hee used as his concubine during good Horvendiles life, in that sort spotting his name with a double vice, and charging his conscience with abhominable guilt, and two-fold impietie, as incestuous adulterie and parricide murther: and that the unfortunate and wicked woman, that had receaved the honour to bee the wife of one of the valiantest and wiseth† princes in the north, imbased her selfe in such vile sort, as to falsifie her faith unto him, and which is worse, to marrie him, that had bin the tyranous murtherer of her lawfull husband; which made divers men thinke that she had beene the causer of the murther, thereby to live in her adultery without controle. But where shall a man finde a more wicked and bold woman, then a great parsonage once having loosed the bands of honor and honestie? This princesse, who at the first, for her rare vertues and courtesses was honored of al men and beloved of her husband, as soone as she once gave eare to the tyrant Fengon, forgot both the ranke she helde among the greatest names, and the dutie of an honest wife on her behalfe. But I will not stand to gaze and mervaile at women, for that there are many which seeke to blase and set them foorth, in which their writings they spare not to blame them all for the faults of some one, or few women. But I say, that either nature ought to have bereaved man of that opinion to accompany with women, or els to endow them with such spirits, as that they may easily support the crosses they endure, without complaining so often and so strangely, seeing it is their owne beastlinesse that overthrowes them. For if it be so, that a woman is so imperfect a creature as they make her to be, and that they know this beast to bee so hard to bee tamed as they affirme, why then are they so foolish to preserve them, and so dull and brutish as to trust their deceitfull and wanton imbraceings. But let us leave her in this extreamitie of laciviousnesse, and proceed to showe you in what sort the yong prince Hamblet behaved himselfe, to escape the tyranny of his uncle.]

[III.]

Slanderers more honoured in court then vertuous persons.

The incestuous marriage of Fengon with his brothers wife.

If a man be deceived by a woman, it is his owne beastlinesse.

XLVIII

[II.]

Grande ruse du jeune prince Amleth.

fier en ses caresses? Geruthe s'estant ainsi oubliee, le Prince Amleth se voyant en danger de sa vie, abandonné de sa mere propre, delaissé de chacun, et que Fengon ne le souffriroit guere longuement sans luy faire tenir le chemin de Horwendille, pour tromper les ruses du tyran, qui le soupçonnoit pour tel, que s'il venoit à perfection d'aage il n'auroit garde se passer de poursuyvre la vengeance de la mort de son pere, il contrefit le fol, avec telle ruse, et subtilité, que faignant d'avoir tout perdu le sens, et souz un tel voile il couvrist ses desseins et defendist son salut, et vie, des trahisons et embusches du tyran. Car tous les jours estant au palais de la Royne, qui avoit plus de soing de plaire à son paillard, que de soucy de venger son mary, ou de remettre son filz en son heritage, il se souilloit tout de vilenie, se veautrant és balieures et immondices de la maison, et se frottant le visage de la fange des rues, par lesquelles il couroit comme un maniacle, ne disant rien, qui ne ressentist son transport de sens, et pure frenaisie, et toutes ses actions, et gestes, n'estoyent que les contenances d'un homme qui est privé de toute raison et entendement, de sorte qu'il ne servoit plus que de passetemps aux pages et courtisans esventez, qui estoyent à la suite de son oncle, et beaupere.

Mais le galant les marquoit avec intention de s'en venger un jour avec tel effort, qu'il en seroit à jamais memoire. Voila un grand traict de sagesse, et bon esprit en un jeune Prince, que de pourvoir avec un si grand defaut à son avancement, et par son abaissement, et mespris, de faciliter la voye, à estre un des plus heureux Roy de son aage: Aussi jamais homme ne fut reputé avec aucune sienne action plus sage et prudent, que Brute, faignant un grand desvoyement de son esprit: veu que l'occasion de telle ruyne fainte de son meilleur, ne proceda d'ailleurs, que d'un bon conseil, et sage deliberation, tant à fin de conserver ses biens, et eviter la rage du tyran le Roy superbe, qu'aussi pour se faire une large voye de chasser Tarquin, et affranchir le peuple oppressé souz le joug d'une grande et miserable servitude.

Aussi tant Brute, que cestuy cy, ausquels vous pouvez adjouster le Roy David, qui faignist le forcené entre les Royteletz de Palestine, pour conserver sa vie, monstrent la leçon à ceux qui malcontents de quelque grand, n'ont les forces suffisantes pour s'en prevaloir, ny se venger de

Chap. II.

[III.]

How Hamblet counterfeited the mad man, to escape the tyrannie of his uncle, and how he was tempted by a woman (through his uncles procurement) who thereby thought to undermine the Prince, and by that meanes to finde out whether he counterfeited madnesse or not: and how Hamblet would by no meanes bee brought to consent unto her, and what followed.

Geruth having (as I sayd before) so much forgotten herself, the prince Hamblet perceiving himself to bee in danger of his life, as beeing abandoned of his owne mother, and forsaken of all men, and assuring himselfe that Fengon would not detract the time to send him the same way his father Horvendile was gone, to beguile the tyrant in his subtilties (that esteemed him to bee of such a minde that if he once attained to mans estate he wold not long delay the time to revenge the death of his father) counterfeiting the mad man with such craft and subtill practises, that hee made shewe as if hee had utterly lost his wittes: and under that vayle hee covered his pretence, and defended his life from the treasons and practises of the tyrant his uncle. And all though bee had beene at the schoole of the Romane Prince, who, because hee counterfeited himselfe to bee a foole, was called Brutus, yet hee imitated his fashions, and his wisedom. For every day beeing in the queenes palace, (who as then was more carefull to please her whoremaster, then ready to revenge the cruell death of her husband, or to restore her sonne to his inheritance), hee rent and tore his clothes, wallowing and lying in the durt and mire, his face all filthy and blacke, running through the streets like a man distraught, not speaking one worde, but such as seemed to proceede of madnesse and meere frenzie; all his actions and jestures beeing no other than the right countenances of a man wholly deprived of all reason and understanding, in such sort, that as then hee seemed fitte for nothing but to make sport to the pages and ruffling courtiers that attended in the court of his uncle and father-in-law. But the yong prince noted them well enough, minding one day to bee revenged in such manner, that the memorie thereof should remaine perpetually to the world.

Beholde, I pray you, a great point of a wise and brave spirite in a yong prince, by so great a shewe of imperfection in his person for advancement, and his owne imbasing and despising, to worke the meanes and to prepare the way for himselfe to bee one of the happiest kings in his age. In like sort, never any man was reputed by any of his actions more wise and prudent then Brutus, dissembling a great alteration in his minde, for that the occasion of such his devise of foolishnesse proceeded onely of a good and mature counsell and deliberation, not onely to preserve his goods, and shunne the rage of the proude tyrant, but also to open a large way to procure the banishment and utter ruine of wicked Tarquinius, and to infranchise the people (which were before oppressed) from the yoake of a great and miserable servitude. And so, not onely Brutus, but this man and worthy prince, to whom wee may also adde king David, that counterfeited the madde man among the petie kings of Palestina to preserve his life from the subtill practises of those kings. I shew this example unto such, as beeing offended with any great personage, have not sufficient meanes to prevaile in their intents, or

Brutus esteemed wise, for counterfeiting the foole. Read Titus Livius and Halicarnassus.

David counterfeited the mad man before king Aches.

[II.] l'injure receue. Or quand je parle de se resentir d'un grand, duquel on aura esté outragé, il le faut entendre de celuy qui ne nous est point souverain, contre lequel ne faut regimber, ny luy tramer aucune trahison, ou conspirer aucunement contre sa vie.

Celuy qui veut suyvre tel chemin, faut qu'il parle, face tout au plaisir de l'homme qu'il veut tromper, loue ses actions, l'estime sur tout autre, et contraire en toute chose à ce qu'il a en son esprit: car c'est veritablement faire le sot, et contrefaire le fol, quand il faut dissimuler, et baiser la main de celuy, que l'on voudroit sçavoir cent piedz souz terre, pour n'en sentir point les aproches.

Amleth donc se façonnant à l'exercice d'une grande folie, faisoit des actes pleins de grande signifiance, et respondoit si à propos, qu'un sage homme eust jugé bien tost de quel esprit est-ce que sortoit une invention si gentile: car estant aupres du feu, et aiguisant des buchettes, en forme de poignars, estocs, quelqu'un luy demanda en riant à quoy servoyent ces

Responce subtile du prince Amleth.

petits bastons, et qu'il faisoit de ces buchettes: J'apreste, dit-il, des dards acerez et sagettes poignantes, pour venger la mort de mon pere. Les fols, comme j'ay dit, acomptoyent cecy à peu de sens, mais les hommes accors, et qui avoyent le nez long, commencerent à soupçonner ce qui estoit, et estimerent que souz ceste folie gisoit, et estoit cachee une grande finesse, et telle qui pourroit estre un jour prejudiciable à leur Prince: disant que sous telle rudesse et simplicité il voiloit une grande et cauteleuse sagesse, et qu'il celoit un grand lustre de bon esprit, souz l'obscurité de ceste fardee subtilité. A ceste cause donnerent conseil au Roy de tenter par tout moyen s'il se pourroit faire, que ce fard fust decouvert, et qu'on s'apperçeust de la tromperie de l'adolescent. Or ne voyoient ils ruse plus propre pour l'atraper, que s'il luy mettoyent quelque belle femme en lieu secret, laquelle taschast de le gaigner avec ses caresses les plus mignardes et attrayantes, desquelles elle se pourroit adviser. D'autant que le naturel de tout jeune homme, mesmement estant nourry à son ayse, est si transporté aux plaisirs de la chair, et se lance avec telle impetuosité à la jouyssance, qui lui est octroyee, de ce qui est excellemment beau, qu'il est presque impossible de couvrir telle affection, ny d'en dissimuler les apprehensions par art, ny industrie quelconque, ny de le fuyr, quelque ruse qu'il usast pour pallier sa malice: veu que s'offrant l'occasion, et icelle secrette de la volupté la plus chatouilleuse, il faudroit que forcé des apetits, il succombast aux efforts, et puissance de la partie sensuelle.

Ruse pour descouvrir les finesses de Amleth.

Ainsi furent deputez quelques courtisans, pour mener le Prince en quelque lieu escarté, dedans le bois, et lesquels luy presentassent ceste femme, l'incitans à se souiller en ses baysers et embrassemens, artifices assez frequens de nostre temps, non pour essayer si les grands sont hors de leur sens, mais pour les priver de force, vertu et sagesse, par le moyen de ses sangsues et infernales Lamies, produites par leurs serviteurs, ministres de corruption. Le povre Prince eust esté en danger de succomber à cest assaut, si un Gentil-homme, qui du vivant de Horwendille, qui avoit esté nourry avec luy, ne se fust plus monstré amy de la neurriture prinse avec Amleth, que affectionné à la puissance du tyran, lequel pourchassoit les moyens de envelopper le fils és pieges, esquels le pere avoit finy ses jours, et lequel s'accompaigna des courtisans deputez

revenge the injurie by them receaved. But when I speake of revenging any injury received upon a great personage or superior, it must be understood by such an one as is not our soveraigne, againste whome wee maie by no meanes resiste, nor once practise anie treason nor conspiracie against his life: and hee that will followe this course must speake and do all things whatsoever that are pleasing and acceptable to him whom hee meaneth to deceive, practise his actions, and esteeme him above all men, cleane contrarye to his owne intent and meaning; for that is rightly to playe and counterfeite the foole, when a man is constrained to dissemble and kisse his hand, whome in hearte hee could wishe an hundred foote depth under the earth, so hee mighte never see him more, if it were not a thing wholly to bee disliked in a christian, who by no meanes ought to have a bitter gall, or desires infected with revenge. Hamblet, in this sorte counterfeiting the madde man, many times did divers actions of great and deepe consideration, and often made such and so fitte answeres, that a wise man would soone have judged from what spirite so fine an invention mighte proceede; for that standing by the fire and sharpning sticks like poynards and prickes, one in smiling manner asked him wherefore he made those little staves so sharpe at the points? I prepare (saith he) piersing dartes and sharpe arrowes to revenge my fathers death. Fooles, as I said before, esteemed those his words as nothing; but men of quicke spirits, and such as hadde a deeper reache began to suspect somewhat, esteeming that under that kinde of folly there lay hidden a greate and rare subtilty, such as one day might bee prejudiciall to their prince, saying, that under colour of such rudenes he shadowed a crafty pollicy, and by his devised simplicitye, he concealed a sharp and pregnant spirit: for which cause they counselled the king to try and know, if it were possible, how to discover the intent and meaning of the yong prince; and they could find no better nor more fit invention to intrap him, then to set some faire and beawtifull woman in a secret place, that with flattering speeches and all the craftiest meanes she could use, should purposely seek to allure his mind to have his pleasure of her: for the nature of all young men, (especially such as are brought up wantonlie) is so transported with the desires of the flesh, and entreth so greedily into the pleasures therof, that it is almost impossible to cover the foul affection, neither yet to dissemble or hyde the same by art or industry, much lesse to shunne it. What cunning or subtilty so ever they use to cloak theire pretence, seeing occasion offered, and that in secret, especially in the most inticing sinne that rayneth in man, they cannot chuse (being constrayned by voluptuousnesse) but fall to naturall effect and working. To this end certaine courtiers were appointed to leade Hamblet into a solitary place within the woods, whether they brought the woman, inciting him to take their pleasures together, and to imbrace one another, but the subtill practises used in these our daies, not to try if men of great account bee extract out of their wits, but rather to deprive them of strength, vertue and wisedome, by meanes of such devilish practitioners, and intefernall† spirits, their domestical servants, and ministers of corruption. And surely the poore prince at this assault had him in great danger, if a gentleman (that in Horvendiles time had been nourished with him) had not showne himselfe more affectioned to the bringing up he had received with Hamblet, then desirous to please the tirant, who by all meanes sought to intangle the sonne in the same nets wherein the father had ended his dayes. This gentleman bare the courtyers (appointed as aforesaide of this treason) company, more desiring to

[III.]

Rom. VIII. 21.

A subtill answere of Prince Hamlet.

Nature corrupted in man.

Subtilties used to discover Hamblets madnes.

Corrupters of yong gentlemen in princes courts and great houses.

[II.]

pour ceste trahison, plus avec deliberation d'instruire le Prince, de ce qu'il avoit à faire, que pour luy dresser des embusches et le trahir, estimant que le moindre indice qu'il donneroit de son bon sens, qu'il suffiroit, pour luy faire perdre la vie. Cestuy-cy avec certains signes fait entendre à Amleth, en quel peril est ce qu'il se metroit, si en sorte aucune il obeyssoit aux mignardes caresses, et mignotises de la Damoyselle, envoyee par son oncle, ce qu'estonnant le Prince, esmeu de la beauté de la fille, fut par elle asseuré encor de la trahison: car elle l'aymoit des son enfance, et eust esté bien marrie de son desastre et fortune, et plus de sortir de ses mains, sans jouyr de celuy qu'elle aymoit plus que soy-mesme. Ayant le jeune seigneur trompé les courtisans, et la fille, soustenant qu'il ne s'estoit avancé en sorte aucune à la violer, quoy qu'il dist du contraire, chacun s'asseura que veritablement il estoit insensé, et que son cerveau n'avoit force quelconque, capable d'apprehension raisonnable. Entre tous les amis

Autre ruse pour tromper Amleth.

de Fengon, en y avoit un qui sur tout autre se doutoit des ruses, et subtilitez de ce fol dissimulé, lequel pour ceste raison dict, qu'il estoit impossible qu'un galant si rusé, que ce plaisant qui contrefaisoit le fol, fust descouvert avec des subtilitez si communes, et lesquelles on pouvoit aisément descouvrir: et que par ainsi il falloit inventer quelque moyen plus accort et subtil, et ou l'astuce fust attrayante, et l'attrait si fort, que le galant ny sceust user de ses accoustumees dissimulations. De cecy il se disoit sçavoir une voye propre pour executer leur dessein, et de surprendre Amleth en ses ruses, et luy faire de luy-mesme se prendre au filet, et declarer quelles sont les conceptions de son ame. Il faut (dit-il) que le Roy Fengon faigne s'en aller en quelque voyage, pour quelque affaire de grande importance, et que cependant on enferme Amleth seul avec sa mere dans une chambre, dans laquelle soit caché quelqu'un au desseu de l'un et de l'autre, pour ouyr et sentir leurs propos, et les complots qu'ils prendront, pour les desseins bastyz par ce fol sage et rusé compagnon. Asseurant le Roy que s'il y avoit rien de sage, ny arresté en l'esprit ny cerveau du jeune homme, que facilement il se descouvriroit à sa mere, sans craindre rien, et qu'il feroit son conseil et deliberation à la foy, et loyauté de celle qui l'avoit porté en ses flancs, et nourry avec si grande diligence.

Cestuy mesme s'offrist pour estre l'espion, et tesmoing des propos

give the prince instruction what he should do, then to intrap him, making
full account that the least showe of perfect sence and wisedome that
Hamblet should make would be sufficient to cause him to loose his life:
and therefore by certain signes, he gave Hamblet intelligence in what danger
hee was like to fall, if by any meanes hee seemed to obaye, or once like
the wanton toyes and vicious provocations of the gentlewoman sent thither
by his uncle. Which much abashed the prince, as then wholy beeing in
affection to the lady, but by her he was likewise informed of the treason,
as being one that from her infancy loved and favoured him, and would
have been exceeding sorrowfull for his misfortune, and much more to
leave his companie without injoying the pleasure of his body, whome she
loved more than herselfe. The prince in this sort having both deceived
the courtiers, and the ladyes expectation, that affirmed and swore that
hee never once offered to have his pleasure of the woman, although in
subtilty hee affirmed the contrary, every man there upon assured themselves that without all doubt he was distraught of his sences, that his
braynes were as then wholly void of force, and incapable of reasonable
apprehension, so that as then Fengons practise took no effect: but for al
that he left not off, still seeking by al meanes to finde out Hamblets
subtilty, as in the next chapter you shall perceive.

[III.]

Chap. III.

How Fengon, uncle to Hamblet, a second time to intrap him in
his politick madnes, caused one of his counsellors to be secretly
hidden in the queenes chamber, behind the arras, to heare what
speeches passed between Hamblet and the Queen; and how Hamblet killed him, and escaped that danger, and what followed.

Among the friends of Fengon, there was one that above al the rest
doubted of Hamblets practises in counterfeiting the madman, who for
that cause said, that it was impossible that so craftie a gallant as Hamblet, that counterfeited the foole, should be discovered with so common
and unskilfull practises, which might easily bee perceived, and that to
finde out his politique pretence it were necessary to invent some subtill
and crafty meanes, more attractive, whereby the gallant might not have
the leysure to use his accustomed dissimulation; which to effect he said
he knewe a fit waie, and a most convenient meane to effect the kings
desire, and thereby to intrap Hamblet in his subtilties, and cause him
of his owne accord to fall into the net prepared for him, and thereby evidently shewe his secret meaning. His devise was thus, that King Fengon
should make as though he were to goe some long voyage concerning
affaires of great importance, and that in the meane time Hamblet should
be shut up alone in a chamber with his mother, wherein some other
should secretly be hidden behind the hangings, unknowne either to him
or his mother, there to stand and heere their speeches, and the complots
by them to bee taken concerning the accomplishement of the dissembling
fooles pretence; assuring the king that if there were any point of wisedome
and perfect sence in the gallants spirit, that without all doubte he would
easily discover it to his mother, as being devoid of all feare that she
would utter or make knowne his secret intent, beeing the woman that
had borne him in her bodie, and nourished him so carefully; and withall offered himselfe to be the man that should stand to harken and beare

Another subtilty used to deceive Hamblet.

[II.]

Cautelle de Amleth.

du fils avec la mere, à fin qu'on ne l'estimast tel qui donnoit un conseil, duquel il refusast estre l'executeur, pour servir son Prince. Le Roy print grand plaisir à ceste invention, comme le seul souverain remede pour guerir le Prince de sa folie: et ainsi en faignant un long voyage, sort du Palais, et s'en va pourmener à la chasse, là ou cependant le conseil entra secrettement en la chambre de la Royne, se cachant souz quelque loudier: un peu au paravant que le fils y fust enclos avec sa mere. Lequel comme il estoit fin et cauteleux, si tost qu'il fut dedans la chambre, se douta de quelque trahison et surprinse: et que s'il parloit à sa mere de quelque cas serieux, il ne fust entendu, continuant en ses façons de faire, folles et niaises, se prist à chanter tout ainsi qu'un coq, et batant tout ainsi des bras, comme cest oyseau fait des aisles, sauta sur ce loudier, ou sentant qu'il y avoit dessous quelque cas caché, ne faillit aussi tost d'y donner dedans à tout son glaive, puis tirant le galant à demy mort, l'acheva d'occir, et le mit en pieces, puis le fait bouillir, et cuit qu'il est le jetta par un grand conduit de cloaque, par ou sortoient les immondicitez, affin qu'il servist de pasture aux pourceaux. Ayant ainsi descouvert l'embusche, et puny l'inventeur d'icelle il s'en revint trouver la Royne, laquelle se tourmentoit et plouroit voyant toute son esperance perdue: car quelque faute qu'elle eust commise, si estoit elle angoissee grandement, voyant que ce seul fils qui luy restoit, ne luy servoit que de mocquerie, chacun luy reprochant sa folie, un trait de laquelle elle en avoit veu devant ses yeux: ce qui luy donna un grand elancement de conscience, estimant que les Dieux luy envoyassent ceste punition, pour s'estre incestueusement accouplee avec le tyran meurtrier de son espoux, et lequel ne laissoit moyen aucun, qu'il ne cherchast pour mettre fin à la vie de son neveu, accusant l'indiscretion naturelle, qui est la guide ordinaire de celles qui ayment tant les plaisirs du corps, que voilant la voye à toute raison, n'advisent ce qui peut s'ensuyvir de leur legereté et grande inconstance, et comme un plaisir de peu de duree suffisoit, pour luy causer un repentir à jamais, et luy faire maudire l'heure que onc ces apprehensions si volages luy avoyent saisi l'esprit, ny bandé les yeux pour rejetter l'honnesteté requise à Dame de son calibre, et à mespriser la saincte institution des Dames, qui l'avoyent precedé, et en sang, et en vertu. Se souvenoit du bon renom, et grandes louanges donnees par tous les Danoys à Rinde fille du Roy Rothere, la plus chaste de son temps, et si pudique, que jamais elle ne voulut entendre à mariage d'aucun Prince, ny Chevalier, surpassant tout ainsi en vertu les Dames de son pays, comme elle les surmontoit en beauté, doux maintien et bonne grace. Mais ainsi que la Royne se tourmentoit, voicy entrer Amleth, lequel ayant visité encor tous les coings de la chambre, comme se deffiant aussi bien de sa mere, que des autres, se voyant seul avec elle luy parla fort sagement en ceste maniere.

Faict cruel d'Amleth sur celuy qui le vouloit trahir.

Repentance de la royne Geruth.

Rinde princesse d'une admirable chasteté.

Harangue d'Amleth à la Royne Geruthe sa mere.

Quelle trahison est ceste-cy, ô la plus infame de toutes celles qui onc se sont prostituees à la volonté de quelque paillard abominable, que souz le fard d'un pleur dissimulé, vous convriez l'acte le plus meschant, et le crime le plus detestable, que homme sçauroit imaginer, ny commettre? Quelle fiance peux-je avoir en vous, qui comme une lascive paillarde,

witnesse of Hamblets speeches with his mother, that hee might not be esteemed a counsellor in such a case wherein he refused to be the executioner for the behoofe and service of his prince. This invention pleased the king exceeding well, esteeming it as the onelie and soveraigne remedie to heale the prince of his lunacie; and to that ende making a long voyage, issued out of his pallace, and road to hunt in the forrest. Meane time the counsellor entred secretly into the queenes chamber, and there hid himselfe behind the arras, not long before the queene and Hamblet came thither, who beeing craftie and pollitique, as soone as hee was within the chamber, doubting some treason, and fearing if he should speake severely and wisely to his mother touching his secret practises he should be unterstood, and by that meanes intercepted, used his ordinary manner of dissimulation, and began to come like a cocke beating with his armes, (in such manner as cockes use to strike with their wings) upon the hangings of the chamber: whereby, feeling something stirring under them, he cried, A rat, a rat! and presently drawing his sworde thrust it into the hangings, which done, pulled the counsellour (halfe dead) out by the heeles, made an end of killing him, and beeing slaine, cut his bodie in pieces, which he caused to be boyled, and then cast it into an open vaulte or privie, that so it mighte serve fore foode to the hogges. By which meanes having discovered the ambushe, and given the inventer thereof his just rewarde, hee came againe to his mother, who in the meane time wepte and tormented her selfe to see all her hopes frustrate, for that what fault soever she had committed, yet was shee sore grieved to see her onely child made a meere mockery, every man reproaching her with his folly, one point whereof she had as then seene before her eyes, which was no small pricke to her conscience, esteeming that the gods sent her that punishment for joining incestuously in marriage with the tyrannous murtherer of her husband, who like wise ceased not to invent all the means he could to bring his nephew to his ende, accusing his owne naturall indiscretion, as beeing the ordinary guide of those that so much desire the pleasures of the bodie, who shutting up the waie to all reason, respect not what maie eusue of their lightnes and great inconstancy, and how a pleasure of small moment is sufficient to give them cause of repentance during their lives, and make them curse the daye and time that ever any such apprehensions entred into theire mindes, or that they closed their eies to reject the honestie requisite in ladies of her qualitie, and to despise the holy institution of those dames that had gone before her, both in nobilitie and vertue, calling to mind the great prayses and commendations given by the danes to Rinde, daughter to king Rothere, the chastest lady in her time, and withall so shamefast that she would never consent to marriage with any prince or knight whatsoever; surpassing in vertue all the ladyes of her time, as shee herselfe surmounted them in beawtie, good behaviour, and comelines. And while in this sort she sate tormenting herselfe, Hamlet entred into the chamber, who having once againe searched every corner of the same, distrusting his mother as well as the rest, and perceiving himselfe to bee alone, began in sober and discreet manner to speak unto her, saying,

What treason ist his, O most infameus woman! of all that ever prostrated themselves to the will of an abhominable whore monger, who, under the vail of a dissembling creature, covereth the most wicked and detestable crime that man could ever imagine, or was committed. Now may I be assured to trust you, that like a vile wanton adultresse, alto-

[III.]

Hamblets subtilty.

A cruell revenge taken by Hamble upon him that'd would have betrait him.

Queens Gernthes repentance.

Rinde a princes of an admirable chastitie.

[II.] desreiglee sur toute impudicité, allez courant les bras tendus apres celuy felon et traistre tyran, qui est le meurtrier de mon pere, et caressez incestueusement le voleur du lict legitime de vostre loyal espoux, mignardez impudiquement celuy qui estoit le pere cher de ce fils miserable, et privé de tout comfort, si les Dieux ne luy font la grace d'eschapper bien tost d'une captivité tant indigne du rang qu'il tient, et de la noble race et illustre famille de ses ancestres et majeurs? Est-ce à une Royne, et fille de Roy, de suyvre les appetits des bestes, et que tout ainsi que les jumens s'accouplent à ceux qui ont vaincu leurs premiers maris, vous suyviez la volonté du Roy abominable, qui a tué un plus vaillant et homme de bien que luy, et a esteint, en massacrant Horwendille, la gloire et honneur des Danoys, lesquels sont aneantis, sans force, coeur ny vaillance, depuis que le lustre de chevalerie a eu pris fin par le plus poltron et cruel vilain de la terre? Je ne veux l'estimer mon parent, et ne puis le regarder comme oncle, ny vous comme mere treschere, l'un n'ayant respecté le sang qui nous devoit unir plus estroittement, qu'avec l'alliance de l'autre, qui aussi ne pouvoit avec son honneur ny sans soupçon d'avoir consenti à la mort de son espoux, s'accorder jamais aux nopces de son cruel ennemy.

Ah Royne Geruthe! c'est à faire aux chiennes à se mesler avec plusieurs, et souhaiter le mariage et accouplement de divers masles: c'est la lubricité seule qui vous a effacé en l'ame la memoire des vaillances et vertus du bon Roy, vostre espoux, et mon pere: c'est un desir effrené qui a conduit la fille de Rorique à embrasser le tyran Fengon, sans respecter les ombres de Horwendille, indigne de si estrange traictement, et que son frere l'occit traistreusement, et que sa femme le trayst laschement, laquelle il a tant bien traictee, et pour l'amour de laquelle il a jadis despouillé Norverge† de richesses, et despeuplé d'hommes vaillans pour accroistre les thresos‡ de Rorique, et rendre Geruthe l'espouse du plus hardy Prince de l'Europe. Ce n'est pas estre femme, et moins Princesse, en laquelle doit reluire toute douceur, courtoisie, compassion et amitié, que laisser ainsi sa chere geniture à l'abandon de fortune, et entre les mains sanglantes et meurtrieres d'un felon et voleur, les bestes plus farouches n'en sont pas ainsi: car les lions, tigres, onces et leopards, combatent pour la deffense de leurs faons, et les oyseaux de bec, griffes et esles resistent à ceux qui veulent voler leurs petits, là où vous m'exposez et livrez à mort en lieu de me defendre. N'est-ce pas me trahir, quand cognoissant la perversité d'un tyran, et ses desseins, pleins de conseil de mort sur la race et image de son frere, vous n'ayez sceu ou daigné trouver les moyens de sauver vostre enfant ou en Suece, ou Norvege, ou plustost l'exposer aux Anglois, que le laisser la proye de vostre infame adultere? Ne vous offensez je vous prie, Madame, si transporté de douleur, je vous parle si rigoureusement, et si je vous respecte moins que de mon devoir: car vous m'ayant oublié, et mis à neant la memoire du deffunct Roy mon pere, ne faut s'esbahir, si aussi je sors des limites de toute recognoissance. Voyez en quelles destresses je suis tombé, et à quel malheur m'a acheminé ma fortune, et vostre trop grande legereté, et peu de sagesse, que je sois contraint de faire le fol, et imite les façons de faire d'un insensé, pour sauver ma vie, en lieu de m'adextrer aux armes, suivre les adventures, et tascher par tout moyen de me faire cog-

LVII

gether impudent and given over to her pleasure, runnes spreading forth [III.] her armes joyfully to imbrace the trayterous villanous tyrant that murthered my father, and most incestuously receivest the villain into the lawfull bed of your loyall spouse, imprudently entertaining him in steede of the deare father of your miserable and discomforted soone†, if the gods grant him not the grace speedilie to escape from a captivity so unworthie the degree he holdeth, and the race and noble familie of his ancestors. Is this the part of a queene, and daughter to a king? to live like a brute beast (and like a mare that yieldeth her bodie to the horse that hath beaten hir companion awaye), to followe the pleasure of an abhominable king that hath murthered a farre more honester and better man then himself in massacring Horvendile, the honor and glory of the Danes, who are now esteemed of no force nor valour at all, since the shining splendure of knighthood was brought to an end by the most wickedest and cruellest villaine living upon earth. I, for my part, will never account him for my kinsman, nor once knowe him for mine uncle, nor you my deer mother, for not having respect to the blud that ought to have united us so * ✓ straightly together, and who neither with your honor nor without suspicion of consent to the death of your husband could ever have agreed to have marryed with his cruell enemie. O, queene Geruthe, it is the part of a bitch to couple with many, and desire acquaintance of divers mastiffes: it is licentiousnes only that hath made you deface ont of your minde the memory of the valor and vertues of the good king your husband and my father: it was an unbrideled desire that guided the daughter of Roderick to imbrace the tyrant Fengon, and not to remember Horvendile (unworthy of so strange intertainment), neither that he killed his brother traiterously, and that shee being his fathers wife betrayed him, * although he so well favoured and loved her, that for her sake he utterly bereaved Norway of her riches and valiant souldiers to augment the treasures of Roderick, and make Geruthe wife to the hardyest prince in Europe: it is not the parte of a woman, much lesse of a princesse, in whome all modesty, curtesse, compassion, and love ought to abound, thus to leave her deare child to fortune in the bloody and murtherous hands of a villain and traytor. Bruite beasts do not so, for lyons, tygers, ounces and leopards fight for the safety and defence of their whelpes; and birds that have beakes, claws, and wings, resist such as would ravish them of their yong ones; but you, to the contrary, expose and deliver mee to death, whereas ye should defend me. Is not this as much as if you should betray me, when you knowing the preversenes of the tyrant and his intents, ful of deadly counsell as touching the race and image of his brother, have not once sought, nor desired to finde the meanes to save your child (and only son) by sending him into Swethland, Norway, or England, rather than to leave him as a pray to youre infamous adulterer? bee not offended, I praye you, Madame, if transported with dolour and griefe, I speake so boldely unto you, and that I respect you lesse then duetie requireth; for you, having forgotten mee, and wholy rejected the memorye of the deceased K. my father, must not bee abashed if I also surpasse the bounds and limits of due consideration. Beholde into what distresse I am now fallen, and to what mischiefe my fortune, and your over great lightnesse, and want of wisdome have induced mee, that I am constrained to playe the madde man to save my life, in steed of using and practising armes, following adventures, and seeking all meanes to make myselfe knowne to bee the true and undoubted heire of the valiant

[II.] noistre pour le vray enfant du vaillant et vertueux Roy Horwendille. Ce n'est sans cause et juste occasion que mes gestes, contenances et parolles resentent le fol, et que je veux que chacun me tienne pour privé de sens et cognoissance, veu que je sçay bien que celuy qui n'a point fait conscience de tuer son propre frere, accoustumé aux meurtres, et alleché au gouvernement sans avoir compaignon, quil luy contrerolle ses meschancetez, et trahisons, ne se souciera gueres de s'acharner avec pareille cruanté, sur le sang et reliques qui sont sorties de son frere par luy massacré: ainsi, il me vaut mieux feindre l'un, que suyvre ce que nature me donne: les clairs et saincts rayons de laquelle j'absconse souz cest ombragement, tout ainsi que le Soleil ses flammes souz quelque grand nuage, durant les ardeurs de l'Esté. Le visage d'un insensé me duit, pour y couvrir mes gaillardises et les gestes d'un fol me sont propres, à fin que sagement me conduisant, je conserve ma vie au pays Danoys, et à la memoire du feu Roy mon pere. Car les desirs de le venger sont tellement gravez en mon coeur que si bien tost je ne meurs, j'espere d'en faire une telle, et si haute vengeance qu'il en sera à jamais parlé en ces terres: toutesfois faut-il attendre le temps et les moyens et occasions, à fin que si je precipitois par trop les matieres, je ne causasse ma ruine trop soudaine, et ne finisse plustost que donner commencement aux effects de ce que mon coeur desseigne.

En grandes entreprises ne faut rien precipiter.

Aussi faut-il que contre un meschant desloyal, cruel et descourtois homme, on use des plus gentiles inventions et forbes, desquelles se peut adviser un bon esprit, pour ne descouvrir point son entreprise, veu que la force n'estant point de mon costé: c'est raison que les ruses, dissimulations, et secrettes menees y donnent ordre.

Au reste, Madame, neplourez point pour l'esgard de ma folie, plustost gemissez la faute que vous avez commise, et vous tourmentez pour celle infamie qui a souillee celle ancienne renommee, et gloire qui rendoit illustre la Royne Geruthe: car ce n'est les vices d'autruy qui doivent élancer nos consciences, ains faut se douloir de nos meffaits et trop grandes folies. Vous advisant au reste sur tout aussi cher que vous avez la vie, que le roy ny autre ne soit en rien informé de cecy, et me laissez faire au reste: car j'espere de venir à bout de mon entreprise.

Faut plorer pour ses fautes, et non pour le vice d'autruy.

Quoy que la Royne se sentist piquer† de bien pres, et que Amleth la touchant vivement où plus elle se sentoit interessee, si est-ce qu'elle oublia tout le desdain qu'elle eust peu concevoir, se voyant ainsi aigrement tencee et reprinse, pour la grand'joye qui la saisit, cognoissant la gentillesse d'esprit de son fils, et ce qu'elle pouvoit esperer d'une telle et si grande sagesse: d'un costé elle n'osoit lever les yeux pour le regarder, se souvenant de sa faute, et de l'autre, elle eust volontiers embrassé son fils, pour les sages admonitions qu'il luy avoit fait, et lesquelles eurent telle efficace, que sur l'heure elle esteignit les flammes de convoitise, qui l'avoyent rendue amye de Fengon, pour planter encor en son coeur le souvenir des vertus de son espoux legitime, lequel elle regretoit en son coeur, voyant la vive image de sa vertu et sagesse en cest enfant, representant le hault coeur de son pere. Ainsi vaincue de ceste honneste passion, et fondant toute en larmes, apres avoir longuement tenu les yeux fichez sur Amleth, comme ravie en quelque grande contemplation, et saisie de quelque estonnement, en fin l'accolant, avec la mesme amitie qu'une

and vertuous king Horvendile. It was not without cause, and juste occasion, that my gestures, countenances, and words, seeme all to proceed from a madman, and that I desire to have all men esteeme mee wholly deprived of sence and reasonable understanding, bycause I am well assured, that he that hath made no conscience to kill his owne brother, (accustomed to murthers, and allured with desire of governement without controll in his treasons), will not spare, to save himselfe with the like crueltie, in the blood and flesh of the loyns of his brother by him massacred: and, therefore, it is better for me to fayne madnesse, then to use my right sences as nature hath bestowed them upon me; the bright shining clearnes thereof I am forced to hide under this shadow of dissimulation, as the sun doth hir beames under some great cloud, when the wether in sommer time overcasteth. The face of a mad man serveth to cover my gallant countenance, and the gestures of a fool are fit for me, to the end that guiding myself wisely therein, I may preserve my life for the Danes, and the memory of my late deceased father; for the desire of revenging his death is so engraven in my heart, that if I dye not shortly, I hope to take such and so great vengeance, that these countryes shall for ever speake thereof. Neverthelesse, I must stay the time, meanes, and occasion, lest by making over great hast, I be now the cause of mine owne sodaine ruine and overthrow, and by that meanes end before I beginne to effect my hearts desire. Hee that hath to doe with a wicked, disloyall, cruell, and discourteous man must use craft and politike inventions, such as a fine witte can best imagine, not to discover his interprise; for seeing that by force I cannot effect my desire, reason alloweth me by dissimulation, subtiltie, and secret practises to proceed therein. To conclude, weepe not (madame) to see my folly, but rather sigh and lament your owne offence, tormenting your conscience in regard of the infamie that hath so defiled the ancient renowne and glorie that (in times past) honoured queene Geruth; for wee are not to sorrowe and grieve at other mens vices, but for our owne misdeedes, and great folloyes. Desiring you, for the surplus of my proceedings, above all things (as you love your owne life and welfare) that neither the king nor any other may by any meanes know mine intent; and let me alone with the rest, for I hope in the ende to bring my purpose to effect.

[II.]

We must use subtiltie to a disloyal person.

Wee must weepe for our owne faults and not for other mens.

Although the queene perceived herselfe neerly touched, and that Hamlet mooved her to the quicke, where she felt herselfe interested, neverthelesse shee forgot all disdaine and wrath, which thereby she might as then have had, hearing herselfe so sharply chiden and reprooved, for the joy she then conceaved, to behold the gallant spirit of her sonne, and to thinke what she might hope, and the easier expect of his so great policie and wisedome. But on the one side she durst not lift up her eyes to behold him, remembering her offence, and on the other side she would gladly have imbraced her son, in regard of the wise admonitions by him given unto her, which as then quenched the flames of unbridled desire that before had moved her to affect K. Fengon, to ingraff in her heart the vertuous actions of her lawfull spouse, whom inwardly she much lamented, when she beheld the lively image and portraiture of his vertue and great wisedome in her childe, representing his fathers haughtie and valiant heart: and so, overcome and vanquished with this honest passion, and weeping most bitterly, having long time fixed her eyes upon Hamlet, as beeing ravished into some great and deepe contemplation, and as it were wholy amazed, at the last imbracing him in her armes (with the like

[II.]

Geruthe à son fils Amleth.

mere vertueusse peut baiser, et caresser sa portee, elle luy usa de ce langage :

Je sçay bien (mon fils) que je t'ay fait tort en souffrant le mariage de Fengon, pour estre le cruel tyran et assassineur de ton pere, et de mon loyal espoux : mais quand tu considereras le peu de moyens de resistence, et la trahison de ceux du Palais, le peu de fiance que nous pouvons avoir aux courtisans tous faicts à sa poste, et la force qu'il preparoit : là où j'eusse fait refus de son alliance, tu m'excuseras plustost que accuser de lubricité, ny d'inconstance, et moins me feras ce tort que de soupçonner que jamais Geruthe ait consenty à la mort de son espoux, te jurant par la haute majesté des Dieux, que s'il eust esté en ma puissance de resister au tyran, et qu'avec l'effusion de mon sang, et perte de ma vie, j'eusse peu sauver la vie de mon seigneur et espoux, je l'eusse fait d'aussi bon coeur, comme depuis j'ay plusieurs fois donné empeschement à l'accourcissement de la tienne, laquelle t'estant ravie, je ne veux plus demeurer en ce monde, puis que l'esprit estant sain, je voy les moyens plus aisez de la vengeance de ton pere. Toutesfois, mon fils, et doux amy, si tu as pitié de toy, et soin de la memoire de ton pere : et si tu veux rien faire pour celle qui ne merite point le nom de mere en ton endroit, je te prie de conduire sagement tes affaires, n'estre hasté, ny trop bouillant en tes entreprinses, n'y t'avancer plus que de raison à l'offect de ton dessein. Tu voys qu'il n'y a homme presque en qui tu te puisses fier, ny moy femme à qui j'osasse avoir dit un seul secret, lequel ne soit soudain raporté à ton adversaire, lequel combien qu'il feigne de m'aimer, pour jouyr de mes embrassemens, si est-ce qu'il se deffie, et craint de moy, à ta cause : et n'est si sot qu'il se puisse bien persuader, que tu sois fol, ou incensé ; or si tu fais quelque acte qui ressente rien de serieux, et prudent, tant secrettement le sçaches tu executer, si est-ce que soudain il en aura les nouvelles, et ne† crains encor que les Demons ne luy signifient ce qui s'est passé à present entre nous, tant fortune nous est contraire, et poursuit nos aises, ou que ce meurtre que tu as commis, ne soit cause de nostre ruine, duquel je feindray ne sçavoir rien, comme aussi je tiendray secrette, et ta sagesse, et ta gaillarde entreprinse. Priant les Dieux (mon fils) que guidans ton coeur, dressans tes conseils, et bienheurans ton entreprinse, je te voye jouyssant des biens qui te sont deuz, et de la couronne de Dannemarch, que le tyran t'a ravie, à fin que j'aye le moyen de me resjouyr en ta prosperité, et me contenter, voyant avec quelle hardiesse tu auras pris vengeance du meurtrier de ton pere, et de ceux qui luy ont donné faveur, et main forte pour l'executer. Madame, respondit Amleth, j'adjousteray foy à vostre dire, et ne veux m'enquerir plus outre de vos affaires : vous priant que selon l'amitié que vous devez à vostre sang, vous ne faciez plus de compte de ce paillard mon ennemy, lequel je feray mourir, quoy que tous les demons le tinssent en leur garde, et ne sera en la puissance de ses courtisans, que je n'en depesche le monde, et qu'eux mesmes ne l'accompaignent aussi bien à sa mort, comme ils ont esté les pervers conseillers de la mort de mon pere,

love that a vertuous mother may or can use to kisse and entertaine her [III.]
owne childe), shee spake unto him in this manner.

I know well (my sonne) that I have done thee great wrong in
marrying with Fengon, the cruell tyrant and murtherer of thy father, and
my loyall spouse: but when thou shalt consider the small meanes of
resistance, and the treason of the palace, with the little cause of confidence we are to expect or hope for of the courtiers, all wrought to his
will, as also the power hee made ready, if I should have refused to like
of him, thou wouldest rather excuse then accuse me of lasciviousnes or
inconstancy, much lesse offer me that wrong to suspect that ever thy
mother Geruthe once consented to the death and murther of her husband:
swearing unto thee (by the majestie of the Gods) that if it had layne in
my power to have resisted the tyrant, although it had beene with the
losse of my blood, yea and my life, I would surely have saved the life
of my lord and husband, with as good a will and desire as, since that time,
I have often beene a meanes to hinder and impeach the shortning of thy
life, which being taken away, I will no longer live here upon earth.
For seeing that thy sences are whole and sound, I am in hope to see an
easie meanes invented for the revenging of thy fathers death. Neverthelesse, mine owne sweet soone, if thou hast pittie of thy selfe, or care of
the memorie of thy father (although thou wilt do nothing for her that
deserveth not the name of a mother in this respect), I pray thee, carie
thine affayres wisely: bee not hastie, nor over furious in thy interprises,
neither yet advance thy selfe more then reason shall moove thee to effect
thy purpose. Thou seest there is not almost any man wherein thou mayest
put thy trust, nor any woman to whom I dare utter the least part of my
secrets, that would not presently report it to thine adversarie, who, although
in outward shew he dissembleth to love thee, the better to injoy his pleasures of me, yet hee distrusteth and feareth mee for thy sake, and is
not so simple to be easily perswaded that thou art a foole or mad; so
that if thou chance to doe any thing that seemeth to proceed of wisedome
or policie (how secretly soever it be done) he will presently be informed
thereof, and I am greatly afraide that the devils have shewed him what
hath past at this present betweene us, (fortune so much pursueth and
contrarieth our ease and welfare) or that this murther that now thou
hast committed be not the cause of both our destructions, which I by no
meanes will seeme to know, but will keepe secret both thy wisedome and
hardy interprise; beseeching the Gods (my good soone) that they, guiding
thy heart, directing thy counsels, and prospering thy interprise, I may see
thee possesse and injoy that which is thy right, and weare the crowne
of Denmarke, by the tyrant taken from thee; that I may rejoyce in thy
prosperitie, and therewith content my self, seeing with what courage and
boldnesse thou shalt take vengeance upon the murtherer of thy father,
as also upon all those that have assisted and favoured him in his murtherous and bloody enterprise. Madame (sayd Hamlet) I will put my
trust in you, and from henceforth meane not to meddle further with your
affayres, beseeching you (as you love your owne flesh and blood) that
you will from hence foorth no more esteeme of the adulterer, mine enemie
whom I will surely kill, or cause to be put to death, in despite of all
the devils in hel: and have he never so manie flattering courtezans to
defend him, yet will I bring him to his death, and they themselves also
shall beare him company therein, as they have bin his perverse counsellors in the action of killing my father, and his companions in his

[II.]

Hothere pere du Roy Rorique.

Ne faut user de loyauté aux traistres et parjures.

Roys sont l'image des Dieux.

Vie miserable qui est accompagnée d'infamie.

L'esprit genereux ne sçait mentir.

et les compagnons de sa trahison, assassinat, et cruelle entreprinse. Aussi est il raison que tout ainsi que traistreusement ils ont faict mourir leur Prince, qu'avec pareille, mais plus juste, finesse, ils payent les interests de leur felonnie. Vous sçavez Madame, comme Hothere vostre ayeul, et pere du bon Roy Rorique ayant vaincu Guimon, le feit brusler tout vif, à cause qu'auparavant ce cruel paillard avoit usé de tel traictement à l'endroit de Gevare son seigneur, qu'il prinst de nuict, et par trahison. Et qui est celuy qui ne sçache que les traistres et parjures, ne meritent point qu'on leur garde foy ny loyauté quelconque, et que les pactes faits avec un assassineur se doivent estimer comme toilles d'araignes, et tenir en mesme rang, comme chose non promise? Mais quand bien j'auray dressé la main contre Fengon, ce ne sera trahison ny felonnie, luy n'estant point mon Roy ny seigneur: ains justement le puniray comme mon vassal, qui s'est forfait desloyaument contre son seigneur, et souverain Prince. Et puis que la gloire est le salaire des vertueux, l'honneur, et le prix de ceux qui font service à leur Prince naturel, pourquoy le blasme n'accompaignera il les traistres, et la mort ignominieuse, ceux qui osent mettre la main violente sur les Roys sacrez, et qui sont les amis et compaignons des Dieux, et ceux qui representent leur majesté, et image? En somme la gloire estant la couronne de vertu, et le prix de la constance, puis qu'elle ne s'accompaigne point avec l'infelicité, et qu'elle fuyt la covardise, et s'esloigne des esprits aviliz, et abatuz, il faut ou qu'une fin glorieuse mette fin à mes jours, ou qu'ayant les armes au poing, chargé de triomphe et victoire, je ravisse la vie à ceux qui rendent la mienne mal-heureuse, et obscurcissent les rayons de celle vertu que je tiens du sang et memoire illustre de mes predecesseurs. Et dequoy sert vivre, où la honte, et l'infamie sont les bourreaux qui tourmentent nostre conscience, et la poltronnerie est celle qui retarde le coeur des gaillardes entreprises, et destourne l'esprit des honnestes desirs de gloire et louange, qui sera à jamais durable? Je sçay que c'est sottement fait, que de cueillir un fruict avant saison, et de tascher de jouyr d'un bien, duquel on ne sçait si la jouyssance nous en est deue: Mais je m'attens de faire si bien, et espere tant en la fortune, qui a guidé jusques icy les actions de ma vie, que je ne mourray ja, sans me venger de mon enemy, et que luy mesme sera l'instrument de sa ruine, et me guidera à executer ce, que de moy-mesme je n'eusse osé entreprendre. Apres cecy Fengon comme s'il fust venu de quelque loingtain voyage arrivé en court, et s'enquerant de celuy qui avoit entreprise la charge d'espion, pour surprendre Amleth en sa sagesse dissimulee, fut bien estonné n'en pouvant ouyr ny vent, ny nouvelle: et pour ceste cause, demanda au fol s'il sçavoit point qu'estoit devenu celuy qu'il luy nomma. Le Prince qui n'estoit menteur, et qui en quelque response que jamais il feit durant sa fainte folie, ne s'estoit onc esgaré de la verité, comme aussi tout esprit genereux est mortel ennemy de la mensonge, luy respondit, que le courtisan qu'il cherchoit s'en estoit allé par les privez, là ou suffoqué par les immondices du lieu, les pourceaux s'y rencontrans en avoyent remply leur

treason, massacre and cruell enterprise. And reason requireth that, even as trayterously they then caused their prince to bee put to death, that with the like (nay well, much more) justice they should pay the interest of their fellonious actions.

You know (Madame) how Hother your grandfather, and father to the good king Roderick, having vanquished Guimon, caused him to be burnt, for that the cruell vilain had done the like to his lord Gevare, whom he betrayed in the night time. And who knoweth not that traytors and perjured persons deserve no faith nor loyaltie to be observed towardes them, and that conditions made with murtherers ought to bee esteemed as cobwebs, and accounted as if they were things never promised nor agreed upon: but if I lay handes upon Fengon, it will neither be fellonie nor treason, hee being neither my king nor my lord, but I shall justly punish him as my subject, that has disloyaly behaved himselfe against his lord and soveraigne prince. And seeing that glory is the rewarde of the vertuous, and the honour and praise of those that do service to their naturall prince, why should not blame and dishonour accompany traytors, and ignominious death al those that dare be so bold as to lay violent hands upon sacred kings, that are friends and companions of the gods, as representing their majestie and persons. To conclude, glorie is the crown of vertue, and the price of constancie; and seeing that it never accompanieth with infelicitie, but shunneth cowardize and spirits of base and trayterous conditions, it must necessarily followe, that either a glorious death will be mine ende, or with my sword in hand (laden with tryumph and victorie), I shall bereave them of their lives that made mine infortunate, and darkened the beames of that vertue which I possessed from the blood and famous memory of my predecessors. For why should men desire to live, when shame and infamie are the executioners that torment their consciences, and villany is the cause that withholdeth the heart from valiant interprises, and diverteth the minde from honest desire of glorie and commendation, which indureth for ever? I know it is foolishly done to gather fruit before it is ripe, and to seeke to iujoy a benefit, not knowing wither it belong to us of right; but I hope to effect it so well, and have so great confidence in my fortune (that hitherto hath guided the action of my life) that I shall not dye without revenging my selfe upon mine enemie, and that himselfe shall be the instrument of his owne decay, and to execute that which of my selfe I durst not have enterprised.

After this, Fengon (as if hee had beene out some long journey) came to the court againe, and asked for him that had received the charge to play the intilligencer, to entrap Hamlet in his dissembled wisedome, was abashed to heare neither newes nor tydings of him, and for that cause asked Hamlet what was become of him, naming the man. The prince that never used lying, and who in all the answers that ever he made (during his counterfeit madnesse) never strayed from the trueth (as a generous minde is a mortal enemie to untruth) answered and sayd, that the counsellor he sought for was gone downe through the privie, where being choaked by the filthynesse of the place, the hogs meeting him had filled their bellyes.

[III.]

Hother, father to Rodericke. Guimon burnt his lord Gevare.

We must observe neither faith fullnesse or fidelitie to traytors or parricides.

ventre. On eust plustot creu toute autre chose, que ce massacre, fait par Amleth: toutesfois Fengon ne se pouvoit asseurer, et luy sembloit tousjours, que ce fol luy joueroit quelque mauvais tour, il l'eust volontiers occis, mais il craignoit le Roy Rorique son ayeul, et qu'aussi il n'osoit offencer la Royne mere du fol, qu'elle aymoit et caressoit, quoy qu'elle monstrast un grand crevecoeur de le voir ainsi transporté de son sens: ainsi voulant s'en depescher, il tascha de s'ayder du ministere d'un estranger, et feit le Roy des Anglois le ministre du massacre de l'innocence simulee, aymant mieux que son amy souillast son renom, avec une telle meschanceté, que de tomber en infamie par l'exploit d'une si grande cruauté. Amleth entendant qu'on l'envoyoit en la grand Bretaigne, vers l'Anglois, se douta tout aussi tost de l'occasion de ce voyage, pour ce ayant parlé à la Royne, la pria de ne faire aucun signe d'estre faschee de ce depart, plustost feignist d'en estre joyeuse, comme deschargee de la presence de celuy, lequel, jaçoit qu'elle l'aymast, si mouroit elle de dueil, le voyant en si piteux estat, et privé de tout usage de raison: encor supplia il la Royne, qu'à son depart elle tapissast la salle, et affichast avec des clouds les tapisseries contre le mur, et luy gardast ces tisons, qu'il avoit aguisez par le bout, lors qu'il dist qu'il faisoit des sagettes pour venger la mort de son pere: en fin l'admonesta, que l'an accomply, elle celebrast ses obseques et funerailles, l'asseurant, qu'en ceste mesme saison, elle le verroit de retour, et tel qu'elle seroit contente et plus que satisfaicto de son voyage. Auquel avec luy furent envoyez deux des fideles ministres de Fengon, portans des lettres, gravees dans du boys, qui portoient la mort de Amleth, ainsi qu'il la commandoit à l'Anglois: mais le rusé Prince Danois, tandis que ses compaignons dormoyent, ayant visité le pacquet, et cogneu la grande trahison de son oncle, et la meschanceté des courtisans qui le conduisoient à la boucherie, rasa les lettres mentionnans sa mort, et au lieu y grava et cisa un commandement à l'Anglois de faire pendre et estrangler ses compaignons: et non content de tourner sur eux la mort ordonnee pour sa teste, il y adjousta que Fengon commandoit au Roy Insulaire de donner au nepovu du Roy sa fille en mariage. Arrivez qu'ils sont en la grand Bretaigne, les messagers se presentent au Roy, et luy donnent les lettres de leur seigneur, lequel voyant le contenu d'icelles, dissimula le tout, attendant son opportunité, de mettre en effect la volonté de Fengon. Cependant il traicta les Danois fort gracieusement, et leur faict cest honneur, que de les recevoir à sa table, d'autant que les Roys d'alors n'estoient pas si superstitieux que maintenant, et ne tenoit† leur presence si chere, et n'estoient si chiches de leur familiarité, qu'on les voit en ce

Ruse et cautelle d'Amleth pour sauver sa vie.

Roys de Perse ne se laissoient voir.

Chap. IV.

[III.]

How Fengon the third time devised to send Hamblet to the king of England, with secret letters to have him put to death: and how Hamblet, when his companions slept, read the letters, and instead of them counterfeited others, willing the king of England to put the two messengers to death, and to marry his daughter to Hamblet, which was effected; and how Hamblet escaped out of England.

A man would have judged any thing, rather then that Hamblet had committed that murther, nevertheless Fengon could not content himselfe, but still his minde gave him that the foole would play him some tricke of liegerdemaine, and willingly would have killed him, but he feared king Rodericke, his grandfather, and further durst not offend the queene, mother to the foole, whom she loved and much cherished, shewing great griefe and heavinesse to see him so transported out of his wits. And in that conceit, seeking to bee rid of him, determined to finde the meanes to doe it by the ayde of a stranger, making the king of England minister of his massacreing resolution, choosing rather that his friende should defile his renowne with so great a wickednesse, then himselfe to fall into perpetuall infamie by an exploit of so great crueltie, to whom he purposed to send him, and by letters desire him to put him to death.

Hamblet, understanding that he should be sent into England, presently doubted the occasion of his voyage, and for that cause speaking to the queene, desired her not to make any shew of sorrow or griefe for his departure, but rather counterfeit a gladnesse, as being rid of his presence; whom, although she loved, yet she dayly grieved to see him in so pittifull estate, deprived of all sence and reason: desiring her further, that she should hang the hall with tapestrie, and make it fast with nayles upon the walles, and keepe the brands for him which hee had sharpened at the points, then, when as he said he made arrowes to revenge the death of his father: lastly, he counselled her, that the yeere after his departure being accomplished, she should celebrate his funerals; assuring her that at the same instant she should see him returne with great contentment and pleasure unto her for that his voyage. Now, to beare him company were assigned two of Fengons faithfull ministers, bearing letters ingraved in wood, that contained Hamlets death, in such sort as he had advertised the king of England. But the subtile Danish prince (beeing at sea) whilst his companions slept, having read the letters, and knowne his uncles great treason, with the wicked and villainous mindes of the two courtyers that led him to the slaughter, raced out the letters that concerned his death, and in stead thereof graved others, with commission to the king of England to hang his two companions; and not content to turne the death they had devised against him upon their owne neckes, wrote further, that king Fengon willed him to give his daughter to Hamlet in marriage. And so arriving in England, the messengers presented themselves to the king, giving him Fengons letters; who having read the contents, sayd nothing as then, but stayed convenient time to effect Fengons desire, meane time using the Danes familiarly, doing them that honour to sit at his table (for that kings as then where not so curiously, nor solemnely served as in these our dayes), for in these dayes

Hamblets craft to save his life.

[II.]

Majesté du Roy des Ethiopiens.

temps, où les Roytelets et Seigneurs de peu de consequence, sont aussi difficiles à estre accostez, qu'estoient jadis les Monarques des Perses, ou comme l'on dict encor du grand Roy de l'Ethiopie, qui ne permet qu'on voye à descouvert sa face, laquelle il couvre ordinairement d'un voile. Comme ses messagers sont à table, et s'esjouyssoient parmy les Anglois, le cauteleux Amleth, tant s'en faut qu'il s'esjouyst avec la troupe, qu'il ne voulut toucher viande, ny breuvage quelconque, qu'on servist à la table Royale, non sans l'esbahissement des assistans, lesquels estoyent estonnez de voir un adolescent estranger ne tenir compte des viandes exquises, ny des breuvages delicieux presentez au banquet, et les avoit tout ainsi rejettez comme chose sale, de mauvais goust, et encor plus mal apprestee. Le Roy qui sur l'heure dissimula ce qui'l en pensoit, feit conduire ses hostes en leur chambre, enjoignant à un sien loyal de se cacher dedans, pour luy rapporter les propos tenuz par les estrangers en se couchant.

Or ne furent ils si tost dans la chambre, que estans sortis ceux qui avoient la charge de les traicter, les compaignons de Amleth ne luy demandassent pour quelle occassion, il avoit desdaigné, et les viandes et la boisson qu'on luy avoit presenté à table, et n'avoit honoré la table d'un si grand Roy qui les avoit recueillis, avec telle honnesteté et courtoisie: disoient en outre qu'il avoit tort, et faisoit deshonneur à celuy qui l'envoyoit, comme s'il mandoit en Bretaigne des hommes, qui se craignoient d'estre empoisonnez par un Roy tant honnorable. Le Prince qui

Subtile responce de Amleth.

n'avoit rien fait sans raison, leur respondit tout soudain: et quoy pensez vous que je vueille manger le pain trempé avec le sang humain: et souiller mon gosier de rouilleure de fer, et user de la chair qui sent la puanteur, et corruption des corps humains, ja tous pourris et corrompus, et qui raporte au goust d'une charongne de long temps jettee à la voyrie? Et comment voulez vous que je respecte le Roy qui a un regard d'esclave, et une Royne, laquelle en lieu d'une grande Majesté a faict trois choses dignes d'une femme de vil estat, et qui sont plus propres à quelque chambrière, qu'a une Dame de son calibre: et ayant dit cecy, il avança plusieurs propos injurieux et piquans, tant contre le Roy, et Royne, que les autres qui avoient assisté à ce banquet et festin, pour la reception des Ambassades de Dannemarch. Amleth ne dit rien qui ne fust veritable,

Pays Septentrionaux pleins d'enchanteurs.

ainsi que pourrez entendre cy apres, veu qu'en ce temps là tous ces pays Septentrionaux, estans souz l'obeyssance de Sathan, il y avoit une infinité d'enchanteurs, et n'estoit fils de bonne mere, qui n'en sçavoit assez pour sa provision, si comme encor en la Gothie et Biarmie, il se trouve infinité qui sçavent plus de choses que la saincteté de la religion Chrestienne ne permet, comme lisant les histoires de Norvege et Gothie, vous verrez assez facilement: et ainsi Amleth, vivant son pere, avoit esté endoctriné en celle science, avec laquelle le malin esprit abuse les hommes, et advertissoit ce Prince (comme il peut) des choses ja passees. Je n'ay affaire icy de discourir des parties de divination en l'homme, et si ce Prince, pour la vehemence de la melancholie, avoit receu ces impressions, devinant ce qu'autre ne luy avoit jamais declaré, ainsi que les Philosophes qui traitent de la judiciaire, donnent la force de telle prediction à ceux, qui influez de Saturne, chantent souvent des choses, lesquelles cessant une telle fureur, ils ne peuvent eux mesmes entendre qui en sont les prononceurs. Et c'est pourquoy Platon dit, plusieurs vaticinateurs et Poëtes, devins, apres que l'effort, et impetuosité de leur fureur se refroidit, à peine entendent ils ce qu'ils escrivent, jaçoit qu'en traitant ces choses durant

meane kings, and lords of small revenewe are as difficult and hard to bee seene, as in times past the monarches of Persia used to bee: or as it is reported of the great king of Aethyopia, who will not permit any man to see his face, which ordinarily hee covereth with a vaile. And as the messengers sate at the table with the king, subtile Hamlet was so far from being merry with them, that he would not taste one bit of meate, bread, nor cup of beare whatsoever, as then set upon the table, not without great wondering of the company, abashed to see a yong man and a stranger not to esteeme of the delicate meates and pleasant drinkes served at the banquet, rejecting them as things filthy, evill of tast, and worse prepared. The king, who for that time dissembled what he thought, caused his ghests to be conveyed into their chamber, willing one of his secret servantes to hide himselfe therein, and so to certifie him what speeches past among the Danes at their going to bed.

Now they were no sooner entred into the chamber, and those that were appointed to attend upon them gone out, but Hamlets companions asked him, why he refused to eate and drinke of that which hee found upon the table, not honouring the banquet of so great a king, that entertained them in friendly sort, with such honour and courtesie as it deserved? saying further, that hee did not well, but dishonoured him that sent him, as if he sent men into England that feared to bee poysoned by so great a king. The prince, that had done nothing without reason and prudent consideration, answered them, and sayd: What, think you, that I will eat bread dipt in humane blood, and defile my throate with the rust of yron, and use that meat that stinketh and savoureth of mans flesh, already putrified and corrupted, and that senteth like the savour of a dead carryon, long since cast into a valt? and how woulde you have me to respect the king, that hath the countenance of a slave; and the queene, who instead of great majestie, hath done three things more like a woman of base parentage, and fitter for a waiting gentlewoman then beseeming a lady of her qualitie and estate. And having sayd so, used many injurious and sharpe speeches as well against the king and queene, as others that had assisted at that banquet for the intertrainment of the Danish ambassadors; and therein Hamblet said trueth, as hereafter you shall heare, for that in those dayes, the north parts of the worlde, living as then under Sathans lawes, were full of inchanters, so that there was not any yong gentleman whatsoever that knew not something therein sufficient to serve his turne, if need required: as yet in those dayes in Gothland and Biarmy, there are many that knew not what the Christian religion permitteth, as by reading the histories of Norway and Gothland, you maie easilie perceive: and so Hamlet, while his father lived, had bin instructed in that devilish art, whereby the wicked spirite abuseth mankind, and adverticeth him (as he can) of things past.

It toucheth not the matter herein to discover the parts of devination in man, and whether this prince, by reason of his over great melancholy, had received those impressions, devining that, which never any but himselfe had before declared, like the philosophers, who discoursing of divers deep points of philosophie, attribute the force of those divinations to such as are saturnists by complection, who oftentimes speake of things which, their fury ceasing, they then alreadye can hardly understand who are the pronouncers; and for that cause Plato saith, many deviners and many poets, after the force and vigour of their fier beginneth to lessen, do hardly understand what they have written, although intreating †

[II.] leur transport, ils discourent si bien de ce qu'ils demeslent, que les auteurs et versez és arts, par ceux là mis en avant en louent le discours, et subtile dispute. Aussi ne me soucie de mettre en jeu, ce que croyent plusieurs qu'une ame toute convertie en raison, devient la maison et domicile des demons moyens, par le moyen desquels il aprend la science et secret des choses naturelles et humaines: et moins tiens je compte des gouverueurs supposez du monde, par les Magiciens, par le moyen desquels ils se vantent d'effectuer des choses merveilleuses: jaçoit que ce soit chose miraculeuse, que Amleth peust deviner, ce que puis apres on veit estre plus que veritable, si (comme je vous ay dit) le diable n'avoit la cognoissance parfaite des choses passees: car de vous accorder que l'advenir luy soit notoire, jamais je ne commettray une faute si lourde, ny ne tomberay en si grand erreur, si vous ne voulez mesurer les predictions faites par conjecture, aussi asseurees que celles qui sont gardees par l'esprit de Dieu, et annoncees par les saincts Prophetes, lesquels ont gousté la science merveilleuse, et à eux seuls declaree† des merveilles, et secrets du tout puissant. Et ne faut que ces impôsteurs, qui veulent tant donner de divinité à l'ennemy de Dieu, et pere de mensonge, que de luy attribuer la verité de ce qui doit succeder aux hommes, me mettent en avant le fait de Saul, avec la devineresse: veu qu'un exemple est en l'escriture, et mesme amené pour la condamnation d'un meschant, n'est puissant pour donner loy de vigueur universelle: car eux mesmes confessent qu'ils peuvent predire non suyvant la cause universelle des choses, mais par les signes empraints és causes semblables, qui sont tousjours mesmes, et peuvent par ces conjectures donner jugement des effets à venir: Mais estant tout cecy appuyé d'un si foible baston, que la conjecture, et ayant un si maigre fondement, que quelque sotte et tardive experience, et les fictions en estant volontaires, ce seroit une grand folie à l'homme de bon esprit, et mesmement à celuy qui embrasse la pureté de la doctrine, et ne cherche que le pur effect de la verité, de s'arrester à pas une reigle de ces verisimilitudes, ou escrits pleins de fallace.

Quant aux operations magiques, je leur en accorderay une partie, voyant les histoires pleines de telles illusions, et que la saincte Bible en fait foy, et en defend l'usage, voyre les loix des gentils, et ordonnances des Empereurs y ont pourveu par leurs ordonnances, tellement que Mahommeth imposteur, et amy des Diables, avec l'astuce desquels il abusa presque tout l'Orient, à estably grosses peines à ceux qui s'adonnoyent à ces arts illicites, et damnables, desquels esloignans le propos, reviendrons à Amleth institué en ces folies, suyvans la coustume de son pays: les compaignons duquel oyans sa response, luy reprochoient sa folie, et disoyent qu'il n'en pouvoit donner plus grand indice, qu'en mesprisant ce qui estoit louable, et rejettant ce que tous recevoyent comme necessaire, et qu'au reste il s'estoit bien lourdement oublié, accusant ainsi un tel, et si excellent homme que le Roy, et vituperer la Royne des plus illustres, et sages princesses, qui fust és isles voysines, le menaçans au reste de le faire chastier, selon le merite de son outrecuidance. Mais luy continuant en sa folie dissimulee, se mocquoit d'eux, et disoit qu'il n'avoit rien fait, ny proposé qui ne fust bon, et plus que veritable. D'autre part le Roy adverty qu'il est de tout cecy, par celui qui les avoit escoutez, jugea soudain que Amleth parlant ainsi ambiguement, ou estoit fol jusque à la haute gamme, ou des plus sages de son temps respondant si soudain, et si à propos à ce que les

of such things, while the spirite of devination continueth upon them, [III.] they doe in such sorte discourse thereof that the authors and inventers of the arts themselves by them alledged, commend their discourses and subtill disputations. Likewise I mean not to relate that which divers men beleeve, that a reasonable soul becometh the habitation of a meaner sort of devels, by whom men learn the secrets of things natural; and much lesse do I account of the supposed governors of the world fained by magitians, by whose means they brag to effect mervailous things. It would seeme miraculous that Hamlet shold divine in that sort, which after prooved so true (if as I said hefore) the devel had not knowledg of things past, but to grant it he knoweth things to come I hope you shall never finde me in so grose an error. You will compare and make equall derivation, and conjecture with those that are made by the spirit of God, and pronounced by the holy prophets, that tasted of that marvelous science, to whome onely was declared the secrets and wondrous workes of the Almighty. Yet there are some imposturious companions that impute so much devinitie to the devell, the father of lyes, that they attribute unto him the truth of the knowledge of thinges that shall happen unto men, alledging the conference of Saul with the witch, although one example out of the Holy Scriptures, specially set downe for the condemnation of wicked man, is not of force to give a sufficient law to all the world; for they themselves confesse that they can devine, not according to the universal cause of things, but by signes borrowed from such like causes, which are all waies alike, and by those conjectures they can give judgement of thinges to come, but all this beeing grounded upon a weake support, (which is a simple conjecture) and having so slender a foundation, as some foolish or late experience the fictions being voluntarie, it should be a great folly in a man of good judgment, specially one that imbraceth the preaching of the gospell, and seeketh after no other but the trueth thereof, to repose upon any of these likelihoods or writings full of deceipt.

As touching magical operations, I will grant them somewhat therein, finding divers histories that write thereof, and that the Bible maketh mention, and forbiddeth the use thereof: yea, the lawes of the gentiles and ordinances of emperors have bin made against it in such sort, that Mahomet, the great hereticke and friend of the devell, by whose subtiltyes hee abused most part of the east countries, hath ordained great punishments for such as use and practise those unlawfull and damnable arts, which, for this time leaving of, let us returne to Hamblet, brought up in these abuses, according to the manner of his country, whose companions hearing his answere reproached him of folly, saying that hee could by no meanes show a greater point of indiscretion, then in despising that which is lawfull, and rejecting that which all men receaved as a necessary thing, and that hee had not† grossely so forgotten himselfe as in that sort to accuse such and so excellent a man as the king of England, and to slander the queene, being then as famous and wise a princes as any at that day raigning in the ilands thereabouts,† to cause him to be punished according to his deserts; but he, continuing in his dissimulation, mocked him, saying that hee had not done any thing that was not good and most true. On the other side, the king being advertised thereof by him that stood to heare the discourse, judged presently that Hamlet, speaking so ambiguously, was either a perfect foole, or else one of the wisest princes in his time, answering so sodainly, and so much to the

[II.] compaignons s'estoyent enquis sur ses façons de faire: et pour en savoir mieux la verité, commanda qu'on feist venir le boulanger qui avoit fait le pain de sa bouche, auquel comme il s'enquist en quel lieu est ce qu'on avoit cueilly le grain, duquel on faisoit le pain pour son ordinaire, et si en ce champ y avoit point aucun signe ny indice de bataille ny combat, pour y avoir du sang humain espars. A quoy fut respondu que non loing de là, estoit un champ tout chargé des ossements d'hommes occis jadis en quelque cruelle rencontre, veu le taz amoncellé qu'on y pouvoit encore apercevoir, et que pour estre la terre plus grasse et fertile à cause de l'humeur et gresse des morts, on y semoit tous les ans le plus beau bled qu'on pouvoit choisir pour son service. Le Roy voyant la verité correspondre aux paroles du jeune Prince, s'enquist encor où est ce qu'on avoit nourry les pourceaux, la chair desquels avoit esté servie sur table, et cogneut qu'estans eschapez de leur test et estable, ilz s'estoyent rassasiez de la charongne et corps d'un larron justicié pour ses forfaicts et demerites. C'est icy que le prince Anglois s'estonne et voulut sçavoir de quelle eau estoit ce que la Biere servie à table avoit esté composee: tellement que faisant creuser bien avant le ruisseau, duquel on s'estoit aydé à faire leur boisson, on trouva des espees et armes rouillees, qui donnoyent ce mauvais goust au breuvage. Il sembleroit advis que je vous feisse icy des comptes de Merlin, que lon feinct avoir parlé avant qu'il eust un an accomply: mais si vous advisez de pres, tout ce qui est desja dit, n'est gure difficile à deviner, quoy que le ministere de satan y eust peu servir, donnant les responces soudaines à cest adolescent: veu qu'il n'y a rien icy que choses naturelles, et telles qui estoyent desja en la cognoissance de ce qui est, et ne falloit songer sur ce qui devoit advenir. Tout cecy espluché, le Roy fut esmeu encor d'une curiosité de savoir pourquoy le seigneur Danoys avoit dit que le Roy avoit regard d'un esclave, car il soupçonnoit que l'autre luy reprochast la vileté de son sang, et qu'il voulust dire que jamais Prince n'avoit esté l'auteur de son engeance: et à fin d'esclercir ce doubte il s'adressa à sa Mere, et l'ayant conduite secrettement en une chambre, laquelle il ferma sur eux, la pria de luy dire sur son honneur à qui il devoit rendre graces d'estre né en ce monde. La bonne Dame asseuree que jamais aucun n'avoit rien sceu de ses amours, ny forfaiture, luy jura que le Roy seul se pouvoit vanter sans autre d'avoir jouy de ses embrassements. Luy qui desja estoit abreuvé de l'opinion des responces veritables du Danois, menace sa mere, de luy faire dire par force, ce que de bon gré ne luy vouloit confesser, entendit qu'elle d'autrefois se soumettant à un esclave, l'avoit rendu le pere du Roy de la grand Bretaigne: dequoy si le Roy fut estonné, et camuz, je le laisse à penser à ceux qui s'estiment plus gens de bien que tout autre, et cuidans qu'il n'y ait rien que reprendre en leur maison, s'enquierent plus qu'il ne faut pour entendre aussi ce que point ne desirent: toutesfois dissimulant son maltalant, et rongeant son frein, pour ne vouloir point se scandaliser en publiant la lubricité de sa mere, ayma mieux laisser un grand peché impuny, que se rendre contemptible à ses subjetz, qui peut estre, l'eussent rejetté, comme ne voulans un bastard qui commandast à une si belle province.

Comme donc il estoit marry de ouir sa confusion†, il print grand plaisir à la subtilité, et gentilesse d'esprit du jeune Prince, le vinst

purpose upon the demaund by his companions made touching his behaviour; [III.] and the better to find the trueth, caused the babler† to be sent for, of whome inquiring in what-place the corne grew whereof he made bread for his table, and whether in that ground there were not some signes or newes of a battaile fought, whereby humaine blood had therein been shed? the babler answered that not far from thence there lay a field ful of dead mens bones, in. times past slaine in a battaile, as by the greate heapes of wounded sculles mighte well appeare, and for that the ground in that parte was become fertiler then other grounds, by reason of the fatte and humours of the dead bodies, that every yeer the farmers used there to have in the best wheat they could finde to serve his majesties house. The king perceiving it to be true, according to the yong princes wordes, asked where the hogs had bin fed that were killed to be served at his table? and answere was made him, that those hogs getting out of the said fielde wherein they were kepte, had found the bodie of a thiefe that had beene hanged for his demerits, and had eaten thereof: whereat the king of England beeing abashed, would needs know with what water the beer he used to drinke of had beene brued? which having knowne, he caused the river to bee digged somewhat deeper, and therin found great store of swords and rustie armours, that gave an ill savour to the drinke. It were good I should heere dilate somewhat of Merlins prophesies, which are said to be spoken of him before he was fully one yeere old; but if you consider wel what hath al reddy been spoken, it is no hard matter to divine of things past, although the minister of Sathan therein played his part, giving sodaine and prompt anweres to this yong prince, for that herein are nothing but natural things, such as were well known to be true, and therefore not needfull to dreame of thinges to come. This knowne, the king, greatly moved with a certaine curiositie to knowe why the Danish prince saide that he had the countenance of a slave, suspecting thereby that he reproached the basenes of his blood, and that he wold affirme that never any prince had bin his sire, wherin to satisfie himselfe he went to his mother, and leading her into a secret chamber, which he shut as soone as they were entred, desired her of her honour to shewe him of whome he was ingendred in this world. The good lady, wel assured that never any man had bin acquainted with her love touching any other man then her husband, sware that the king her husband onely was the man that had enjoyed the pleasures of her body; but the king her sonne, alreadie with the truth of the Danish princes answers, threatned ∗ his mother to make her tell by force, if otherwise she would not confesse it, who for feare of death acknowledged that she had prostrated her body to a slave, and made him father to the king of England; whereat the king was abashed, and wholy ashamed. I give them leave to judge who esteeming themselves honester than theire neighbours, and supposing that there can be nothing amisse in their houses, make more enquirie then is requisite to know the which they would rather not have knowen. Neverthelesse dissembling what he thought, and biting upon the bridle, rather then he would deprive himselfe by publishing the lasciviousnes of his mother, thought better to leave a great sin unpunished, then thereby to make himselfe contemptible to his subjects, who peradventure would have rejected him, as not desiring to have a bastard to raigne over so great a kingdome.

But as he was sorry to hear his mothers confession, on the other side he tooke great pleasure in the subtilty and quick spirit of the yong

[II.] trouver, et s'enquist de luy pourquoy est ce qu'il avoit repris en la Royne trois choses plus requises à un esclave, et resentans leur servitude, que rien*de Roy, et qui eust une majesté propre pour une grande Princesse. Ce Roy non content d'avoir receu un grand desplaisir, pour se savoir estre bastard, et d'avoir ouy avec quelles injures il attaquoit celle que le plus il aimoit en ce monde, voulut aussi entendre ce qui luy despleut autant que son malheur propre, à sçavoir que la Royne sa femme estoit fille d'une chambrière, et luy specifia quelques sottes contenances d'icelle, qui declaroyent assez non seulement de quel sang, et condition elle estoit sortie, ains encor que ses humeurs correspondoyent à la vilenie et vileté de ses parens, la mere de laquelle il luy asseura estre encor detenue en servitute. Le Roy, admirant ce jeune homme, et contemplant en luy quelque cas de plus grand que le commun des hommes, luy donna sa fille en mariage, suyvant les tablettes falsifiees par le cauteleux Amleth, et des l'endemain il feit pendre les deux serviteurs du Roy Fengon, comme satisfaisant à la volonté de son grand amy: mais Amleth, quoy que le jeu luy pleust, et que l'Anglois ne luy peust faire chose plus agreable, feignit d'en estre fort marry, et mença† le Roy de se ressentir de l'injure: pour lequel appaiser, l'Anglois luy donna une grande somme d'or, que le Prince feit fondre, et mettre dans des bastons qu'il avoit fait creuser pour cest effect, et pour s'en servir ainsi qu'orrez cy apres: car de toutes les Royales richesses, il n'emporta rien en Dannemarch, que ces bastons, prenans son chemin à son pays, si tostque l'an fut accomply, ayant plustost obtenu congé du Roy son beau pere, avec promesse de revenir le plustost pour accomplir le mariage d'entre luy, et la Princesse Angloise. Arrivé qu'il fut en la maison et palais de son oncle, dans lequel on celebroit ses propres funerailles et entrant en la sale, où le dueil estoit demené, ce ne fut sans donner un grand estonnement à chacun, n'y ayant personne qui ne le pensast estre mort, et d'entre lesquels la pluspart n'en fussent joyeux, pour le plaisir qu'ils sçavoyent que Fengon recevoit d'une si plaisante perte, et peu qui se contristoyent, se souvenant de la gloire du deffunct Horwendille, les victoires duquel ils ne pouvoyent oublier, et moins effacer de leur memoire rien qui sortist du sien, lesquels s'esjouirent grandement, voyans que le renom avoit failly à ceste fois, et que le tyran n'auroit encor le passetemps du vray heritier de Jutie, mais que plustost les Dieux luy rendroyent son bon sens, pour le bien de sa Province.

L'esbahissement converty que fut en risee, chacun de ceux qui assistoyent au banquet funebre de celuy qu'on tenoit pour mort, se moquoit

prince, and for that cause went unto him to aske him, why he had [III.]
reproved three things in his queene convenient for a slave, and savouring
more of basenes then of royaltie, and far unfit for the majesty of a great
prince? The king, not content to have receaved a great displeasure by
knowing him selfe to be a bastard, and to have heard with what injuries
he charged her whom hee loved best in all the world, would not content
himself untill he also unterstood that which displeased him, as much as
his owne proper disgrace, which was that his queen was the daughter
of a chambermaid, and with all noted certaine foolish countenances she
made, which not onely shewed of what parentage she came, but also
that hir humors savored of the basenes and low degree of hir parents,
whose mother, he assured the king, was as then yet holden in servitude.
The king admiring the young prince, and beholding in him some matter
of greater respect then in the common sort of men, gave him his daughter
in marriage, according to the counterfet letters by him devised, and the
next day caused the two servants of Fengon to be executed, to satisfie,
as he thought, the king's desire. But Hamlet, although the sport plesed
him wel, and that the king of England could not have done him a greater
favour, made as though he had been much offended, threatning the king
to be revenged, but the king, to appease him, gave him a great sum of
gold, which Hamlet caused to be molten, and put into two staves, made
hollow for the same purpose, to serve his tourne there with as neede *
should require; for of all other the kings treasures he took nothing with
him into Denmark but onely those two staves, and as soone as the yeare
began to bee at an end, having somewhat before obtained licence of the
king his father in law to depart, went for Denmarke; then, with all the *
speed he could to returne againe into England to marry his daughter,
and so set sayle for Denmarke.

Chap. V.

How Hamblet, having escaped out of England, arrived in Denmarke
  the same day that the Danes were celebrating his funerals,
  supposing him to be dead in England; and how he revenged his
  fathers death upon his uncle and the rest of the courtiers; and
  what followed.

Hamblet in that sort sayling into Denmark, being arrived in the
contry, entered into the pallace of his uncle the same day that they
were celebrating his funeralls, and going into the hall, procured no small
astonishment and wonder to them all, no man thinking other but that
hee had beene deade: among the which many of them rejoyced not a
little for the pleasure which they knew Fengon would conceave for so
pleasant a losse, and some were sadde, as remembering the honourable
king Horvendile, whose victories they could by no meanes forget, much
lesse deface out of theire memories that which apperteined unto him,
who as then greatly rejoyced to see a false report spread of Hamlets
death, and that the tyrant had not as yet obtained his will of the heire
of Jutie, but rather hoped God would restore him to his sences againe
for the good and welfare of that province. Their amazement at the last
beeing tourned into laughter, all that as then were assistant at the funerall
banquet of him whome they esteemed dead, mocked each at other, for

[II.] de son compaignon pour avoir esté si amplement deceuz, et gaussans le Prince, de ce que avec le voyage, il n'avoit rien reconvert de son bon sens, luy demanderent qu'estoyent devenuz ceux qui avoyent voyagé avec luy en la grande Bretaigne, ausquels il respondit, en monstrant les deux bastons creusez, où il avoit mis l'or fondu, que Anglois luy donna pour l'appaiser sur le meurtre de ses compaignons, voicy et l'un et l'autre de ceux qui m'ont accompaigné.

Plusieurs qui cognoissoyent desja les humeurs du pelerin s'asseurent soudain qu'il leur avoit joué quelque tour de maistre, et que pour se delivrer de peril, les avoit lancez dans la fosse, pour luy preparee: si que craignant de suyvre leurs voyes, et courir quelque mauvaise fortune, s'absenterent du Palais, et bien pour eux, veu les esplanades de ce Prince le jour de ses funerailles, qui fut le dernier pour ceux, qui s'esjouyssoyent pour sa ruine. Car comme chacun fust entif à faire grand chere, et semblast que l'arrivee d'Amleth leur donnast plus d'occassion de hausser le gobelet, le Prince faisoit aussi l'estat, et office d'eschanson et gentil-homme servant, ne laissant jamais les hanaps unides [3]): et abbreuva la Noblesse de telle sorte, que tous estans chargez de vin, et offusquez de viandes, fallut que se couchassent au lieu mesme où ils avoyent prins le repas, tant les avoit abestis et privez de sens, et de force de trop boire, vice assez familier, et à l'Alemand, et à toutes ces nations et peuples Septentrionaux: Amleth, voyant l'opportunité si grande pour faire son coup, et se venger de ses adversaires, et ensemble laisser, et les actions, et le geste et l'abillement d'un insensé, ayant l'occasion à propos, et qui luy offroit la chevelure, ne faillit de l'empoigner, ains voyant ces corps assoupis de vin, gisans par terre comme pourceaux, les uns dormans, les autres vomissans le trop de vin que par trop gouleusement ils avoyent avallé, feit tomber la tapisserie tendue par la sale sur eux, laquelle il cloua par le pavé de la sale, qui estoit tout d'aiz, et aux coignz il mist les tisons qu'il avoit aiguisez, et desquelz a esté parlé cy dessus, qui servoyent d'attaches, les liant avec telle façon, que quelque effort qu'ils feissent, il leur fut impossible de se despestrer, et soudain il mit le feu par les quatre coins de la maison Royale: de sorte que de ceux qui estoyent en la sale, il n'en eschappa pas un seul, qui ne purgeast ses fautes par le feu, et ne dessechast le trop de liqueur, qu'il avoit avallee, mourans trestous enveloppez dans l'ardeur inevitable des flammes. Ce que voyant l'Adolescent, devenu sage, et sachant que son oncle s'estoit retiré avant la fin du banquet, en son corps de logis, separé du lieu exposé aux flammes, s'en y alla, si que entrant en sa chambre, se saisit de l'espee du meurtrier de son pere, et y laissa la sienne au lieu, qu'on luy avoit clouee avec le fourreau, durant le banquet: puis s'adressant à Fengon, lui dist: Je m'estonne, Roy desloyal, comme tu dors ainsi à ton aise, tandis que tout Palais est tout en feu, et que l'embrasement d'iceluy a bruslé tous les courtisans, et ministres de tes cruautez et detestables tyrannies, et ne sçais comme tu es si asseuré de ta fortune, que de reposer, voyant Amleth si pres de toy, et armé des espieux qu'il aiguisa, il y a long temps, et qui à present est tout prest de se venger du tort et injure traitresse par toy faite à son seigneur et

---

[3]) Lies uides d. i. vides, wie auch der englische Übersetzer las.

having beene so simply deceived, and wondering at the prince, that in [III.]
his so long a voyage he had not recovered any of his sences, asked what
was become of them that had borne him company into Greate Brittain?
to whome he made answere (shewing them the two hollow staves, wherein
he had put his molten golde, that the king of England had given him
to appease his fury, concerning the murther of his two compauions), and
said, Here they are both. Whereat many that already knew his humours,
presently conjectured that hee had plaide some tricke of legerdemane,
and to deliver himselfe out of danger, had throwne them into the pitte
prepared for him; so that fearing to follow after them and light upon
some evil adventure, they went presently out of the court. And it was
well for them that they didde so, considering the tragedy acted by him
the same daie, beeing accounted his funerall, but in trueth theire last
daies, that as then rejoyced for their† overthrow; for when every man
busied himselfe to make good cheare, and Hamlets arivall provoked them
more to drinke and carouse, the prince Hamlet at that time played the
butler and a gentleman attending on the tables, not suffering the pots
nor goblets to bee empty, whereby hee gave the noble men such store of
liquor, that all of them being ful laden with wine and gorged with meate, *Drunkenes a vice*
were constrained to lay themselves downe in the same place where they *overcommon in*
had supt, so much their sences were dulled, and overcome with the fire *the north partes*
of over great drinking (a vice common and familiar among the Almaines, *of the world.*
and other nations inhabiting the north parts of the world) which when
Hamlet perceiving, and finding so good opportunitie to effect his purpose
and bee revenged of his enemies, and by the means to abandon the
actions, gestures and apparel of a mad man, occasion so fitly finding his
turn, and as it were effecting it selfe, failed not to take hold therof,
and seeing those drunken bodies, filled with wine, lying like hogs upon
the ground, some sleeping, others vomiting the over great abundance of
wine which without measure they had swallowed up, made the hangings
about the hall to fall downe and cover them all over; which he nailed
to the ground, being boorded, and at the ends thereof he stuck the brands,
whereof I spake before, by him sharpned, which served for prickes,
binding and tying the hangings in such sort, that what force soever they
used to loose themselves, it was unpossible to get from under them:
and presently he set fire in the foure corners of the hal, in such sort,
that all that were as then therein not one escaped away, but were forced
to purge their sins by fire, and dry up the great aboundance of liquor
by them received into their bodies, all of them dying in the inevitable
and mercilesse flames of the whot and burning fire: which the prince
perceiving, became wise, and knowing that his uncle, before the end of *
the banquet, had withdrawn himselfe into his chamber, which stood apart *A strange revenge*
from the place where the fire burnt, went thither, and entring into the *taken by Hamlet.*
chamber, layd hand upon the sword of his fathers murtherer, leaving
his own in the place, which while he was at the banket some of the
courtiers had nailed fast into the scaberd, and going to Fengon said:
I wonder, disloyal king, how thou canst sleep heer at thine ease, and
al thy pallace is burnt, the fire therof having burnt the greatest part of
thy courtiers and ministers of thy cruelty, and detestable tirannies; and
which is more, I cannot imagin how thou sholdst wel assure thy self and *A mocke but yet*
thy estate, as now to take thy ease, seeing Hamlet so neer thee armed *sharp and sting-*
with the shafts by him prepared long since, and at this present is redy *ing, given by Ham-*
to revenge the traiterous injury by thee done to his lord and father. *let to his uncle.*

10*

[II.]

Fengon occis par Amleth son neveu.

pere. Fengon congnoissant à la verité la descouverte des ruses de son nepveu, et l'oyant parler de sens rassis: et qui plus est, luy voyant le glaive nud en main, que desja il haussoit pour le priver de vie sauta legerement du lict, jettant la main à l'espee clouee de son neveu, laquelle comme il s'esforçoit de desgainer, Amleth luy donna un grand coup sur le chinon du col, de sorte qu'il luy feit voler la teste par terre, disant: C'est le salaire deu à ceux qui te ressemblent, que de mourir ainsi violemment: et pource va, et estant aux enfers, ne faulx de compter à ton frere, que tu occis meschamment, que c'est son fils qui te fait faire ce message, à fin que soulagé par ceste memoire, son ombre s'appaise parmy les esprits bien heureux, et me quitte de celle obligation, qui m'astraignoit à poursuyvre ceste vengeance sur mon sang mesme, puis que c'estoit par luy, que j'avois perdu ce qui me lioit à telle consanguinité et alliance.

Louange d'Amleth tuant le tyran.

Homme pour vray hardy et courageux, et digne d'eternelle louange, qui s'armant d'une folie cauteleuse, et dissimulant accortement un grand desvoyement de sens, trompa sous telle simplicité les plus sages, fins et rusez: conservant non seulement sa vie des efforts et embusches du tiran, ains qui plus est, vengeant avec un nouveau genre de punition, et non excogité supplice la mort de son pere, plusieurs annees apres l'execution: de sorte que conduisant ses affaires avec telle prudence, et effectuant ses desseins avec une si grande hardiesse, et constance: il laisse un jugement indecis entre les hommes de bon esprit, lequel est le plus recommandable

Vengeance juste où est ce que doit estre consideree.

en luy, ou sa constance et magnanimité, ou la sagesse, en desseignant et accortisé en mettant ses desseins au parfait accomplissement de son oeuvre, de long temps premedité. Si jamais la vengeance sembla avoir quelque justice, il est hors de doute, que la pieté et affection qui nous lie à la souvenance de nos peres poursuyvis injustement, est celle qui nous dispense à cercher les moyens de ne laisser impunie la trahison, et effort outrageux et proditoire: veu que jaçoit que David fut un sainct et juste Roy, homme simple, et courtois, et debonnaire: si est-ce que mourant, il encharga à son fils Salomon, luy succedant à la couronne, de ne laisser descendre au tombeau quelque certain, qui l'avoit outragé, non que le Roy, et prochain de la mort, et prest à rendre compte devant Dieu, fust soigneux, ny desireux d'ancune vengeance: mais à fin de donner ceste leçon à ceux qui viendroyent apres eux, que où le public est interessé, le desir de vengeance ne peut porter, tant s'en faut tiltre de condemnation, que plustost il est louable et digne de recommandation et recompense. De cecy font foy les loix Atheniennes, erigeans des statues, eu l'honneur de ceux, qui vengeans le tort et injure faits à la Republique, massacroyent hardiment les tyrans, et ceux qui troubloyent l'aise des citoyens. Le Prince Dannois s'estant vengé si hautement, n'osa de prime face declarer son dessein au peuple, ains delibera d'user de ruses, pour luy faire entendre ce qu'il avoit executé, et la raison qui l'avoit esmeu à ce faire: si que accompagné de ceux qui restoyent encor des amis de feu son pere, il attendoit ce que le peuple feroit sur ceste si soudaine et effroyable occurrence. Les villes voisines desirans congnoistre d'où procedoyent les flammes qu'on avoit veu la nuict, viennent le matin, et voyant la maison

Fengon, as then knowing the truth of his nephews subtile practise, [III.] and hering him speak with stayed mind, and which is more, perceived a sword naked in his hand, which he already lifted up to deprive him of his life, leaped quickly out of the bed, taking holde of Hamlets sworde, that was nayled into the scaberd, which as hee sought to pull out, Hamlet gave him such a blowe upon the chine of the necke, that hee cut his head cleane from his shoulders, and as he fell to the ground sayd, This just and violent death is a just reward for such as thou art: now go thy wayes, and when thou commest in hell, see thou forget not to tell thy brother (whom thou trayterously slewest), that it was his sonne that sent thee thither with the message, to the ende that beeing comforted thereby, his soule may rest among the blessed spirits, and quit mee of the obligation that bound me to pursue his vengeance upon mine owne blood, that seeing it was by thee that I lost the chiefe thing that tyed me to this aliance and consanguinitie. A man (to say the trueth) hardie, couragious, and worthy of eternall comendation, who arming himself with a crafty, dissembling, and strange shew of beeing distract out of his wits, under that pretence deceived the wise, pollitike, and craftie, thereby not onely preserving his life from the treasons and wicked practises of the tyrant, but (which is more) by an new and unexpected kinde of punishment, revenged his fathers death, many yeeres after the act committed: in no† such sort that directing his courses with such prudence, and *Commendation of Hamlet for killing the tyrant.* effecting his purposes with so great boldnes and constancie, he left a judgement to be decyded among men of wisdom, which was more commendable in him, his constancy or magnanimitie, or his wisdom in ordring his affaires, according to the premeditable determination he had conceaved.

If vengeance ever seemed to have any shew of justice, it is then, *How just vengeance ought to be considered.* when pitie and affection constraineth us to remember our fathers unjustly murdered, as the things wherby we are dispensed withal, and which * seeke the means not to leave treason and murther unpunished: seeing David a holy and just king, and of nature simple, courteous, and debonaire, yet when he dyed he charged his soone Salomon (that succeeded him in *Davids intent in commanding Salomon to revenge him of some of his enemies.* his throane) not to suffer certaine men that had done him injurie to escape unpunished. Not that this holy king (as then ready to dye, and to give account before God of all his actions) was carefull or desirous of revenge, but to leave this example unto us, that where the prince or countrey is interessed†, the desire of revenge cannot by any meanes (how small soever) beare the title of condemnation, but is rather commendable and worthy of praise: for otherwise the good kings of Juda, nor others had not pursued them to death, that had offended their predecessors, if God himself had not inspired and ingraven that desire within their hearts. Hereof the Athenian lawes beare witnesse, whose custome was to erect images in remembrance of those men that, revenging the injuries of the commonwealth, boldly massacred tyrants and such as troubled the peace and welfare of the citizens.

Hamblet, having in this manner revenged himselfe, durst not presently declare his action to the people, but to the contrary determined to worke by policie, so to give them intelligence, what he had done, and the reason that drewe him thereunto: so that beeing accompanied with such of his fathers friends that then were rising†, he stayed to see what the people would doe when they shoulde heare of that sodaine and fearefull action. The next morning the townes bordering there aboutes, desiring to know from whence the flames of fire proceeded the night before they

[II.] du Roy toute en cendre, et les corps demi bruslez, parmi les ruines de l'edifice, il n'y eut citoyen qui ne se trouvast grandement esbahy, appercevant que de tout le bastiment n'y paroissoit rien plus que les flammes n'eussent devoré jusques aux fondemens. Plus les estonna, voyant le corps du Roy tont ensanglanté, et le tronc d'iceluy d'un costé, et la teste de l'autre: c'est icy que les uns s'aigrissent, sans sçavoir contre qui, les autres larmoyent, voyans un spectacle si piteux: d'autres s'esjouyssoyent, sans en oser faire semblant: les uns detestoyent la cruauté, et d'autres plaignoyent le desastre de leur Prince: mais la pluspart se souvenans du meurtre commis en Horweudille, recognoissoyent un juste jugement d'en-haut qui avoit accablé la teste superbe de ce tyran: ainsi estans diverses *Deffiance empesche souvent les combats.* les opinions de ceste multitude, chacun ignorant quelle seroit l'issue de ceste tragedie, nul ne bougea, ou attenta de faire esmotion quelconque, chacun craignant sa peau, et se defiant de son voisin, l'estimant estre consentant à la conjuration et massacre. Amleth voyant ce peuple ainsi coy, et les plus grans sans s'esmouvoir, et tous ne cerchans que de sçavoir simplement la cause de ceste ruine et deffaite, ne voulant laisser couler le temps, ains s'aidant de la commodité d'iceluy s'avança avec sa suite: et estant en l'assemblee des citoyens, leur parla en ceste sorte.

Harangue d'Amleth aux Danois.

S'il y a quelqu'un d'entre vous, Messieurs de Dannemarch, qui aye encore fraische memoire du tort faict au puissant Roy Horwendille, qu'il ne s'esmeuve en rien, voyant la face confuse et hideusement espouvantable de la presente calamité: S'il y a aucun qui aye la fidelité pour recommandee, et cherisse l'affection qu'on doit à ses parens, et trouve bonne la souvenance des outrages faits à ceux, qui nous ont produits au monde, que celuy ne s'esbahisse, contemplant un tel massacre, et moins s'offense en advisant une si effroyable ruine, et d'hommes, et des plus superbes edifices de tout le pays: car la main qui a executé ceste justice, ne pouvoit en chevir à meilleur marché, et ne luy estoit loisible d'autrement se prevaloir, qu'en ruinant, et l'insensible, et le sensible, pour garder la memoire d'une si equitable vengeance. Je voy bien, Messieurs, (et suis joyeux de cognoistre une telle vostre si affectionnee devotion) que vous estes marris, ayans devant vos yeux Fengon ainsi mutilé, et celuy sans teste, que d'autresfois vous avez recogneu pour chef: mais je vous prie penser que ce corps n'est le corps d'un Roy, ains d'un tyran execrable, et d'un parricide plus detestable. Ah! Danois, le spectacle estoit bien plus hideux, lors que vostre Roy Horwendille fut massacré par un sien frere: quoy frere? mais bien plustost par le bourreau, le plus abominable que le Soleil contemple. C'est vous qui avez veu les membres d'Horwendille mutilez, et qui avec larmes et souspirs, avez accompaigné au cercueil son corps deffiguré, blessé en mille lieux et bourrellé en cent mille sortes. Et qui doubte

had seene, came thither, and preceiving the kings pallace burnt to ashes, and many bodyes (most part consumed) lying among the ruines of the house, all of them where much abashed, nothing being left of the palace but the foundation. But they were much more amased to beholde the body of the king all bloody, and his head cut off lying hard by him; whereat some began to threaten revenge, yet not knowing against whom; others beholding so lamentable a spectacle, armed themselves, the rest rejoycing, yet not daring to make any shewe thereof; some detesting the crueltie, others lamenting the death of their Prince, but the greatest part calling Horvendiles murther to remembrance, acknowledging a just judgement from above, that had throwne downe the pride of the tyrant. And in this sort, the diversities of opinions among that multitude of people being many, yet every man ignorant what would be the issue of that tragedie, none stirred from thence, neither yet attempted to move any tumult, every man fearing his owne skinne, and distrusting his neighbour, esteeming each other to bee consenting to the massacre. [III.]

Chap. VI.

How Hamlet, having slaine his Uncle, and burnt his Palace, made an Oration to the Danes to shew them what he† done; and how they made him King of Denmark; and what followed.

Hamlet then seeing the people to be so quiet, and most part of them not using any words, all searching onely and simply the cause of this ruine and destruction, not minding to loose any time, but ayding himselfe with the commoditie thereof, entred among the multitude of people, and standing in the middle spake unto them as followeth.

If there be any among you (good people of Denmark) that as yet have fresh within your memories the wrong done to the valiant king Horvendile, let him not be mooved, nor thinke it strange to behold the confused, hydeous, and fearfull spectacle of this present calamitie: if there be any man that affecteth fidelitie, and alloweth of the love and dutie that man is bound to shewe his parents, and find it a just cause to call to remembrance the injuryes and wrongs that have been done to our progenitors, let him not be ashamed beholding this massacre, much lesse offended to see so fearfull a ruine both of men and of the bravest house in all this countrey: for the hand that hath done this justice could not effect it by any other meanes, neither yet was it lawfull for him to doe it otherwise, then by ruinating both sensible and unsensible things, thereby to preserve the memorie of so just a vengeance.

I see well (my good friends) and am very glad to know so good attention and devotion in you, that you are sorrie (before your eyes) to see Fengon so murthered, and without a head, which heeretofore you acknowledged for your commander; but I pray you remember this body is not the body of a king, but of an execrable tyrant, and a parricide most detestable. Oh Danes! the spectacle was much more hydeous when Horvendile your king was murthered by his brother. What should I say a brother! nay, rather by the most abhominable executioner that ever beheld the same. It was you that saw Horvendiles members massacred, and that with teares and lamentations accompanied him to the grave; his body disfigured, hurt in a thousand places, and misused in ten times

[II.] (puis que l'experience vous l'a fait congnoistre) que le tyran en accablant vostre Roy legitime, ne tendoit qu'à ruiner et abbatre la liberté ancienne de ses concitoyens? Aussi fut-ce une seule main, laquelle s'acharnant sur Horwendille, le despouilla de vie cruellement, et par mesme moyen, injustement vous osta la liberté, et anciennes franchises. Qui est celuy si despourveu de sens, qui ayme mieux choisir une miserable servitude, et se plaist plus d'en estre accablé, que d'embrasser la face joyeuse de quelque liberté proposee, et livree, sans qu'il luy faille rien aventurer pour avoir la jouyssance? Est qui est l'insensé, qui se delecte plus en la tyrannie de Fengon, que en la douceur et courtoisie renouvellee d'Horwendille? S'il est ainsi, que par clemence et affabilité les coeurs plus rogues et farouches sont adoucis et rendus traitables, et que le mauvais traittement rend un peuple insuportable et seditieux: que ne voyez vous la debonnaireté du premier, pour la parangonner aux cruautez et insolences de ce second, autant cruel et barbare, que son frere a esté doux, plaisant et accostable? Souvienne vous, Dannois, souvienne vous, quelle estoit l'amitié d'Horwendille envers vous, avec quelle equité il a gouverné les affaires du royaume, et avec quelle humanité, et courtoisie, il vous a deffendus, et cheris: et lors je m'asseure que le plus grossier d'entre vous, se souviendra et congnoistra qu'on luy a osté un Roy trespaisible, et pere tresjuste, et equitable, pour mettre en sa place un tyran, et asseoir sur son trosne meurtrier de son frere, lequel a perverti tout droict, aboly les loix de nos majeurs, souillé la memoire de nos ancestres, et pollu par sa meschanceté l'integrité de ceste province, sur le col de laquelle il a mis le joug fascheux d'une lourde servitude, abolissant celle liberté, en laquelle Horwendille vous maintenoit, et vous souffroit vivre à vostre aise. Et serez vous marris de voir la fin de vos malheurs, et que ce miserable, accablé du fardeau de ses forfaits paye à present l'usure du parricide, commis en la personne de son frere, et soit luy mesme le vengeur de l'outrage, faict au fils d'Horwendille, qu'il vouloit priver de son heritage, ostant au pays de Dannemarch, un successeur legitime, pour en saisir quelque voleur estranger, et captiver ceux que mon pere a jettez hors de misere et servitude? Et qui est l'homme, jouyssant le moins du monde de quelque prudence, qui acompte un bien fait à injure, et mesure les plaisirs à l'esgal de quelque tort, et evident outrage? Ce seroit bien grand folie et temerité aux Princes et vaillans chefs de guerre, de s'exposer à peril et hazard de leur vie, pour le soulagement d'un peuple, si pour toute recompense et action de graces, ils n'en raportoient que la haine, et indignation de la multitude, qui n'eust servy à Hercule d'accabler le tyran Baldere, si pour et au lieu de recognoissance, les Sueons et Danois l'eussent chassé, pour caresser les successeurs de celuy qui ne pourchassoit que leur ruine? Qui sera celuy, ayant si peu de sentiment, de raison et justice, qui soit marri de voir que la trahison paye son autheur, et qu'un forfaict face sentir la penitence de sa felonnie, à celuy mesme qui en aura esté l'occasion? Qui fut onc dolent de veoir exterminé le cruel meurtrier des innocens, ou qui pleure sur le juste massacre, faict en un tyran usurpateur, meschant, et sanguinaire? Je vous voy tous attentifs et estonnez, pour ignorer l'autheur de vostre delivrance: et marris, que ne sçavez à qui vous devez rendre graces d'un tel, et si grand benefice, que l'accablement d'un tyran, et la ruine du lieu, qui estoit le magazin de ces meschancetez, et le vray asile et retraicte

La douceur des Rois dompte les coeurs des peuples farouches.

LXXXI

as many fashions. And who doubteth (seeing experience hath taught you) [III.] that the tyrant (in massacring your lawfull king) sought onely to infringe the ancient liberties of the common people? and it was one hand onely, that murthering Horvendile, cruelly dispoyled him of life, and by the same meanes unjustly bereaved you of your ancient liberties, and delighted * more in oppression then to embrace the plesant countenance of prosperous libertie without adventuring for the same. And what mad man is he that delighteth more in the tyrany of Fengon then in the clemencie and renewed courtesie of Horvendile? If it bee so, that by clemencie and affabilitie the hardest and stoutest hearts are molified and made tractable, and that evill and hard usage causeth subjects to be outragious and unruly, why behold you not the debonair cariage of the first, to compare it with the cruelties and insolencies of the second, in every respect as cruell and barbarous as his brother was gentle, meeke, and courteous? Remember, O you Danes, remember what love and amitie Horvendile shewed unto you; with what equitie and justice he swayed the great affaires of this kingdome, and with what humanitie and courtisie he defended and cherished you, and then I am assured that the simplest man among you will both remember and acknowledge that he had a most peaceable, just, and righteous king taken from him, to place in his throane a tyrant and murtherer of his brother: one that hath perverted all right, abolished the aunctient lawes of our fathers, contaminated the memories of our ancestors, and by his wickednesse polluted the integritie of this kingdome, upon the necke thereof having placed the troublesome yoak of heavie servitude, abolishing that libertie wherein Horvendile used to maintaine you, and suffered you to live at your ease. And should you now bee sorrie to see the ende of your mischiefes, and that this miserable wretch, pressed downe with the burthen of his offences, at this present payeth the usury of the parricide committed upon the body of his brother, and would not himselfe be the revenger of the outrage done to me, whom he sought to deprive of mine inheritance, taking from Denmark a lawfull successor, to plant a wicked stranger, and bring into captivitie those that my father had infranchised and delivered out of misery and bondage? And what man is he, that having any sparke of wisdom, would esteem a good deed to be an injury, and account pleasures equal with wrongs and evident outrages? It were then great folly and temerity in princes and valiant commanders in the wars to expose themselves to perils and hazards of their lives for the welfare of the common people, if that for a recompence they should reape hatred and indignation of the multitude. To what end should Hother have punished Balder, if, in steed of recom- * pence, the Danes and Swethlanders had banished him to receive and accept the successors of him that desired nought but his ruine and overthrowe? What is hee that hath so small feeling of reason and equitie, that would be grieved to see treason rewarded with the like, and that an evill act is punished with just demerit in the partie him- selfe that was the occasion? who was ever sorrowfull to behold the murtherer of innocents brought to his end, or what man weepeth to see a just massacre done upon a tyrant, usurper, villaine, and bloody per- sonage?

I perceive you are attentive, and abashed for not knowing the author of your deliverance, and sorry that you cannot tell to whom you should bee thankefull for such and so great a benefit as the destruction of a tyrant, and the overthrow of the place that was the storehouse of his

[II.] de tous les voleurs, et traistres de ce Royaume: mais voicy devant vous celuy, qui a effectué un bien tant necessaire. C'est moy (messieurs) c'est moy, qui confesse avoir pris vengeance, pour l'outrage faict à monseigneur, et Pere, et pour l'assujettissement et servitude, en laquelle je voyois reduite la Province, de laquelle je suis le juste successeur, et heritier legitime. C'est moy qui a mis à effect tout seul l'oeuvre, auquel vous me deviez tenir la main, et m'y donner faveur et aide, et seul ay accomply, ce que vous tous pouviez justement parachever, avec raison, et sans tiltre aucun de felonnie. Il est vray que je me fie tant de vostre bonne volonté, envers le deffunct Horwendille, et que la memoire de ses vertus, est encor si vivement imprimee en vostre ame, que si je vous eusse requis de secours, vous n'eussiez ja refusé vostre assistance, et moyens à vostre naturel Prince. Mais il m'a pleu de le faire tout seul, me semblant tres bon de punir les meschans, sans hazarder la vie de mes amis, et loyaux citoyens, ne voulant soumettre les espaules d'autruy, à supporter ce faix, puis que je m'en faisois fort d'en venir à bout, sans exposer personne en peril, et gaster, en le publiant, le dessein que j'ay mis à fin avec si grande felicité. J'ay redigé en cendre les courtisans, compaignons des forfaits et trahisons du tiran, mais j'ay laissé Fengon, afin que ce soit vous qui punissez le tronc, et charoigne morte, puis que vivant il n'est peu tomber en vos mains, pour en faire entiere la punition et vengeance, et rassasier vostre colere, sur les oz de celuy qui s'est repeu de voz richessses, et a espandu le sang de vos freres, et amis. Courage donc, mes bons amis, courage, dressez le bucher pour ce Roy usurpateur, bruslez son corps abhominable, cuisez ses membres lascifs, et espandez en l'air les cendres de celuy, qui a esté nuisible à tout le monde, chassez loing de vous ses estincelles impitoyables, afin que ny la cruche d'argent, ou cristal, ny un sacre tombeau soient le repos des reliques, et ossemens d'un homme si detestable. Faites qu'on ne voye une seule trace de parricide, et que vostre pays ne soit pollu de la seule presence du moindre membre qui soit de ce tyran sans pieté, que les voisins n'en sentent point la contagion, et nostre terre l'infection pollue d'un corps condemné pour ses demerites: j'ay faict mon debvoir en le vous rendant tel, c'est à vous à mettre fin à l'oeuvre, et adjouster la derniere main au debvoir à quoy vostre office vous appelle: car c'est ainsi qu'il faut honorer les Princes abhominables. Et telles doivent estre les funerailles d'un tyran parricide, et usurpateur, et du lict et du patrimoine qui ne luy appartenoit en rien: lequel ayant desnué son pays de liberté, c'est raison que sa terre luy refuse giste, pour l'eternel repos de ses ossemens. Ah! mes bons amis, puis que vous sçavez le tort qu'on ma faict, quelles sont mes angoisses, en quelle misere j'ay vescu depuis la mort du Roy mon seigneur, puis que mieux que moy toutes ces choses vo'avez cogneues et goustees, lors que encore je ne pouvoye gouster parfaictement l'outrage que je soufroy: que me servira-il de le vous reciter? De quel proufit en sera le discours, devant ceux qui le sçachans, crevoient de despit de veoir si grand mon

villanies, and the true receptacle of all the theeves and traytors in this kingdome: but beholde (here in your presence) him that brought so good an enterprise to effect. It is I (my good friends), it is I, that confesse I have taken vengeance for the violence done unto my lord and father, and for the subjection and servitude that I perceived in this countrey, whereof I am the just and lawfull successor. It is I alone, that have done this piece of worke, whereunto you ought to have lent me your handes, and therein have ayded and assisted me. I have only accomplished that which all of you might justly have effected, by good reason, without falling into any point of treason or fellonie. It is true that I hope so much of your good willes towards the deceased king Horvendile, and that the remembrances of his vertues is yet so fresh within your memories, that if I had required your aide herein, you would not have denied it, specially to your naturall prince. But it liked mee best to doe it my selfe alone, thinking it a good thing to punish the wicked without hazarding the lives of my friends and loyall subjects, not desiring to burthen other mens shoulders with this weight; for that I made account to effect it well inough without exposing any man into danger, and by publishing the same should cleane have overthrowne the device, which at this present I have so happily brought to passe. I have burnt the bodyes of the courtiers to ashes, being companions in the mischiefs and treasons of the tyrant; but I have left Fengon whole, that you might punish his dead carkasse (seeing that when hee lived you durst not lay hands upon him), to accomplish the full punishment and vengeance due unto him, and so satisfie your choller upon the bones of him that filled his greedy hands and coffers with your riches, and shed the blood of your brethren and friends. Bee joyfull, then (my good friends); make ready the nosegay f) for this usurping king: burne his abhominable body, boyle his lascivious members, and cast the ashes of him that hath beene hurtfull to all the world into the ayre: drive from you the sparkes of pitie, to the end that neither silver, nor christall cup, nor sacred tombe may be the restfull habitation of the reliques and bones of so detestable a man: let not one trace of a parricide be seene, nor your countrey defiled with the presence of the least member of this tyrant without pity, that your neighbors may not smell the contagion, nor our land the polluted infection of a body condemned for his wickedness. I have done my part to present him to you in this sort; now it belongs to you to make an end of the worke, and put to † the last hand of dutie whereunto your severall functions call you; for in this sort you must honor abhominable princes, and such ought to be the funerall of a tyrant, parricide, and usurper, both of the bed and patrimony that no way belonged unto him, who having bereaved his countrey of liberty, it is fit that the land refuse to give him a place for the eternal rest of his bones.

O my good friends, seeing you know the wrong that hath bin done unto mee, what my griefs are, and in what misery I have lived since the death of the king, my lord and father, and seeing that you have both known and tasted these things then, when as I could not conceive the outrage that I felt, what neede I recite it unto you? what benefit would

[III.]

---

f) Sollte der englische Übersetzer — da r und t im Druck des französischen Originals sehr ähnlich und schwer zu unterscheiden sind — hier das bucher in buchet verlesen und dies für bouquet genommen haben?

[II.] desastre et malheur, et despitoient la fortune, qui accabloit ainsi un enfant Royal, que de le priver de sa majesté, jaçoit que pas un de vous n'osoit faire semblant de tristesse? Vous sçavez comme mon beau pere a conspiré ma mort, et a tasché en plusieurs sortes de m'accabler, comme j'ay esté abandonné laschement par la Royne ma mere, et mocqué de mes amis, mesprisé de mes propres subjets, j'ay jusque icy vescu chargé de dueil, et tout confit en larmes, ayant le temps de ma vie tousjours accompagné de craintes et soupçons, et n'attendant à tout propos que l'heure que le glaive trenchant mist fin et à ma vie et à mes angoisses et soucis, en tout miserables.

Combien de fois, faignant l'insensé, vous ay-je ouy plaindre mon desastre, et vous lamenter en secret de me veoir desherité, et sans aucun, qui vengeast la mort de mon pere, ou punist le forfait de mon incestueux oncle, et beau pere plein de meurtres, et massacres? Ceste charité me donnoit coeur, et ces voz affectionnees complaintes me faisoient veoir evidemment vostre bon vouloir, qui aviez presente la calamité de vostre Prince, et engravé en vostre coeur le desir de vengeance de la mort de celuy, qui meritoit de vivre plus longuement.

Et quel sera le coeur si dur et peu maniable, ny l'esprit tant severe, cruel, et rigoureux qui ne s'amollisse par la souvenance de mes passions, et angoisses, et n'aye pitié d'un enfant orphelin, et ainsi abandonné de tout le monde? Quels seront les yeux si taris et sans humeur, qui encor ne distilleront quelques larmes, voyans un pauvre Prince assailly des siens, trahy par sa mere, poursuivy par son oncle, et si fort accablé, que le peuple qui l'ayme n'ayt osé luy monstrer les effects de sa charité, et devotion bien affectionnee? Ah! messieurs, ayez compassion de celuy que vous avez nourry, et que vostre coeur sente quelque elancement pour la memoire de mes infortunes.

Je parle à vous, qui estes innocens de toute trahison, et ne souillastes onc ny voz mains, ny vostre esprit, ou desir du sang du grand et vertueux Roy Horwendille. Ayez pitié de la Royne jadis vostre Dame, et ma treshonoree mere, forcee par le tyran, et soyez joyeux de veoir finy, et esteint l'object de son deshonneur, et lequel la contraignoit à estre peu pitoyable à l'endroit de son mesme sang, voire d'embrasser le meurtrier de son cher espoux, portant sur elle un double fardeau d'infamie, et d'inceste, et de souffrance, pour l'avilissement de sa moytié, et ruine de sa race.

C'a esté l'occasion, Messieurs, pour laquelle j'ay fainte ceste sottise, et ay voilé mes desseins souz le fard d'une grande folie, laquelle a couvé ma sagesse et prudence pour esclorre le fruit de ceste vengeance, laquelle si elle est d'assez d'efficace, et si est parvenue à son parfait accomplissement, vous en serez les juges. Car de cecy, et de toute autre chose concernant mon prouffit, et le maniement des affaires, c'est à vostre sage advis et conseil que je m'en raporte, et souz lequel je pretens me assujettir. Aussi estes vous ceux qui foulez aux pieds les estincelles meurtrieres de mon pere, et mesprisez les cendres de celuy qui a pollu, et violé la femme, et espouse de son frere, par luy massacré, qui a commis felonnie contre son seigneur, qui a traistreusement assailly la majesté de son Roy, et esclavé injustement sous une grande servitude son pays, et vous ses loyaux citoyens, à qui ravissant la liberté, n'a craint d'ajouster inceste au parricide detesté par tout le monde. C'est aussi à vous que le devoir et raison commandent de garantir, et defendre Amleth, qui est

it be to discover it before them that knowing it would burst (as it were
with despight) to heare of my hard chance, and curse Fortune for
so much imbasing a royall prince, as to deprive him of his majesty,
although not any of you durst so much as shew one sight of sorrow or
sadnes? You know how my father in law conspired my death, and sought
by divers meanes to take away my life; how I was forsaken of the queen
my mother, mocked of my friends, and dispised of mine own subjects:
hetherto I have lived laden with griefe, and wholy confounded in teares,
my life still accompanied with fear and suspition, expecting the houre
when the sharp sword would make an ende of my life and miserable
anguishes. How many times, counterfeiting the mad man, have I heard
you pitty my distresse, and secretly lament to see me disinherited? and
yet no man sought to revenge the death of my father, nor to punish the *
treason of my incestuous uncle, full of murthers and massacres. This
charitie ministred comfort, and your affectionate complaints made me
evidently see your good wills, that you had in memorie the calamity of
your prince, and within your harts ingraven the desire of vengeance for
the death of him that deserved a long life. And what heart can bee so
hard and untractable, or spirit so severe, cruel, and rigorous, that would
not relent at the remembrance of my extremities, and take pitty of an
orphan child, so abandoned of the world? What eyes were so voyd of
moysture but would distill a field g) of tears, to see a poore prince
assaulted by his owne subjects, betrayed by his mother, pursued by his
uncle, and so much oppressed that his friends durst not shew the effects
of their charitie and good affection? O (my good friends) shew pity to
him whom you have nourished, and let your harts take some compassion
upon the memory of my misfortunes! I speak to you that are innocent
of al treason, and never defiled your hands, spirits, nor desires with the
blud of the greate and vertuous king Horvendile. Take pity upon the
queen, sometime your soveraign lady, and my right honorable mother,
forced by the tyrant, and rejoyce to see the end and extinguishing of the
object of her dishonor, which constrained her to be lesse pitiful to her own
blood, so far as to imbrace the murtherer of her own dear spouse, charging her selfe with a double burthen of infamy and incest, together with
injuring and disannulling of her house, and the ruine of her race. This hath
bin the occasion that made me counterfet folly, and cover my intents under
a vaile of meer madnes, which hath wisdom and pollicy therby to inclose
the fruit of this vengeance, which, that it hath attained to the ful point
of efficacy and perfect accomplishment, you yourselves shall bee judges;
for touching this and other things concerning my profit, and the man-
aging of great affairs, I refer my self to your counsels, and therunto am
fully determined to yeeld, as being those that trample under your feet the
murtherers of my father, and despise the ashes of him that hath polluted
and violated the spouse of his brother, by him massacred; that hath
committed felony against his lord, traiterously assailed the majesty of his
king, and odiously thralled his contry under servitude and bondage, and
you his loyall subjects, from whom he, bereaving your liberty, feared not *
to ad incest to parricide, detestable to al the world. To you also it
belongeth by dewty and reason commonly to defend and protect Hamlet,

[III.]

---

g) Collier vermutet a flood of tears.

[II.] le ministre et executeur de si juste vengeance, et qui jaloux de son honneur, et de vostre reputation, s'est ainsi hazardé, esperant que vous luy servirez de peres et deffenseurs, serez ses tuteurs, et le regardans en pitié luy rendrez son bien, et legitime heritage.

Ce'st moy qui ay osté le diffame de mon pays, et estaint le feu qui embrasoit voz fortunes, j'ay lavé les taches, qui denigroient la reputation de la Roine, accablant et le tyran, et la tyrannie, et trompant les ruses du plus cauteleux affineur de l'univers, ay par mesme moyen donné fin à ses meschancetez, et imposture. J'estois marry de l'injure faite, et à mon pere, et à ma chere patrie, et ay occis celuy qui usoit de commandement plus rigoureux sur vous qu'il n'est juste ny seant qu'on en use sur les hommes, qui ont commandé aux plus braves nations de la terre.

Estant donc tel envers vous, c'est raison que vous recognoissiez le plaisir, et me sçachez gré du bien que j'ay fait à la posterité, et que reverant mon esprit et sagesse, vous m'eslisez pour Roy, s'il vous semble que j'en sois digne. Vous me voyez auteur de vostre salut, heritier de l'Empire de mon pere, ne forlignant et devoyant aucunement de ses vertueux actes: non meurtrier, violateur, ny parricide, ny homme qui jamais n'offensay aucun que les vicieux, legitime successeur du Royaume, et juste vengeur d'un crime sur tout autre le plus grief et punissable. C'est à moy, à qui vous devez le benefice de vostre liberté recouvree, et de l'avilissement de celle tyrannie qui tant vous affligeoit, qui ay foulé aux pieds le joug du tyran, et ruiné son trosne, et osté le sceptre des mains à celuy, qui abusoit d'une saincte puissance. Mais c'est à vous à recompenser ceux qui ont bien merité: vous sçavez quel est le salaire et retribution d'un tel merite, et estant en vos mains à le distribuer, c'est aussi de vous que je redemande le pris deu de ma vertu, et la recompence de ma victoire.

Ceste harangue du jeune Prince esmeut de telle sorte le coeur des Danois, et gaigna si bien les affections de la noblesse que les uns plouroient de pitié, les autres de grand'joye, voyans la sagesse et gaillardise d'esprit d'Amleth: et ayans mis fin à leur tristesse tous d'un consentement le declarerent Roy de Jutie, et Chersone, ce qui est à present le propre pays qu'on nomme Dannemarch.

Ayans celebré les festes de son couronnement, et receu les hommages, et fidelitez de ses subjets, il passa en la grande Bretaigne pour aller querir son espouse, et se resjouyr avec son beau pere sur sa presente bonne fortune: mais il s'en fallut bien peu que l'Anglois parfist ce à quoy jamais Fengon n'avoit sçeu attaindre avec toutes ses ruses: Car des que Amleth fut en Bretaigne, il racompta les moyens qu'il avoit tenus à regaigner sa perte, si que l'Anglois entendant la mort de Fengon, demeura

the minister and executor of just vengeance, who being jealous of your [III.] honour and your reputation, hath hazarded himself, hoping you will serve him for fathers, defenders, and tutors, and regarding him in pity, restore him to his goods and inheritances. It is I that have taken away the infamy of my contry, and extinguished the fire that imbraced your fortunes. I have washed the spots that defiled the reputation of the queen, overthrowing both the tirant and the tiranny, and beguiling the subtilties of the craftiest deceiver in the world, and by that meanes brought his wickednes and impostures to an end. I was grieved at the injurie committed both to my father and my native country, and have slaine him that used more rigorus commandements over you, then was either just or convenient to be used unto men that have commaunded the valiantest nations in the world. Seeing, then, he was such a one to you, it is * reason that you acknowledge the benefit, and thinke wel of for the good I had done your posterity, and admiring my spirit and wisdome, chuse me your king, if you think me worthy of the place. You see I am the author of your preservation, heire of my fathers kingdome, not straying in any point from his vertuous action, no murtherer, violent parricide, nor man that ever offended any of you, but only the vitious. I am lawfull successor in the kingdom, and just revenger of a crime above al others most grievous and punishable: it is to me that you owe the benefit of your liberty receaved, and of the subversion of that tyranny that so much afflicted you, that hath troden under feete the yoke of the tirant, and overwhelmed his throne, and taken the scepter out of the hands of him that abused a holy and just authoritie; but it is you that are to recompence those that have well deserved, you know what is the reward of so greate desert, and being in your hands to distribute the same, it is of you that I demand the price of my vertue, and the recompence of my victory.

This oration of the yong prince so mooved the harts of the Danes, and wan the affections of the nobility, that some wept for pity, other for joy, to see the wisedome and gallant spirit of Hamlet; and having made an end of their sorrow, al with one consent proclaimed him king of Jutie and Chersonnese, at this present the proper country of Denmarke. And having celebrated his coronation, and received the homages and fidelities of his subjects, he went into England to fetch his wife, and rejoyced h) with his father in law touching his good fortune; but it wanted little that the king of England had not accomplished that which Fengon with all his subtilties could never attaine.

Hamlet king of one part of Denmark.

Chap. VII.

How Hamlet, after his coronation, went into England; and how the king of England secretly would have put him to death; and how he slew the king of England, and returned againe into Denmarke with two wives; and what followed.

Hamlet, being in England, shewed the king what meanes hee had wrought to recover his kingdom; but when the king of England under-

---

h) Wieder aus dem Verlesen des Übersetzers ein t für r, resjouyt für resjouyr zu erklären.

[II.] estonné, et confuz en son ame, se sentant assailly de deux puissantes passions, veu que jadis luy et Fengon, ayans esté compagnons d'armes s'estoyent juré reciproquement la foy, que s'il advenoit que l'un d'eux fust occis par quiconque ce fust, que l'autre (espousant la querelle) ne cesseroit tant qu'il en eust pris la vengeance, ou se fust mis en devoir de ce faire. Or l'amitié juree, et le serment incitoyent ce Roy Barbare à massacrer Amleth, puis l'alliance se presentant devant ses yeux, et contemplant l'un mort, quoy que son amy l'autre en vie, et l'espoux de sa fille, il effaçoit ce desir de vengeance: mais à la fin le devoir et conscience d'un serment, et foy promise gaignerent le dessus, et conclud ce Roy en son esprit la mort de son gendre, laquelle entreprise fut cause de sa mort, et du saccagement de toute l'Isle Angloise, par la cruauté, et despit esmeu du Roy des Danois. J'ay laissé le discours de ceste bataille tout à oscient, pour ne servir de guere à nostre propos, et que aussi je ne veux vous detenir si longuement, me contentant de vous faire voir quelle fut la fin de ce vaillant et sage Roy, qui se vengeant de tant d'ennemis, et descouvrant toutes les trahisons brassees contre son salut, et vie, en fin servit de jouet à fortune, et d'exemple aux grans, qui se fient trop és felicitez de ce monde, lesquelles ont bien peu de stabilité, et sont de peu de duree.

Or l'Anglois voyant que peu facilement il pourroit se prevaloir du Roy son gendre, et qu'aussi il ne vouloit violer les droits et loix d'hospitalité, il delibera de faire qu'un estranger seroit le vangeur de son injure, et accompliroit le serment juré à Fengon, sans qu'il souillast ses mains du sang du mary de sa fille, ny pollust sa maison, en massacrant traistreusement son hoste.

A lire ceste histoire il sembleroit veoir en Amleth un Hercule envoyé ça et la par Euristee, (sollicité par Junon) de tous costez du monde, là où il sçauroit estre quelque peril evident, pour l'y precipiter, et luy faire perdre la vie: ou bien que ce fust un Bellerophon mandé à Jobatez, pour l'exposer à la mort, ou (laissant les fables) un Urie destiné par David pour servir de but pour faire passer la colere des Barbares.

Bellerophon envoyé portant les lettres de sa mort.

Car l'Anglois (estant freschement morte sa femme) quoy qu'il ne se souciast point de se lier à femme quelconque, pria son gendre, de faire un voyage pour luy en Escosse, et l'amadoua avec ce mot, que sa singuliere prudence l'avoit induit à le preferer à tout autre en telle legation, s'asseurant qu'il estoit impossible, que Amleth, le plus subtil, et accort homme du monde, sceust rien entreprendre, sans le conduire à son effect.

Arrogante chasteté d'Hermethrude Royne d'Escosse.

Or la Royne d'Escosse fille vierge, et d'un hautain courage, mesprisoit les nopces de chacun, et n'estimoit homme digne de son accointance, de sorte qu'avec ceste si arrogante opinion, il n'y venoit amoureux aucun pour la solliciter, à qui elle ne feit perdre la vie.

Mais la fortune du Prince Danois fut si bonne, que Hermethrude (car tel estoit le nom de la Royne Escossoise) oyant parler d'Amleth, et comme il venoit pour l'Anglois la demander à mariage, oublia tout son orgueil, et despouilla son naturel farouche, avec intention de rendre sien

stood of Fengons death, he was both abashed and confused in his minde, [III.]
at that instant feeling himselfe assailed with two great passions, for that
in times past he and Fengon having bin companions together in armes,
had given each other their faith and promises, by oath, that if either of
them chanced to bee slaine by any man whatsoever, hee that survived
(taking the quarrel upon him as his owne) should never cease till he
were revenged, or at the leaste do his endeavour. This promise incited
the barbarous king to massacre Hamlet, but the alliance presenting it
selfe before his eies, and beholding the one deade, although his friend,
and the other alive, and husband to his daughter, made him deface ¹) his
desire of revenge. But in the end, the conscience of his oath and promise obtained the upper hand, and secretly made him conclude the death
of his sonne in law, which enterprise after that was cause of his own
death, and overrunning of the whole country of England by the cruelty
and despight conceived by the king of Denmarke. I have purposely
omitted the discourse of that battaile, as not much pertinent to our
matter, as also, not to trouble you with too tedious a discourse,
being content to shew you the end of this wise and valiant king Hamlet,
who revenging himselfe upon so many enemies, and discovering all the
treasons practised against his life, in the end served for a sport to
fortune, and an example to all great personages that trust overmuch
to the felicities of this world, that are of small moment, and lesse
continuance.

The king of England perceiving that hee could not easilie effect his
desire upon the king, his son in lawe, as also not being willing to break
the laws and rights of hospitality, determined to make a stranger the
revenger of his injury, and so accomplish his oath made to Fengon
without defiling his handes with the blood of the husband of his daughter,
and polluting his house by the traiterous massacring of his friend. In
reading of this history, it seemeth, Hamlet should resemble another Hercules, sent into divers places of the world by Euristheus (solicited by
Juno) where he knew any dangerous adventure, thereby to overthrow
and destroy him; or else Bellerophon sent to Ariobatus to put him to
death; or (leaving prophane histories) an other Urias, by king David
appointed to bee placed in the fore front of the battaile, and the man
that should bee first slain by the barbarians. For the king of Englands
wife being dead not long before (although he cared not for marrying an
other woman) desired his sonne in lawe to make a voyage for him into
Scotland, flattering him in such sort, that he made him beleeve that his
singular wisdome caused him to preferre him to that ambassage, assuring
himselfe that it were impossible that Hamlet, the subtillest and wisest
prince in the worlde, should take any thing in the world in hand without
effecting the same.

Now the queen of Scots beeing a maid, and of a haughty courage,
despised marriage with al men, as not esteeming any worthy to be her
companion, in such manner that by reason of this arrogant opinion there
never came any man to desire her love but she caused him to loose his
life: but the Danish kings fortune was so good, that Hermetrude (for
so was the queens name) hearing that Hamlet was come thither to intreat
a marriage between her and the king of England, forgot all her pride,

---

¹) Collier vermutet deferre; aber das Französische weist auf efface.

[II.]

Hermeths vde devient amoureuse d'Amleth.

le Prince le plus accomply, duquel elle eust jamais ouy parler, et priver la Princesse Angloise d'un mariage, que seule elle se pensoit meriter. Ainsi ceste Amazone sans amitié, parant l'estomach à Cupidon, et se soumettant de son gré aux assaux de sa concupiscence, arrivé le Danois, voulut veoir les lettres du vieillard d'Angleterre, et se moquant des fols appetis de celuy duquel le sang estoit à demy glacé, tenoit l'oeil fiché sur ce jeune et plaisant Adonis de Septentrion, s'estimant bienheureuse, qu'une telle proye luy fut tombeé en main, et de laquelle elle se faisoit forte d'avoir les despouilles. Et elle qui jamais n'avoit peu estre vaincue par la grace, gentilesse, vaillance, ny richesses d'aucun Prince, ny chevalier, grand seigneur, est à present mise à bas par le seul renom des ruses du Danois, lequel, sachant avoir fiancé la fille de l'Anglois, elle arraisonna luy parlant ainsi.

Je n'eusse jamais attendu un si grand heur, ny des Dieux, ny de la fortune que de voir en mes terres le Prince plus accomply, qui soit en toutes les marches Septentrionales, et lequel s'est rendu louable et estimé parmy toutes les nations, tant voisines qu'estrangeres, pour le seul respect de sa vertu, sagesse, et bon-heur, luy servans beaucoup en la poursuite et effect des choses par luy desseignees, et me sens grandement redevable au Roy Anglois, quoy que sa malice ne cherche ny mon avancement, ny le bien de vous, Monsieur, de m'avoir tant honnoree, que de m'envoyer un si excellent homme, pour capituler avec moy du mariage d'entre luy, qui est ja vieux et cassé, et ennemy mortel des miens, avec moy qui suis telle que chacun voit, et qui ne desire m'accointer d'homme de si basse qualité que celuy que vous avez dit estre filz d'un esclave.

Mais d'autre costé, je m'esbahis que le fils d'Horwendille, et petit fils du grand Roy Rorique, celuy qui par sa folle sagesse et feinte sottise a surmonté les forces et ruses de Fengon, et s'est emparé du Royaume de son adversaire, se soit avili jusques à là, qu'ayant esté bien sage et advisé en toutes ses actions, au chois de la compagne de son lict, il se soit fourvoyé: et luy qui par son excellence et lustre, surpassa l'humaine capacité, se soit abaissé jusques à prendre pour femme, celle qui sortant d'une race servile, a beau avoir un Roy pour pere, veu que tousjours la vilité de son sang, luy fera monstrer quelles sont les vertus, et noblesse ancienne de sa race.

Les mariages se doivent mesurer a la vertu et race, et non à la beauté.

Est-ce à vous, Monsieur, à ignorer, que la liaison maritale, ne doit estre mesuree par quelque folle opinion d'une beauté exterieure, mais plustost par le lustre de la vertu, et antiquité de race, honnoree pour sa prudence, et qui jamais ne degenera de l'integrité de ses ancestres? Aussi la beauté exterieure n'est rien, où la perfection de l'esprit ne donne accomplissement, et orne ce qui au corps se flestrit, et perd par un accident et occurrence de peu d'effect: joinct que telles mignotises en ont decen plusieurs, et les attrayans, comme gluantes amorces, les ont percipitez és abismes de leur ruyne, deshonneur, et accablement.

La beauté a ruiné plusieurs.

C'estoit à moy à qui cest advantage estoit deu, qui suis Royne, et telle qui me puis esgaller en noblesse, avec les plus grans de l'Europe, qui ne suis en rien moindre, soit en antiquité de sang, ou valeur des parens, et abondance de richesses.

and dispoiling herselfe of her sterne nature, being as then determined to make him (being the greatest prince as then living) her husband, and deprive the English princesse of her sponse, whome shee thought fit for no men ᵏ) but herself; and so this Amazon without love, disdaining Cupid, by her free wil submitted her haughtie mind to her concupiscence. The Dane arriving in her court, desired she to see the old king of Englands letters, and mocking at his fond appetites, whose blood as then was half congealed, cast her eies upon the yong and plesant Adonis of the North, esteeming her selfe happy to have such a pray fallen into her hands, wherof she made her ful account to have the possession: and to conclude, she that never had been overcome by the grace, courtesie, valor, or riches of anie prince nor lord whatsoever, was as then vanquished with the onelie report of the subtilties of the Dane; who knowing that he was already fianced to the daughter of the king of England, spake unto him and said: I never looked for so great a blisse, neither from the gods nor yet from fortune, as to behold in my countries the most compleate prince in the North, and he that hath made himselfe famous and renowned through all the nations of the world, as well neighbours as strangers, for the only respect of his vertue, wisdom, and good fortune, serving him much in the pursuite and effect of divers thinges by him undertaken, and thinke myselfe much beholding to the king of England (although his malice seeketh neither my advancement nor the good of you, my lord) to do me so much honor as to send me so excellent a man to intreate of a marriage (he being olde, and a mortal enemy to me and mine) with mee that am such a one as every man seeth, is not desirous to couple with a man of so base quality as he, whom you have said to be the son of a slave. But on the other side, I marvel that the son of Horvendile, and grand-child to king Roderick, he that by his foolish wisedom and fained madnesse surmounted the forces and subtilties of Fengon, and obtained the kingdom of his adversary, should so much imbase himselfe (having otherwise bin very wise and wel advised in all his actions) touching his bedfellow; and hee that for his excellency and valor surpasseth humane capacity, should stoope so lowe as to take to wife her that, issuing from a servile race, hath only the name of a king for her father, for that the basenes of her blood will alwaies cause her to shewe what are the vertues and noble qualities of her ancestors. And you, mylord, said she, are you so ignorant as not to know that mariage should not bee measured by any foolish opinion of an outward beautie, but rather by vertues, and antiquitie of race, which maketh the wife to be honored for her prudence, and never degenerating from the integritie of his ancestors: exterior beauty also is nothing, where perfection of the mind doth not accomplish and adorn that which is outwardly seen to be in the bodie, and is lost by an accident and occurrence of small moment: as also such toyes have deceived many men, and drawing them like enticing baits, have cast them headlong into the gulf of their ruine, dishonor, and utter overthrow. It was I to whom this advantage belonged, being a queen, and such a one as for nobility may compare my selfe with the greatest princes in Europe, being nothing inferiour unto any of them,

[III.]

ᵏ) Collier will, wohl mit Recht, no one für no men lesen; aber seine Conjectur (2 Zeilen weiter) desired her to see für desired she to see wird vom Französischen widerlegt.

[II.] Et ne suis seullement Royne, mais telle que recevant qui bon me semblera pour compagnon de ma couche, je peux luy faire porter tiltre de Roy et luy donner, avec mes embrassemens, la jouyssance d'un beau Royaume et grande Province. Advisez, Monsieur, combien j'estime vostre alliance, qui ayant de coustume de poursuyvre, avec le glaive, ceux qui s'osoyent enhardir de pourchasser mon accointance, c'est à vous seul à qui je fais present, et de mes baisers, et accollade, et de mon sceptre, et couronne. Qui est l'homme, s'il n'est de marbre, qui refusast un gage si precieux, que Hermethrude avec le Royaume d'Escosse? Acceptez, gentil Roy, acceptez ceste Royne, qui avec une si grande amitié vous pourchasse tant de bien, et peut vous donner plus d'aise en un jour, que jamais l'Angloise ne sauroit vous appresster de contentement et plaisir toute sa vie: et quoy qu'elle me surpasse en beauté, si est-ce que le sang en estant vil et roturier, il est plus seant à un tel Roy que vous de choisir Hermethrude moins belle, mais noble et illustre, que l'Angloise de grand beauté, mais sortie d'une race incognue, et sans nom quelconque.

La fille d'Angleterre à son espoux, l'ayant laissee pour une autre.
Or pensez si le Danois oyant des raisons si vallables, et se sentant attaindre au poinct que luy mesme avoit descouvert, puis esmeu de courroux, pour la trahison de son beau pere, qui l'avoit là envoyé pour le faire mourir, et en fin caressé, baisé et mignardé par ceste Royne, et jeune, et passablement belle, s'il ne fut assez facile à estre converty, et à oublier l'affection de sa premiere espouse, pour avec ceste cy empieter l'Escosse, et se faire la voye à estre seigneur de toute la grand Bretaigne. Tant y a qu'il l'espousa, et l'emmena avec luy à la court de l'Anglois, ce qui esmout d'avantage l'autre à chercher le moyens de le faire mourir, et l'eust mis à effect, si sa fille, et l'espouse d'Amleth plus soigneuse de celuy qui l'avoit mesprisee, que du salut de son pere, ne luy eut descouvert l'entreprinse en luy disant: Je say bien, Monsieur, que les allechemens d'une effrontee, et les attraiz d'une femme sans vergongne quelconque estans plus lascifs, que les chastes embrassemens d'une femme legitime et pudique, sont plus chatouilleux, et de tant plus charment les sens des jeunes hommes: mais je ne puis prendre pour argent content ce vostre mespris, qui me laissa sans aucune raison, ny faute precedente cogneue en vostre loyalle espouse, avez trouvee† bonne l'alliance de celle, qui un jour sera cause de vostre ruyne. Or quoy qu'une juste jalousie, et courroux raisonnable me dispense à ne tenir non plus de compte de vous, que vous faictes de moy, qui ne suis digne qu'on mesprise de telle sorte, si est-ce que la charité maritale aura bien plus de force en mon endroit, que non pas le desdain conceu, pour veoir qu'une concubine tienne ma place, et qu'une femme estrangere jouysse en ma presence des embrassemens de mon loyal espoux. Ceste injure, Monsieur, quoy que grande, et pour laquelle venger plusieurs Dames de grand renom ont jadis causé la mort et ruyne de leurs marys, ne me gardent de vous advertir de ce que l'on trame contre vous, et vous prier de vous tenir sur vos gardes: veu qu'on ne machine rien moins que vostre mort, laquelle advenant, je ne sauroiz gueres plus vous suyvre. [4]) Plusieurs raisons m'induisent à vous cherir, et icelles de grande consequence, mais sur

---

[4]) Es ist wohl eine que nach plus ausgefallen, so dass die englische Übersetzung I shall not long live after you das Richtige hat.

neither for antiquitie of blood, nobilitie of parents, nor abundance of riches; and I am not only a queene, but such a one as that, receiving whom I will for my companion in bed, can make him beare the title of a king, and with my body give him possession of a great kingdome, and goodly province. Think then, my Lord, how much I account of your alliance, who being accustomed with the sword to pursue such as durst imbolden themselves to win my love, it is to you only to whom I make a present both of my kisses, imbracings, scepter, and crown: what man is he, if he be not made of stone, that would refuse so precious a pawn as Hermetrude, with the kingdome of Scotland? accept, sweete king, accepte this queene, who with so great love and amitie, desireth your so great profit, and can give you more contentment in one day then the princesse of England wold yeeld you pleasure during her life: although shee surpass me in beauty, her bloud beeing base it is fitter for such a king as you are to chuse Hermetrude, lesse beautiful but noble and famous, rather then the English lady with great beawtie, but issuing from an unknown race, without any title of honor.

Now think if the Dane, hearing such forcible resons and understanding that by her which he half doubted[1]), as also moved with choller for the treason of his father in law, that purposely sent him thether to loose his life, and being welcomed, kist, and playd withal by this queen, yong and reasonable fair, if he were not easie enough to be converted, and like to forget the affection of his first wife, with this to enjoy the realme of Scotland, and so open the waie to become king of all Greate Britain: that, to conclude, he marryed her, and led her with him to the king of Englands court, which moved the king from that time forward much more to seek the meanes to bereave him of his life; and had surely done it, if his daughter, Hamlets other wife, more careful of him that had rejected her then of her fathers welfare, had not discovered the enterprise to Hamlet, saying: I know well, my Lord, that the allurements and perswasions of a bold and altogether shameles woman, being more lascivious then the chast imbracements of a lawful and modest wife, are of more force to intice and charm the sences of yong men; but for my part, I cannot take this abuse for satisfaction, to leave mee in this sorte without all cause, reason, or precedent faulte once known in mee, your loyall spouse, and take more pleasure in the aliance of her who one day will be the cause of your ruine and overthrow. And although a just cause of jealousye and reasonable motion of anger, dispence with mee at this time to make no more account of you then you do of me, that am not worthy to be so scornfully rejected; yet matrimoniall charitie shal have more force and vigour in my hart, then the disdaine which I have justly conceived to see a concubine hold my place, and a strange woman before my face injoy the pleasures of my husband. This injury, my Lord, although great and offensive, which to revenge divers ladies of great renown have in times past sought and procured the death of their husbands, cannot so much restrain my good wil, but that [I] may not chuse but advertise you what treason is devised against you, beseeching you to stand upon your guard, for that my fathers onely seeking is to bereave you of your life, which if it happen, I shall not long live after you. Manie reasons induce me to love and cherish you, and those of great

---

[1]) Soll wohl heiszen: had doubted, oder had detected.

[II.] tout me soigne-je de vous, me sentant un gage de vostre fait, remuer dans mes entrailles, pour le respect duquel (sans tant vous oublier) vous devez plus faire de compte de moy, que non de vostre concubine: laquelle j'aimeray, puis que vous luy portez amitié, me suffisant que vostre fils l'ait en haine, et detestation, pour le tort qu'elle fait à sa mere: car il est impossible, que passion, ny trouble aucun de l'ame puisse amortir ces premieres flammes d'amour, qui m'ont faite vostre, ny que j'oublie voz anciens desirs, à poursuivre tant instamment la fille du Roy d'Angleterre: et n'est en la puissance de l'ennie de ma laronnnesse de vostre coeur, ny de la cholere de mon pere, de m'empescher de vous contregarder, aussi bien de vostre serourge†, comme par cy devant vous avez, en faignant, obvié aux desseins, et machinations traitresses de vostre oncle Fengon, estant le complost arresté sur la ruine de vous, et des vostres. Sans cest advertissement, c'estoit fait de la vie du Danois, et des troupes Escossoyses qui l'avoient accompaigné: car le Roy Anglois conviant son gendre, avec les caresses les plus grandes qu'un amy sçauroit faire, à celuy qu'il cherist autant que soymesme, avoit dressé le piege pour l'attraper, et luy faire dancer un piteux bal, pour l'accomplissement des noces de luy, et de sa nouvelle Dame. Mais Amleth y alla couvert d'armes, et ses gens aussi armez sous leurs habits, qui causa que le Danois eschapa avec une playe bien legere de cest estour lequel fut la voye toute desfrichee de la bataille mentionnee cy devant, et en laquelle le Roy Anglois perdant la vie, son pays fut pillé, et saccagé, pour la troisiesme fois, par les Barbares des Isles, et du pays de Dannemarch.

Wiglere tyran occupe Dannemarch. Amleth victorieux, et chargé de despouilles, accompaigné de ces deux femmes, reprenant la route de son pays, entendit comme Wiglere son oncle, et fils de Rorique, ayant osté les thresors royaux à Geruthe sa soeur, et mere d'Amleth, s'estoit aussi saisi du Royaume, disant que Horwendille ny les siens ne le tenoyent que par usufruict, et que c'estoit à luy (en estant le proprietaire) d'en donner la charge à qui bon luy sembleroit. Amleth, qui ne vouloit avoir que celle,⁵) avec le fils de celuy, duquel les predecesseurs avoyent prins leur grandeur, et avancement, feit de si beaux et riches presens à Wiglere, que se contentant, il se retira du pays, et terres du fils de Geruthe. Mais au bout de quelque temps, Wiglere, desireux de tenir tout le pays en sa subjection, affriandé par la conqueste de Scanie et Sialandie: et que aussi Hermethrude (que Amleth aymoit plus que soi-mesme) avoit intelligence avec luy, et luy avoit promis mariage, pourveu qu'il l'ostast des mains de celuy qui la detenoit, envoya deffier Amleth, et luy denoncer la guerre à toute outrance. Ce bon et sage Prince aymant son peuple, eust voulu chercher les moyens d'eviter ceste guerre, mais la refusant il voyoit une grande tache pour

⁵) Soll jedenfalls heiszen avoir querelle, wie die englische Übersetzung es giebt.

consequence, but especially and above all the rest, I am and must bee carefull of you, when I feele your child stirring in my wombe; for which respecte, without so much forgetting yourselfe, you ought to make more account of me then of your concubine, whome I will love because you love her, contenting my selfe that your sonne hateth her, in regard of the wrong she doth to this mother; for it is impossible that any passion or trouble of the mind whatsoever can quench those fierce passions of love that made me yours, neither that I shold forget your favours past, when loyallie you sought the love of the daughter of the king of England. Neither is it in the power of that thiefe that hath stoln your heart, nor my fathers choller, to hinder me from seeking to preserve you from the cruelty of your dissembling friend (as heeretofore by counterfetting the madman, you prevented the practises and treasons of your uncle Fengon), the complot being determined to be executed upon you and yours. Without this advertisement, the Dane had surely been slain, and the Scots that came with him; for the king of England, inviting his son in law to a banquet, with greatest curtesies that a friend can use to him whom he loved as himselfe, had the meanes to intrap him, and cause him dance a pittiful galliard, in that sort to celebrate the marriage betweene him and his new lady. But Hamlet went thither with armour under his clothes, and his men in like sort; by which means he and his escaped with little hurt, and so after that hapned the battaile before spoken of, wherein the king of England losing his life, his countrie was the third time sacked by the barbarians of the ilands and countrie of Denmark.

[III.]

Chap. VIII.

How Hamblet, being in Denmarke, was assailed by Wiglerus his Uncle, and after betrayed by his last wife, called Hermetrude, and was slaine: after whose death she marryed his enemie, Wiglerus.

Hamlet having obtained victory against the king of England, and slaine him, laden with great treasures and accompanied with his two wives, set forward to saile into Denmarke, but by the way hee had intelligence that Wiglere, his uncle, and sonne to Rodericke, having taken the royall treasure from his sister Geruth (mother to Hamblet) had also seazed upon the kingdome, saying, that neither Horvendile nor any of his helde it but by permission, and that it was in him (to whom the property belonged) to give the charge therof to whom he would. But Hamblet, not desirous to have any quarrell with the sonne of him from whom his predecessors had received their greatnes and advancement, gave such and so rich presents to Wiglere, that he, being contented, withdrew himselfe out of the countrey and territories of Geruths sonne. But within certaine time after, Wiglere, desirous to keepe all the countrey in subjection, intyced by the conquest of Scanie and Sialandie, and also that Hermetrude (the wife of Hamlet, whom he loved more then himselfe) had secret intelligence with him, and had promised him marriage, so that he would take her out of the handes of him that held her, sent to defie Hamlet, and proclaimed open warre against him. Hamlet, like a good and wise prince, loving especially the welfare of his subjects, sought by all meanes to avoyde that warre; but againe refusing it, he perceived

Hermetrude betrayeth Hamlet her husband.

[II.]

Une mort honorable plus à choisir que une vie contemptible.

son honneur, et l'acceptant sa fin luy paroissoit certaine: le desir de conserver sa vie l'esguillonnoit d'une part, et l'honneur le poussoit de l'autre, mais à la fin se souvenant que jamais peril quelconque ne l'avoit esbranlé de sa vertu et constance, ayma mieux choisir la necessité de sa ruyne, que perdre le loz immortel que acquierent les hommes vaillans és entreprises de la guerre. Aussi il y a autant de difference entre une vie sans honneur, et une mort honorable, comme la gloire a d'excellence par dessus le mespris et contemnement. Mais le pis qui gastoit ce vertueux Prince, estoit le trop de fiance qu'il avoit en sa femme Hermethrude, et l'amitié trop vehemente qui luy portoit, ne se repentant du tort faict à son espouse legitime, et pour lequel (peut estre) ceste infortune luy estoit survenue, et n'eust jamais estimé, que celle qu'il cherissoit sur toute chose chere, l'eust trahy si laschement, et ne luy souvenoit des propos de l'Angloyse, qui luy predit que les embrassemens de ceste autre, seroyent aussi bien cause de sa ruine, comme ils luy avoyent ravy le meilleur de son sens, et assoupy en luy celle grande prudence, qui le rendoit admirable, par les pays voisins de l'Ocean Septentrional, et en toutes les Allemagnes. Or le plus grand regret qu'eust ce Roy affolé de sa femme, estoit la separation de celle qu'il idolatroit, et s'asseurant de son desastre, eust voulu, ou qu'elle luy eust tenu compagnie à la mort, ou luy trouver mary qui l'aimast, luy trespassé, à l'esgal de l'extreme amour qu'il luy portoit: mais la desloyale avoit desja pourveu à ses nopces, sans que son mary fallust qui se meit en peine pour luy en pratiquer: lequel elle voyant triste pour l'amour d'elle, et se devant absenter de sa compagnie, elle, pour le coiffer d'avantage, et l'encourager d'aller à sa deffaitte, luy promit de le suyvre par tout, et de jouyr de mesme fortune que luy, fust elle mauvaise, ou telle qu'il la souhaitoit, qu'il [6]) luy feroit cognoistre de combien elle surpassoit l'Angloyse en affection en son endroit, et que la femme estoit malheureuse, laquelle craignoit de suyvre, et accompaigner son mary à la mort: si qu'à l'ouyr parler, on eust dit que c'estoit l'espouse d'un Mithridate, ou Zenobie Royne des Palmireniens, tant elle s'affectionnoit à la matiere, et faisoit parade de sa constance, et ferme amitié. Mais à l'effect on voit combien vaine fut la promesse de ceste volage Princesse, et combien mal s'esgaloit la suitte de ceste Escoçoise, à celle rigueur de chasteté, qu'elle gardoit, avant qu'avoir savouré les embrassemens d'un mary: car Amleth ne fut pas si tost au camp, qu'elle trouva les moyens de voir Wiglere: et la bataille estant donnee, et le miserable Danoys mis à mort, Hermethrude se rendit avec les despouilles de son mary mort, entre les mains du tyran, lequel plus que content de ses metamorphoses tant desirees, donna ordre que soudain fut solemnisé le mariage, acheté avec le sang et richesses du fils de Horwendille.

Dissimulation de la Royne Hermethrude.

Zenobie vaillante Royne Asiatique.

Desloyauté de Hermethrude.

Ainsi n'est deliberation de femme, que une bien petite incommodité de fortune ne desmolisse, et face alterer et changer, et que le changement du temps ne pervertisse, tellement que les cas fortuits, subjects à la sagesse d'un homme constant, esbranlent et ruent bas la loyauté naturellement glissante de ce sexe variable, et sans nulle asseurance ne fermeté. Veu que tout ainsi que la femme est facile à promettre, aussi est elle pesante et paresseuse à tenir, et effectuer ce qu'elle aura promis,

Inconstance des femmes.

---

[6]) Auch hier giebt der englische Übersetzer das Richtige: qu'elle.

a great spot and blemish in his honor, and, accepting the same, [III.] he knewe it would bee the ende of his dayes. By the desire of preserving his life on the one side, and his honor on the other side pricking him forward, but, at the last, remembering that never any danger whatsoever had once shaken his vertues and constancy, chose rather the necessitie of his ruine, then to loose the immortall fame that valiant and honourable men obtained in the warres. And there is as much difference betweene a life without honour and an honourable death, as glory and renowne is more excellent then dishonour and evil report.

But the thing that spoyled this vertuous prince was the over great trust and confidence hee had in his wife Hermetrude, and the vehement love hee bare unto her, not once repenting the wrong in that case done to his lawfull spouse, and for the which (paradventure that misfortune had never hapned unto him, and it would never have bin thought that she, whom he loved above all things, would have so villainously betrayed him), hee not once remembring his first wives speeches, who prophesied unto him, that the pleasures hee seemed to take in his other wife would in the end be the cause of his overthrowe, as they had ravished him of the best part of his senses, and quenched in him the great prudence that made him admirable in all the countries in the ocean seas, and through all Germany. Now, the greatest grief that this king (besotted on his wife) had, was the separation of her whom he adored, and, assuring himselfe of his overthrowe, was desirous either that she might beare him company at his death, or els to find her a husband that should love her (he beeing dead) as well as ever hee did. But the disloyall queene had already provided herself of a marriage to put her husband out of trouble and care for that, who perceiving him to be sad for her sake, when shee should have absented her selfe from him, she, to blind him the more and to incourage him to set forward to his owne destruction, promised to follow him whether soever he went, and to take the like fortune that befell to him, were it good or evil, and that so shee would give him cause to know how much shee surpassed the English woman in her affection towardes him, saying, that woman is accursed that feareth to follow and accompany her husband to the death: so that, to heare her speake, men would have sayd that shee had been the wife of Mithridates, or Zenobia queene of Palmira, shee made so greate a show of love and constancy. But by the effect it was after easily perceived howe vaine the promise of this unconstant and wavering princesse was; and howe uncomparable the life of this Scottish queene was to the vigor of her chastitie, being a mayd before she was marryed. For that Hamlet had no sooner entred into the field, but she found meanes to see Wiglere, and the battel begun, wherein the miserable Danish prince was slaine; but Herme- *Hamlet slaine.* trude presently yeelded her self, with all her dead husbands treasons, into the hand of the tyrant, who, more then content with that metamorphosis so much desired, gave order that presently the marriage (bought with the blood and treason of the sonne of Horvendile) should bee celebrated.

Thus you see that there is no promise or determination of a woman, but that a very small discommoditie of fortune mollifieth and altereth the same, and which time doeth not pervert; so that

[II.] comme celle qui est sans fin, ny limite en ses desirs, se chatouillant en la diversité de ses aises, et prenant plaisir en choses nouvelles, desquelles tout aussi tost elle perd la souvenance: et en somme, telles qu'en toutes ses actions elle est precipitee, convoiteuse et ingrate, quelque bien ou service qu'on luy sçache faire. Je m'esgare, à ce que voy, en mes discours, vomissant choses indignes de ce sexe; mais les vices de Hermethrude, m'ont fait plus dire que je ne pensois: joinct que l'autheur d'où j'ay pris ceste histoire, me forçoit presque à suyvre sa trace, tant il y a de douceur et nayveté à poursuyvre ce propos: et tant il me sembloit estre veritable, veu le succez miserable du pauvre roy Amleth. Telle fut la fin d'Amleth, fils d'Horwendille, Prince de Jutie, auquel si la fortune eust esgallé ce qu' il avoit de bon en soy naturellement, je ne sçay lequel des Grecs et Romains eussent eu l'honneur de l'avantager en vertu et excellence: mais son desastre le suyvant en toutes les actions, et luy vainquant la malice du sort, avec l'effert[1]) de sa constance, il nous laisse un exemple notable de grandeur de courage, digne d'un grand Prince, se fortifiant d'espoir és choses mesmes qui estoyent sans couleur d'aucune esperance et qui en tout s'est rendu admirable si une seule tache n'eust obscurcy une bonne partie de ses louanges. D'autant que la plus grande

Quelle est la plus grande victoire en l'homme. victoire que l'homme peut acquerir est celle qui le fait seigneur et dompteur de ses affections, et laquelle chastie les efforts desreiglez du sens affolé en ses convoitises: car l'homme a beau estre fort et sage, que si les chatouillemens de la chair le surmontent, il s'avillira, et arrestera apres ses beautez, et deviendra fol et insensé à la poursuite des femmes. De telle faute a esté chargé le grand Hercule, des Hebrieux Samson, et le plus sage d'entre les hommes, suyvant ce train, y a fait diminution de son sens, et la pluspart des grans, sages, vaillans et discrets par apparence, de nostre temps, dançans une pareille note, donnent de beaux indices de leur gaillardise, prudence et saincteté. / Mais vous qui lisez cecy, je vous prie ne ressembler l'araigne qui se repaist de la corruption qui est és fleurs et fruicts dans un verger, la où l'abeille recueille son miel des fleurs les plus soueſves, et mieux flairantes qu'elle sçait choisir: car l'homme bien né, faut qu'il lise la vie du paillard

Pourquoy on lit histoires. yvroigne, cruel, voleur, et sanguinaire, non pour l'ensuyvir, ny souiller son ame de telles immondices: ains pour eviter la paillardise, fuir le desbord et superfluité és banquets, et suyvre la modestie, continence, et courtoisie, qui recommande Amleth en ce discours, lequel parmy les banquets des autres, demeuroit sobre, et où chacun se penoit d'accumuler thresor, cestuy-cy simplement, n'esgalant les richesses à l'honneur, il consentoit de faire un amas

---

[1]) Der englische Übersetzer las, wohl richtig, effort.

XCIX

the misfortunes subject to a constant man shake and overthrowe [III.]
the naturall slipperie loyaltie of the variable steppes of women,
wholy without and † any faithfull assurance of love, or true
unfained constancy: for as a woman is ready to promise, so is
shee heavy and slowe to performe and effect that which she hath
promised, as she that is without end or limit in her desires, flattring her selfe in the diversitie of her wanton delights, and taking
pleasure in diversitie and change of newe things, which as soone
shee doth forget and growe weary off: and, to conclude, such
shee is in all her actions, she is rash, covetous, and unthankefull,
whatsoever good or service can bee done unto her. But nowe I
perceive I erre in my discourse, vomitting such things unworthy
of this sects †; but the vices of Hermetrude have made mee say
more then I meant to speake, as also the author, from whence I
take this Hystorie, hath almost made mee hold this course, I find
so great a sweetnesse and livelinesse in this kinde of argument;
and the rather because it seemeth so much the truer, considering
the miserable successe of poore king Hamlet.

Such was the ende of Hamlet, sonne to Horvendile, prince of
Jutie; to whom, if his fortune had been equall with his inward and
naturall giftes, I know not which of the auncient Grecians and Romans
had been able to have compared with him for vertue and excellencie:
but hard fortune following him in all his actions, and yet hee vanquishing the malice of his time with the vigour of constancy, hath left us
a notable example of haughtie courage, worthy of a great prince,
arming himselfe with hope in things that were wholy without
any colour or shewe thereof, and in all his honorable actions
made himselfe worthy of perpetuall memorie, if one onely spotte
had not blemished and darkened a good part of his prayses.
For that the greatest victorie that a man can obtaine is to make
himselfe victorious and lord over his owne affections, and that
restraineth the unbridled desires of his concupiscence; for if a
man be never so princely, valiant, and wise, if the desires and
inticements of his flesh prevaile, and have the upper hand, hee
will imbase his credite, and, gasing after strange beauties, become
a foole, and (as it were) incensed, dote on the presence of women.
This fault was in the great Hercules, Sampson; and the wisest
man that ever lived upon the earth, following this traine, therein
impaired his wit; and the most noble, wise, valiant, and discreet
personages of our time, following the same course, have left us
many notable examples of their worthy and notable vertues.

But I beseech you that shall reade this Hystorie not to
resemble the spider, that feedeth of the coruption that shee findeth
in the flowers and fruites that are in the gardens, whereas the
bee gathereth her hony out of the best and fayrest flower shee
can finde: for a man that is well brought up should reade the
lives of whoremongers, drunkards, incestuous, violent, and bloody
persons, not to follow their steps, and so to defile himselfe with
such uncleannesse, but to shunne paliardize, abstain the superfluities and drunkennesse in banquets, and follow the modestie,
courtesie, and continencie that recommendeth Hamlet in this
discourse, who, while other made good cheare, continued sober;
and where all men sought as much as they could to gather together riches and treasure, hee, simply accounting riches nothing
comparable to honor, sought to gather a multitude of vertues

[II.] de vertus, qui l'esgallassent à ceux qu'il estimoit Dieux, n'ayant encor receu la lumiere de l'Evangile: à fin qu'on voye, et parmy les Barbares, et entre ceux qui estoyent esloignez de la cognoissance d'un seul Dieu, que nature estoit esguillonnee à suyvre ce qui est bon, et poussee à embrasser la vertu, n'y ayant jamais eu nation, tant farouche fut elle, qui n'ayt prins plaisir à faire quelque chose ressentant le bien, pour en acquerir louange, lequel nous avons dit estre le salaire de la vertu et bonne vie. Je prens plaisir à toucher ces histoires estrangeres, et de peuple non baptisé, à fin que la vertu de ces grossiers donne plus de lustre à la nostre, qui les voyans si accomplis, sages, prudens, et advisez à la suitte de leurs affaires, tascherons non de les imiter, estant l'imitation peu de chose: mais à les surmonter, ainsi que nostre Religion surpasse leur superstition, et nostre siecle est plus purgé, subtil et gaillard, que la saison qui les conduisoit.

FIN.

that might make him equall to [III.] those that by them were esteemed as gods; having not as then received the lighte of the gospell, that men might see among the barbarians, and them that were farre from the knowledge of one onelye God, that nature was provoked to follow that which is good, and those forward to imbrace vertue, for that there was never any nation, how rude or barbarous soever, that tooke not some pleasure to do that which seemed good, therby to win praise and commendations, which wee have said to be the reward of vertue and good life. I delight to speak of these strange histories, and of people that were unchristned, that the vertue of the rude people maie give more splendor to our nation, who seeing them so compleat, wise, prudent, and well advised in their actions, might strive not only to follow (imitation being a small matter), but to surmount them, as our religion surpasseth their superstition, and our age more purged, subtill, and gallant, then the season wherin they lived ane made their vertues knowne,

FINIS.

NACHTRÄGE.

I. Zu der Erzählung des Saxo Grammaticus.

Für die Übersetzung und Schlußanmerkung wurde seiner Zeit benutzt: Quellen des Shakespeare, hrsg. v. Echtermeyer, Hentschel und Simrock; 1. Aufl. (Berlin 1831), und Shakespeare's Hamlet, hrsg. von Elze, (Leipzig 1857); jetzt sind weiter herbeizuziehen: Simrock, Quellen des Shakespeare, 2. Auflage, 2 Bde., Bonn 1870, und Ettmüller, Altnordischer Sagenschatz, Leipzig 1870; auch Zinzow, Die Hamletsage an und mit verwandten Sagen erläutert, Halle 1877. — Die Übersetzung Simrocks (mit einem Anhange „zur Sagenvergleichung") bricht bei Amleths Königsernennung ab, die Ettmüllers (mit Anmerkungen und Erläuterungen) dagegen geht bis zu dessen Tode, nur seine große Volksrede und die Beschreibung des Schildes auslassend; Zinzow giebt bloß einen längeren Auszug.

S. XIV a Z. 8 v. u. ließe sich *paleum* wohl dem Zusammenhange nach verständlicher, mit Simrock und Ettmüller, übersetzen: *ein rotblühendes Halmgewächs*, „einen Hahnenbart (ein rotblühendes Gewächs; die rote Farbe zeigt Amleth, daß er Blut und Leben wage);" nur scheint das folgende *stramine* doch mehr auf „Strohhalm" zu weisen.

S. XVII b Z. 4 v. u. lies *lange* statt *Tag* für *Tag*

S. XIX b Z. 22 v. u. lies lieber mit Simrock: *Seine Begleiter, die in alle dem nichts als Spuren seiner alten Geistesverwirrung sahen, spotteten seiner* u. s. w.

S. XXI b Z. 8 v. o. lies: *erstens, daß sie wie eine Magd den Kopf mit dem Mantel bedeckt, zweitens, daß sie das Kleid beim Gehen aufgenommen, drittens, daß sie die Überbleibsel der Speisen aus den Zähnen gestochert und dann noch einmal gekaut habe. Er berichtete auch, daß ihre Mutter einmal durch Kriegsgefangenschaft in Dienstbarkeit geraten sei, ihre Fehler also nicht etwa bloß für anerzogene, sondern für angeborene zu halten wären.*

S. XXIII a Z. 14 v. o. lies *popularium* statt *populariam*

S. XXIV a Z. 2 v. u. lies *negotio, si* statt *negotio. si*

S. XXV b Z. 17 v. o. lies: *Keine Spur soll bleiben von dem Brudermörder, keine Stätte im Vaterlande soll seinen schandbefleckten Gliedern zuteil werden, keine Nachbarschaft sollen sie verpesten.*

S. XXVIII a Z. 19 v. o. lies *districto* statt *discricto* und Z. 1 v. u. *cognoscit e* statt *cognoscite*.

S. XXXIV b Z. 3 v. o. könnte *lacessentibus solis radiis* vielleicht heißen sollen: *die den blendenden Strahlen der (dem Feinde entgegenstehenden) Sonne*. — Ebenda a Z. 7 v. u. lies *duas* statt *duas -*, Z. 3 v. u. *periculum, si* statt *periculum si.*

S. XXXV. Der Schlußanmerkung ist (nach Simrock, 1, 133) beizufügen, daß in *Maurers Isländischen Volkssagen, Leipzig* 1860, die Erzählung von Brian dieselben Grundzüge wie Saxos Erzählung hat. — Den Namen *Amleth* erklärt Ettmüller. (S. 118) als *altnordisch Amhlôdhi, d. i. der mit Mühe Sammelnde, Anhäufende, der unausgesetzt Thätige*; aber an anderer Stelle (S. 358 vgl. S. VI) soll *Amlôdhi* (sic) *einen unentschlossenen, mutlosen, thatscheuen Menschen* bezeichnen, wo indes die Bedeutung *dummer Mensch, Narr* wohl ausreicht, so daß doch an dieser festzuhalten sein dürfte. Der von Simrock (S. 130) angeführten Meinung, *Hamlet=Hamleik* solle ausdrücken, *daß er den geistig Verstümmelten eben nur spiele*, kann Simrock selbst keinen großen Wert beimessen.

II. Zu der Erzählung des Belleforest.

Unsern, der Ausgabe: Lyon 1581 entnommenen Abdruck nachträglich nochmals nach dem Originale zu revidiren, ist mir nicht möglich gewesen, da jene Ausgabe mir jetzt leider nicht mehr zugänglich war. Dagegen erhielt ich durch die Güte des Herrn Bibliothekar Dr. Köhler von der Grofsherzoglichen Bibliothek zu Weimar jetzt die früher nicht zu Gebote stehende Ausgabe: Paris 1582 (Bd. 5 der ersten Gesamtausgabe der Histoires tragiques Paris 1580—82), deren genaue Durchsicht mir eine bedeutende Anzahl für den vorliegenden Zweck — die vergleichende Zusammenstellung des französischen und des englischen Textes — wichtiger Varianten ergeben hat. Denn aus ihnen geht hervor, dafs alles Erhebliche, was in der Hystorie of Hamblet, gegen die Ausgabe von 1581 gehalten, als Abweichung oder Zusatz erschien — mit alleiniger Ausnahme der Stellen S. LIII u. LV: behind the arras ... A rat, a rat! ... hangings — nicht vom englischen Übersetzer herrührt, sondern sich im französischen Originale von 1582 vorfindet; selbst die Marginalien stimmen, soweit nicht der Übersetzer diese oder jene, vorzüglich gegen das Ende hin, weggelassen hat. Danach wird also die S. XXXVI Anm. 2) aufgestellte Vermutung, der Hystorie liege die Lyoner Ausgabe von 1581 zu Grunde, entschieden hinfällig; sie stammt vielmehr zweifellos aus dem „durchgesehenen, verbesserten und vermehrten" Text, wie er in der ersten Gesamtausgabe der Histoires tragiques, Paris, 7 Bde. 1580—82, vorliegt und wahrscheinlich auch in der folgenden, Rouen 1603—4, enthalten ist. Da somit der englische Übersetzer entweder die Pariser Ausgabe von 1582 selbst, oder eine von ihr abgeleitete benutzt hat, wird es — um die Abhängigkeit der englischen Erzählung von der französischen ins rechte Licht zu stellen — nötig sein, die in jener gefundenen Varianten, soweit irgend von Belang, hier aufzuführen (wobei einige kleine offenbare Druckfehler stillschweigend corrigirt sein mögen). Der Titel der in Rede stehenden Ausgabe lautet:

Le
CINQUIESME
TOME DES HISTOIRES TRAGIQUES,
Contenant plusieurs Discours memorables,
la plus part recueilly des histoires advenues de nostre temps.
Le tout reveu, corrigé et augmenté, outre les precedentes impressions: Par
F. DE BEL-LEFOREST *Commingeois.*
A PARIS,
chez Gabriel Buon, au clos Bruneau, à l'enseigne de sainct Claude.
1582.
AVEC PRIVILEGE DU ROY.

Diese hat nun:

S. XXXVI, Z. 1 v. o. *d'aujourdhuy*
   Z. 6 v. u. *amis* Druckfehler für *ames*, wie die Lyoner Ausg. 1581 richtig hat u. wie auch der englische Übersetzer (in der Ausg. Rouen 1603—4?) richtig las.
   Z. 2 v. u, fehlt *desja*.
S. XXXVIII, Z. 21 v. o. *ou ne pouvoient parvenir*
   Z. 25 v. o. *qu'on s'est attaché à son sang le plus proche pour se faire grand: et qu'il y en a eu que* (statt *qui*) *ne pouvans*
S. XL, Z. 9 v. u. *aussi la vengeance*
   Z. 17 v. u. *obliger*
   Z. 14 v. u. *la France d'autant que souvent la faulte vient plustost d'eux que non des grands, lesquels ont d'autres affaires qui les destournent de chose qui semble de peu de consequence. Joinct que je me tiens pour plus que satisfait*
   Z. 6 v. u. *mes oeuvres. Et y en a plusieurs qui les admirent: comme d'autres, qui poussez d'envie blasment et calomnient, ausquels je ne* (lies *me*, wie auch der engl. Übers. las) *confesse estre grandement obligé. En-tant qu'ils sont cause que je veille d'avantage, et que par mon travail je suis plus aymé et honoré que jamais, qui est le plaisir plus grand que j'aye,*
   Z. 4 v. u. *tresors les plus grands*
S. XLII, Z. 4 v. o. *fust en leurs biens on en l'honneur,*
   Z. 5 v. u. *au combat*

— CIII —

S. XLIV, Z. 11 v. o. *tacha avec une grande faveur, et courtoisie et se* (lies *de se le*) *rendre à jamais obligé:*
Z. 17 u. 18 v. o. *Fengon* und *de despit.*
Z. 11 v. u. *divinité. Ne voila pas un fin et rusé Conseiller? mais il devoit penser que la mere sachant les desseins du mary ne mettroit son fils en adventure de mort. Ainsi Fengon*
S. XLVI, Z. 21 v. o. *s'accoupler*
Z. 11 v. u. *les plus grands*
Z. 10 v. u. *pour le faut de sa partie.* (? — aber vgl. das Englische.)
Z. 8 u. 7 v. u. *Bien diray-je que, ou faudroit*
S. XLVIII, Z. 3 v. o. *et asseuré que Fengon*
Z. 7 v. o. *qu'il faignit*
Z. 9 v. o. *du tyran. Et bien qu'il eust esté à l'Escole du Prince Romain, qui pour se faindre fol, fut nommé Brute, si est-ce qu'il en imitoit les façons, et la sagesse. Car*
Z. 12 v. u. *Roys*
Z. 9 v. u. *ne proceda jamais d'ailleurs,*
S. L, Z. 7 v. o. *et contrarie*
Z. 10 v. o. *les approches. Si cela n'estoit du tout esloigné de la perfection du Chrestien, qui ne doibt avoir le fiel amer, ny les desirs confits en vengeance.*
Z. 15 v. o. *poignars, et estocs,*
Z. 4 v. u. *Horwendille, avoit esté*
Z. 1 v. u. *jours. Cestuy s'accompagna*
S. LII, Z. 3 v. o. *sens, suffiroit*
Z. 4 v. o. *feit entendre*
Z. 11 v. o. *soustenans*
Z. 4 v. u. *et qu'il fieroit son conseil* (die englische Übersetzung ist hier sehr frei).
S. LIV, Z. 10 v. o. *continuant*
Z. 12 v. o. *sur ce lourdier*
Z. 4 u. 5 v. o. *qui souz le fard d'un plus* (? — aber vgl. das Englische) *dissimulé vous couvriez*
S. LVI, Z. 4 v. o. fehlt *ce* — vgl. das Englische.
Z. 12 v. o. *sans force ny coeur de vaillance*
Z. 25 v. u. *le trahit laschement,*
Z. 23 v. u. *jamais* (statt *jadis* — aber vgl. das Englische) *despouillé Norvege*
Z. 22 v. u. *les thresors*
Z. 6 v. u. *je sors*
S. LVIII, Z. 6 v. o. *qui lui contrerolles*
Z. 9 v. o. *ainsi il vaut mieux faindre l'un* (etwa zu lesen *l'asne ?* — der Engländer übersetzt *to fayne madnesse*).
Z. 16 v. u. *piquer* kann richtig sein, obwohl das folgende *interessee* für *piquee* zu sprechen scheint.
Z. 15 v. u. *touchast*
S. LX, Z. 18 v. u. *les nouvelles: et me crains*
S. LXII, Z. 15 v. u. *nous*

S. LXIV, 11 v. o. *cruauté* (:) *vers lequel se resoulut de l'envoyer, et le prier par lettre d'en despecher le monde. Amleth entandant*
Z. 9 v. u. *nepveu*
Z. 2 u. 1 v. u. *tenoyent* u. *chere, n'y n'estoient*
S. LXVI, Z. 3 v. u. *Poetes devins*
S. LXVIII, Z. 12 v. o. *jamais je ne trouveray* (?)
Z. 20 v. o. *estant en l'escriture*
Z. 15 v. u. *a establiy*
S. LXX, Z. 14 v. o. *de leur tect*
Z. 2 v. u. auch *confusion* (statt *confession*).
S. LXXII, Z. 18 v. o. *menaça*
S. LXXIV, Z. 5 v. o. *que l'Anglois*
Z. 8 v. o. *cognoissent*
Z. 17 v. o. *vuides*
Z. 2 v. u. *pieux*
S. LXXVI, Z. 24 v. o. *et accortise, en mettant*
Z. 26 v. o. *quelque face et forme de justice*
Z. 11 v. u. *recompense. Car autrement ny les bons Roys de Juda, ny autres apres eux, eussent poursuivy la mort de ceux qui avoient offencez leurs majeurs, si Dieu mesme n'eut en eux inspiré et gravé ce desir. De cecy*
S. LXXX, Z. 22 v. o. *le meurtrier*
Z. 27 v. o. *vous marris*
Z. 20 v. u. *saisir*
Z. 12 v. u. *qui eust servy à Hothere.*
S. LXXXII, Z. 9 v. o. *Il est bien vray*
Z. 4 v. u. *vous avez* (während sonst öfter die Abkürzung *voz.*).
S. LXXXIV, Z. 3 v. o. *n'osast*
S. LXXXVI, Z. 4 v. o. *et par mesme*
Z. 8 v. n. *pays*
Z. 4 u. 3 v. u. *ne parfeit* u. *Car dés*
S. LXXXVIII, Z. 5 v. o. *son amy, l'autre*
Z. 15 v. o. *ne veux vous tenir*
Z. 15 v. u. *pour servir de butte et de blanc pour faire passer*
S. XC, Z. 9 v. o. *Et de fait elle qui jamais*
Z. 6 v. n. *precipitez*
S. XCII, Z. 23 v. u. *les moyens.*
S. XCIV, Z. 11 v. o. *de vostre faint hoste, comme*
Z. 21 v. o. *estour, lequel fut la voye toute desfichee* (?)
Z. 17 v. u. *de ses*
Z. 11 v. u. *avoir querelle,*
S. XCVI, Z. 8 v. o. *Mais le pris*
Z. 11 v. u. *despoilles*
S. XCVIII, Z. 15 v. o. *l'effort*
Z. 24 v. o. *apres les beautez*
S. C, Z. 8 v. o. *que la saison en laquelle ils ont vescu. Et fait paroistre leur vertu. Fin de la Troisiesme histoire.*

III. Zur Hystorie of Hamblet. ✓

Ähnlich wie für Belleforest liegt auch für die Hystorie jetzt eine *andere* Ausgabe vor, unsern Abdruck nach ihr zu revidiren.

Als derselbe entstand, konnte er nur nach *Collier: Shakespeare's Library*, London (1843) gegeben werden. Mittlerweile hat aber Hazlitt dieses Werk von neuem 'vermehrt und verbessert' herausgegeben (*Shakespeare's Library.* — Second edition, carefully

revised and greatly enlarged. The text now first formed from a new collation of the original copies. Part I, 4 vols. Part II, 2 vols. London 1875), und hier ist die Hystorie of Hamblet (Part I, vol. II, p. 211—279), wie es scheint treuer als bei Collier, aus dem Cambridger Original-Exemplar (nicht als 'Reprint of Collier' wie Furnefs, Hamlet vol. II, p. 398 irrtümlich sagt, sich deswegen in dem von ihm gegebenen, übrigens am Anfang und Ende gekürzten Abdruck, nur an Collier haltend) abgedruckt. Letzteres geht nicht blofs aus den angeführten Titelworten, sondern auch aus inneren Kennzeichen, wie aus der sehr mangelhaften (von Collier verbesserten) Interpunktion und Orthographie, aus den beibehaltenen Abkürzungen und auch aus den hier und da sich zeigenden kleinen Abweichungen in den Textesworten hervor. Demnach entstand für mich die Frage, ob ich eine genaue Vergleichung des Collier'schen und des Hazlitt'schen Textes vorzunehmen und die sich ergebenden Varianten hier anzugeben habe. Ich habe indes geglaubt, mich dieser Aufgabe überheben zu dürfen; denn die Abweichungen, die ich bei einer teilweisen Collation auffand, zeigten sich doch als gar zu unbedeutende, durchaus unwesentliche; auch hatte ihre Mitteilung keinen mir erkennbaren weiteren Zweck. Dann aber fühlte ich mich auch nicht sicher genug, ob Hazlitts Abdruck das Original überall wirklich völlig treu wiedergebe. Hat derselbe doch unter der Überschrift „Mr. Collier's Introduction" dessen gewifs richtige Meinung (p. VI), dafs Saxo Grammaticus unmittelbar oder mittelbar Belleforest's Quelle gewesen sei, *ganz stillschweigend* dahin verkehrt, dafs es nun — sicher falsch, aber sehr zuversichtlich — heifst (p. 215); „his (Belleforest's) story of Amleth was of course copied from Bandello"! Danach zu urteilen, konnte ich nicht wissen, ob Hazlitt sich nicht etwa auch Freiheiten mit dem Texte der „Hystorie" genommen habe.

R. G.

Errata.

Pag. XXXIX, Zeile 17 von oben (statt: wealh) lies: wealth.
„ XLII, Randglosse zu 12 u. 13 (statt: Rorikue) lies: Rorique.
„ XLVI, Z. 10 v. o., pag. L, Z. 17 v. u., pag. LXVI, Z. 12 v. o. (statt: qui'l) lies: qu'il.
„ L, Z. 25 v. u. (statt: decouvert) lies: descouvert.
„ „ Z. 18 v. u. (statt: excellement) lies: excellemment.
„ LIII, Z. 11 v. o. (statt: she) lies: shee.
„ „ Z. 7 v. u. (statt: accomplishement) lies: accomplishment.
„ LV, Z. 5. v. u. (statt: ist his) lies: is this.
„ LVII, Z. 22 v. o. (statt: ont of) lies: out of.
„ LIX, Z. 6 v. u. (statt: behed) lies: beheld.
„ LXIII, Z. 18 v. u. (statt: injoy) lies: enjoy.
„ LXV, Z. 31 v. u., pag. LXXIII, Z. 27 v. o. (statt: be) lies: hee.
„ LXVII, Z. 26 v. u. (statt: me) lies: mee.
„ „ Z. 21 v. u. (statt: intertrainment) lies: intertainment.
„ LXVIII, Z. 14 v. o. (statt: asseurrees) lies: asseurees. Z. 27 v. u. (statt: ces) lies: ses.
„ LXXIV, Z. 24 v. o. (statt: la) lies: sa.
„ LXXIII, Z. 1 v. u. (statt: bourrellé) lies: bourrelé.
„ LXXIX, Z. 1 v. o. (statt: preceiving) lies: perceiving. Z. 3 v. o. (statt: where) lies: were.
„ LXXX, Z. 9 v. o. (statt: Est) lies: Et. Z. 1 v. u. (statt: ces) lies: ses.
„ LXXXVII, Z. 23 v. o. (statt: afficted) lies: afflicted.
„ XCIV, Z. 8 v. o. (statt: poursuivre) lies: poursuyvre. Z. 9 v. o. (statt: l'enuie) lies: l'envie. Z. 25 v. o. (statt: de ces) lies: de ses. Randglosse zu Z. 26 u. 27 v. o. (statt: Wiylere) lies: Wiglere.
„ XCV, Z. 6 v. u. (statt: this mother) lies: his mother.
„ „ Z. 20 v. u. (statt: obtained victory) lies: obtained the victory.

SHAKESPEARE-MUSEUM.

EINE SAMMLUNG

NEUER UND ALTER, EIGENER UND FREMDER

PROSAISCHER UND POETISCHER

BEITRÄGE ZUR SHAKESPEARE-LITERATUR.

HERAUSGEGEBEN

VON

MAX MOLTKE.

BAND-AUSGABE.

LEIPZIG

VERLAG VON JOH. AMBR. BARTH.

1881.

W. DRUGULIN'S BUCH- UND KUNSTDRUCKEREI IN LEIPZIG.

VOR- UND ZUGLEICH NACHWORT.

Nachdem äufsere Umstände mich genötigt haben, dieses ursprünglich als Zeitschrift angelegte Sammelwerk aufzugeben und abzubrechen, noch bevor alle für den ersten Band zugesagten Aufsätze zum Abdruck gelangt sind, übergebe ich die vorliegenden, ihrer Zeit lieferungsweise erschienenen zwanzig Bogen hiermit der Shakespeare-Gemeinde in einem Gesamtband vereinigt, in der sicheren Überzeugung, dafs der mannigfaltige und reiche Inhalt, durch ein vollständiges Materienregister zugänglicher gemacht, in der vorliegenden Form sich manche neue Freunde erwerben werde.

Ein noch so flüchtiger Blick auf das Inhaltsverzeichnis wird dem Shakepeare-Forscher genügenden Beweis liefern, dafs das vorliegende Buch, wenn auch nicht seinem vielleicht zu hochgegriffenen ursprünglichen Haupttitel, so doch dem neu hinzugefügten Nebentitel wirklich und wörtlich entspricht, dafs es nämlich in der That eine bunte Reihe neuer und alter, eigener und fremder prosaischer und poetischer Beiträge zur Shakespeare-Literatur in sich vereinigt; und wer näher zusieht, wird finden, dafs nicht nur erlauchte Namen der deutschen und englischen Literatur mit interessanten Gelegenheits-Aussprüchen darin vertreten, sondern auch viele verborgene und abgelegene Quellen auf den shakespearologischen Goldsand, den sie mit sich führen, geprüft und ausgebeutet sind. Aber obwohl sich das Buch seiner ganzen Anlage nach aus Excerpten heterogenster Literaturwerke und Zeitschriften zusammensetzt, so enthält es doch auch mehrere selbständige Aufsätze und Abhandlungen, die vorher nur als Einzelschriften oder als Schülprogramme gedruckt waren und entweder niemals in den Buchhandel gekommen oder längst vergriffen sind, z. B.: „An Evening-hour with Shakespeare. Being the Original of a public Lecture, delivered in the German Language at Weimar," von J(ames) M(arshall); ferner: „A few Observations on Shakespeare and his 'Merchant of Venice'," von Henry A. Franklin; und auch die „Berichtigungen zur Schlegel-Tieck'schen Shakespeare-Übersetzung," von Karl Hagena.

Aus meiner eigenen, mit dem ersten Akte abgebrochenen kritischen Hamlet-Biglotte habe ich den Excurs über die Hamlet-Stelle A. I. Sc. 1; R. 44. Z. 4 und 5 unter dem Titel „Pole-axe oder Polacks, Streitaxt oder Polacken" dem Shakespeare-Museum einverleibt, was ich deshalb besonders erwähne, um daran die Bemerkung zu knüpfen, dafs von dem ersten Akte jener mit zahlreichen und ausführlichen Noten versehenen

Hamlet-Biglotte*) noch broschirte Exemplare bei mir selbst zu haben sind, der besonders paginirte Quellen-Text aber als selbständige Broschüre**) in den Verlag des Herrn Joh. Ambr. Barth hierselbst übergegangen ist. Bei dieser Gelegenheit darf ich wohl auch die Mitteilung machen, dafs ich erst kürzlich im Verlage des Herrn Otto Lenz in Leipzig eine vollständige englisch-deutsche Hamlet-Biglotte im kleinsten Taschen-Format herausgegeben habe, die sich im englischen Text durch wesentliche Emendationen der umstrittensten Stellen z. B. „He smote his leaded pole-axe on the ice;" — „And wit, no less nobility of love . . . Do I impart toward you;" — „He's hot, and out of breath" etc. und demzufolge auch in dem deutschen Texte der beibehaltenen Schlegel'schen Übersetzung von allen andern englischen und deutschen Ausgaben der Hamlet-Tragödie vielleicht nicht unvorteilhaft unterscheidet. Wie in dieser Miniatur-Biglotte bin ich auch im Titel und Vorwort des vorliegenden Sammelwerkes zu der altherkömmlichen Schreibung des Namens Shakespeare zurückgekehrt, während ich für das Inhaltsverzeichnis die im Werke selbst durchgeführte Schreibung (ohne das Schluss-e) glaubte beibehalten zu müssen.

Mit diesem räumlichen Vor- und zeitlichen Nachwort mein Shakespeare-Museum abschliefsend, hoffe ich, dafs dasselbe für manchen Shakespeare-Forscher etwelche Seiten oder Blätter enthalte, um derentwillen der ganze Band ihm besitzenswert erscheine.

Leipzig, im Juni 1881.

Max Moltke.

---

*) **Shakespeare's Hamlet**, Akt I, englisch und deutsch, neu emendirt, übersetzt und erläutert von Max Moltke. 84 S. gr. 8⁰. Preis 1 Mk. 50 Pf.
) **Shakespeare's Hamlet-Quellen: Saxo Grammaticus (lateinisch und deutsch), Belleforest und the Hystorie of Hamblet, zusammengestellt und mit Vorwort, Einleitung und Nachträgen von weiland Dr. Robert Gericke herausgegeben von Max Moltke. 108 S. gr. 8⁰. Preis 3 Mk.

INHALTS-VERZEICHNIS.

David Asher.
Conjectur zu 1 King Henry IV 14
Eine Glosse zur Shakespear-Sprache . . 46
Shakespearologischer Brief aus Deutschland, abgedruckt in „The Jewish Chronicle" 302

Eduard von Bauernfeld.
Shakespear. Ein Gedicht als Einleitung zur Biographie 65

Friedrich Bodenstedt.
„Nicht dass dein Name uns erwecke Neid." (Metrische Uebersetzung von Ben Jonsons Gedicht auf Sh. 49
„Wozu braucht meines Shakespear behr Gebein." Metrische Uebersetzung von John Miltons Gedicht auf Sh. 68
Ausspruch über Shakespears Werke . . 81

Roderich Benedix.
Ueber Lönig Lear 254

Ludwig Börne.
Aussprüche über Shakespear 50. 230

Bouterwek.
Ausspruch über Sh's. dramatisches Genie 81

Friedrich Bülau.
Uebersetzung von Macaulays Urteil über Sh. 163

A. Deetz.
Versuch zur Beseitigung des scheinbaren Widerspruchs im Character Lears 215

Robert Dorr.
Apollo und Shakespear. Sonett. 129

Kuno Fischer.
Shakespears Menschenkenntnis 261

K. Francke.
Antwort an Hagena über zwei Stellen in „Was ihr wollt" 181

Henry A. Franklin.
A few Observations on Shakespear and his „Merchant of Venice" 165. 224

Ferdinand Freiligrath.
Deutschland ist Hamlet. Gedicht. (Vgl. auch Amlethiana 4) 92

Hermann Frhr. v. Friesen.
Eine Anfrage (an Prof. Julius Saupe) . . 46

Fritsche.
Ein Shakespear-Portrait in Königsberg 31

Frederick J. Furnivall.
The new Shakspere Society 294

Emanuel Geibel.
Distichen auf Shakespear 17
Kaufmann von Venedig. (Distichen). . . 163

Robert Gericke.
Eine Shakespear-Frage 43
„König Lear. Eine psychiatrische Shakespear-Studie für das gebildete Publikum" 128

Gerstenberg.
Ausspruch über Sh's. Dramen 81
Etwas über Shakespear 100

Gerth.
Warum hat Sh. seinem Lear keinen glücklichen Ausgang gegeben? 262

Gervinus.
Shakespear ein deutscher Dichter . . . 81

Göthe.
Shakespear und kein Ende 6
Kronos als Kunstrichter 17
Shakespeariana aus dem Briefwechsel zwischen Schiller und Göthe 19

Karl Hagena,
Berichtigung der Schlegel-Tieck'schen Shakespear-Uebersetzung
1) König Johann 139
2) „ Richard II. 143
3) „ Heinrich IV. Erster Teil. 144
4) „ dgl. Zweiter Teil 145
5) „ Heinrich V. 147
6) „ Heinrich VI. Erster Teil 147
7) „ dgl. Zweiter Teil 149
8) „ dgl. Dritter Teil 150
9) „ Richard III. 151
10) Romeo und Julia 152
11) Sommernachtstraum . . . 154
12) Julius Caesar 155

INHALTS-VERZEICHNIS.

13) Was ihr wollt 178
14) Zwischen-Bemerkungen . . . 210
15) König Lear 299
16) *Neither = auch nicht; aber auch = auch* 301

J. M. Hales.
Shakespear's pastoral Names . . . 320

H. Harberts.
Sonett auf Shakespear 33

Karl Häser.
Prolog zum 300jährigen Geburtstags-Feste Sh's. auf dem Hoftheater zu Kassel . 257

Herder.
Seine Uebersetzungen Shakespear'scher Lieder:
1) Aus Measure for Measure („Wend, o wende diesen Blick") 75
2) Morgengesang aus Cymbeline („Horch, horch! die Lerch' am Himmelstor singt") 76
3) Einige Zauberlieder aus The Tempest 76
4) Waldgesang aus As you like it . 77
5) Waldlied aus As you like it . . 77
6) Grablied eines Landmanns aus Cymbeline 77
7) Liedchen der Desdemona aus Othello 77
8) Süszer Tod aus Twelfth Night 78
9) Opheliens verwirrter Gesang um ihren erschlagenen Vater, aus Hamlet 79

Samson von Himmelstiern.
Sh's. Humor und Pathos . 261

Luise Hoffmann.
Festdichtung zur Shakespear-Feier im Literarischen Verein zu Nürnberg . . 225

William Howitt.
Freiligraths Gedicht: „Deutschland ist Hamlet", metrisch ins Englische übersetzt 92

Rudolf von Jhering.
Ein Rechtsgutachten zu Gunsten Shylocks 190

Ben Jonson.
To the Memory of my beloved, the author, Master William Shakespear, and what he hath left us. — Gedicht nebst metrischer Uebersetzung von Friedrich Bodenstedt 49

Wilhelm Jordan.
Zeitalter Shakespears 129

M. M. Kalisch.
Distichen auf Shakespear 33

Wilhelm König.
Ueber den Titel von Sh's. „As you like it" 317

Wilh. Aug. Lampadius.
Widmungs-Sonette an die Geliebte zu Uebersetzungen Shakespear'scher Dramen:

1) Zum Wintermärchen 160
2) Zum Sommernachtstraum 160
3) Zu Romeo und Julia 160

Hermann Lingg.
Drei Sonette zu Sh's. dreihundertjähriger Geburtstagsfeier 193

A. Freiherr von Loën.
Die Shakespear-Kenntnis im heutigen Frankreich 231

Otto Ludwig.
Abgerissene Aussprüche über Sh's. „König Lear" 191

Thomas Babington Macaulay.
Urteil über Sh. (englisch nebst deutscher Uebersetzung von Friedrich Bülau) 163

James Marshall.
An Evening-hour with Shakespear. Being the Original of a public Lecture, delivered in the German Language at Weimar 196

Bruno Meyer.
Erläuterung zum König Lear, nach einem Carton von Adolf Schmitz . . 221

John Milton.
An epitaph on the admirable dramatic Poet, W. Shakespear. (Nebst metrischer Uebersetzung von Fr. Bodenstedt) . 68

Paul Möbius.
Ausspruch über Shakespear . 163

Modlinger.
Anmerkung zu Hamlet A. I. Sc. 5. R. 18. Z. 15: 64

Max Moltke.
Blatt-Weihe. Gedicht 1
Vorbemerkung zu Göthes Abhandlung: „Shakespear und kein Ende" 6
Die Shakespearhaltigen Bibliotheken Deutschlands; Anmerkung 13
Anmerkung zu einer Conjectur des Dr. D. Asher 14
Ein königlicher Shakespear-Kämpe (Sonett) 15
Hamlet in Leipzig. 15
Doubtful Plays of William Shakespear 15
Anachronismen auf Kosten Shakespears 16
Pole-axe oder Polacks; Streitaxt oder Polacken.
Ein Excurs über die Hamlet-Stelle A. I. Sc. 44. Z. 4 u. 5. . . . . 23. 37. 56.
Ueber die Diener-Scene in Coriolanus A. IV. Sc. 5 29
Ob Hamlet wahnsinnig war 32
Ein paar deutsche und englische Shakespear-Erwähnungen aus der zweiten Hälfte des 17. Jahrhunderts 48
Epistel von der Shakespear'schen Muse Fürtrefflichkeit und Eigenschaften. (Frei nach dem Bibeldeutsch des Dr. Martin Luther. 1. Corinther Cap. 13, Vers 1—13.) Von L, Komet, Shakespear-Spürer . . . 62

INHALTS-VERZEICHNIS.

The Works of William Shakespear. From the Text of the Rev. Alexander Dyce's Second Edition. (Complete in seven volumes. Leipzig 1868. Bernhard Tauchnitz.) 62
Mitteilung von Herders Shakespear-Uebersetzungen 75
A. W. Schlegels Verdienste um Shakespear 93
Shakespeariana in Schulprogrammen . . 95
Die erste Lear-Scene, neu emendirt und übersetzt 130
Eine Leipziger Shakespear-Feier im Jahre 1866 251

Peucer.
Uebersetzung eines anonymen französischen Ausspruchs über Shakespear . . . 194

Adolf Pichler.
Distichen auf Sh 17

August Graf von Platen.
Sechs kleine Gedichte auf Sh.:
1) Zu einer Anthologie 195
2) Griechen und Britten 195
3) Epos und Drama 195
4) An Shakespears Lobredner . . . 195
5) Shakespear und Sophokles . . . 195
6) Shakespear in seinen Sonetten 195

Rabel.
Ausspruch über Shakespear 34

Leopold Ranke.
Urteil über Shakespear 2

Moritz Rapp.
Das Ewige in der dramatischen Kunst Sh's. 230

Friedrich von Raumer.
Aristoteles über Calderon und Shakespear 94

Christian Schad.
Vom Klingenwald. Sieben Sonette zu William Shakespears dreihundertjähriger Jubelfeier 98

Johannes Scherr.
Urteil über Shakespear 4

Schiller.
Shakespears Schatten 18
Homer und Shakespear 19
Shakespeariana aus dem Briefwechsel zwischen Schiller und Göthe 19

Schipper.
Ausspruch über Sh's Hamlet 261

Aug. Wilh. von Schlegel.
Seine Shakespear-Poesien:
1) Sh's. Sonette und übrige Jugendgedichte 87
2) Zueignung der Trauerspiele Romeo und Julia 87

3) Trost bei einer schwierigen Unternehmung 87
4) Macbeth, für das Weimarische Hoftheater eingerichtet von Schiller 87
5) Die veredelte Hexenzucht . . . 87
6) Die Uebersetzer-Familie . . . 87
7) Wienerischer Nachdruck 88
8) Variationen auf den Refrain des Hexengesangs im Macbeth . . 88
9) An Kotzebue 88

Karl Simrock.
Shakespears Dramen. (Zwei Gedichte) 97

Stahr.
Sh's. Bedeutung für die poetische Nationalliteratur der Deutschen 81

Ludwig Tieck.
Briefe über Shakespear . . 34. 51. 69. 82

Benno Tschischwitz.
Ueber King Richard II. A. 1. Sc. 3. R. 44: 31
Sh's. Schöpfungen 261

E. W.
Recension der Schrift des Frhrn. v. Friesen: „Das Buch: Shakespere von Gervinus. Ein Wort über dasselbe" 25

P. J. Willatzen.
Sonett auf Shakespear 161

Paul Wislicenus.
Macbeth 211

Ernst Ziel.
Erläuterung zu Aug. v. Heckels Lear-Illustration (Verstoszung der Cordelia) in der „Gartenlaube" 318

Amlethiana,
mitgeteilt vom Herausgeber:
1) Das Urbild des Hamlet 88
2) Hamlet auf der deutschen Bühne 89
3) Friedrich Haase als Hamlet . . 90
4) „Deutschland ist Hamlet." Gedicht von Ferdinand Freiligrath, nebst metrischer englischer Uebersetzung von William Howitt 92

Deutsche Shakespear-Gesellschaft.
Generalversammlung derselben von 1870: 32. 61
Satzungen und Regulativ, die Discussions-Abende betreffend 47
Jahrbuch derselben, fünfter Band . . 48
Zehnter Geburtstag derselben i. J. 1874 253

Hermann Lindes.
Shakespear-Recitationen 305

Miscellen und Notizen.
Shakespear-Ausgabe, für Taubstumme bearbeitet 48

INHALTS-VERZEICHNIS.

Shakespear-Gallerie von Friedrich Pecht 80
Stimmen der Presse über das Shakespear-
Museum 95
Das Straszburger Münster und Shakespear 159
Eine Äuszerung Varnhagens 159
Shakespearologische Vorlesungen an deutschen
Universitäten 160
Zu Sh's. Biographie 192
Ein Shakespear-Bildnis 192
Die Widmungs-Adresse zu Sh's. Sonetten 221
Shakespear und Calderon 223
Neuer Shakespear-Verein in England 253

Shakespear-Aufführungen.

Macbeth-Aufführung in Leipzig . . . 183
Cymbelin-Aufführung in Oldenburg . . 187
Romeo und Julia in Bremen 256

Shakespear-Bibliographie.

1) Selbständige Schriften und Text-Aus-
gaben 155. 189. 250
2) Shakespeariana in Zeitschriften 157. 189. 251
3) Shakespeariana-Recensionen 157. 189. 251

Shakespear-Stellen.

King Henry IV. P. 1. A. I. Sc. 1. R. 5. Z. 8: 44
Hamlet A. I. Sc. 1. R. 44. Z. 4—5 . . 23
Coriolanus A. IV. Sc. 5 29
King Richard II. A. I. Sc. 3. R. 44 . . 31
Hamlet A. I. Sc. 5. R 18. Z. 15 64
King Lear A. I. Sc. 1. R. 35. Z. 8 130. 133

Shakespeariana auf deutschen Bibliotheken.

1) Shakespeariana auf der Stadtbibliothek
zu Leipzig. 12
2) auf der Königl. öffentlichen Bibliothek
zu Dresden . . . . 41. 59.
3) auf der Leipziger Universitäts-
Bibliothek 123

Shakesperiana-Recensionen.

Shakespears Julius Caesar ins Lateinische
übersetzt von *Hilgers* 127
König Lear. Eine psychiatrische Shakespear-
Studie für das gebildete Publikum, be-
sprochen von R. G. 128
Shakespearomanie (zur Abwehr.) Von Rode-
rich Benedix 158. 252. 273. 303
Shakespear-Prometheus. Phantastisch-sati-
risches Zauberspiel vor dem Höllenrachen.
Ohne Raum und ohne Zeit im Dämmer-
schein der Ewigkeit. Von Oswald Mar-
bach 312
Vormerkungen für die Bücherschau . . . 14

Druckfehler-Berichtigungen: Seite 224

www.ingramcontent.com/pod-product-compliance
Lightning Source LLC
Chambersburg PA
CBHW020136170426
43199CB00010B/770